CAROUSEL™ COOKING

from

SHARP

The New Deluxe Carousel Microwave Oven

COOKBOOK

SHARP ELECTRONICS CORPORATION

SHARP ELECTRONICS CORPORATION
10 Keystone Place, Paramus, New Jersey 07652

Dear Sharp Customer:

We sincerely hope you will enjoy your new Sharp Carousel Microwave Oven and the exciting world of microwave cooking. This cookbook will help you explore the many benefits of Microwave Cooking and make meal preparation easier and more convenient than ever before possible.

Please read your cookbook thoroughly. Recipes from all categories of food preparation—family favorites to gourmet recipes—are included, as well as basic information on microwave cooking. The versatility of your Sharp Microwave Oven is apparent by just scanning the Table of Contents.

Use your Sharp Microwave Oven every time you prepare a meal. It saves time, energy, and is easy to operate. As you become better acquainted with your new oven, you will find additional uses for it and learn to easily convert your own favorite recipes to microwave cooking.

Feel free to share your ideas with us. We will be happy to hear from you. When writing, please indicate the model number of your oven, your complete mailing address and telephone number.

If we can be of any further assistance, do not hesitate to contact us. We are pleased that you chose a Sharp product and hope you will enjoy using it.

Sincerely,

SHARP ELECTRONICS CORPORATION

Susan Edwards

Susan Edwards
Sharp Test Kitchen
10 Keystone Place
Paramus, NJ 07652

CONTENTS

INTRODUCTION

Precautions To Avoid Possible Exposure To Excessive Microwave Energy

(a) Do not attempt to operate this oven with the door open since open-door operation can result in harmful exposure to microwave energy. It is important not to defeat or tamper with the safety interlocks.

(b) Do not place any object between the oven front face and the door or allow soil or cleaner residue to accumulate on sealing surfaces.

(c) Do not operate the oven if it is damaged. It is particularly important that the oven door close properly and that there is no damage to the:
(1) door (bent), (2) hinges and latches (broken or loosened), (3) door seals and sealing surfaces.

(d) The oven should not be adjusted or repaired by anyone except properly qualified service personnel.

What Is Microwave Energy? How Does It Work?

Electronic or microwave energy is a type of high frequency radio wave. This energy in the form of invisible waves enters the cavity from the top of the oven and is guided down to the food which is placed on a turntable which rotates the food while it cooks.

Cooking with microwave energy differs from conventional energy in that there is no direct application of heat or process of heat penetration to cook the food. Heat energy is absorbed by the food when cooking conventionally; this is a slow process. As microwaves pass through to the food in the oven, the microwaves cause the water molecules within the food to vibrate at extremely high speeds. This friction produces the intense heat which cooks the food. The high speed of vibration accounts for the dramatic savings in the cooking time. Cooking by microwaves can reduce regular cooking times by up to 75%. Microwaves are odorless and tasteless; they cannot affect the flavors of the foods you cook. Microwave cooked foods will usually taste better than the foods cooked conventionally since microwave cooking is more rapid and there is less vitamin and flavor loss.

Microwave energy will either be reflected, absorbed, or will be allowed to pass through the utensils used for cooking. Metal reflects microwaves. The water molecules within the food will absorb the microwaves and thus the food is heated. Glass, plastic, porcelain, china, wood, wicker and paper are good utensils to use for microwave cooking since the waves are allowed to pass through and go directly to the food that you want to cook.

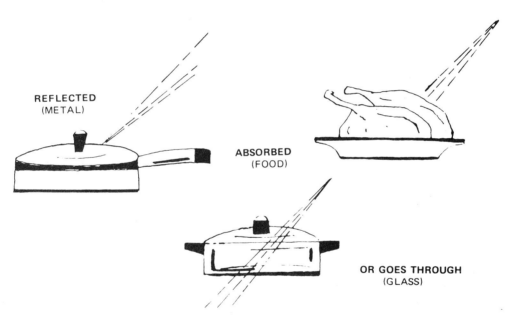

REFLECTED
(METAL)

ABSORBED
(FOOD)

OR GOES THROUGH
(GLASS)

Cleaning And Care of Your Microwave Oven

Exterior:

The outside surface of the unit is painted metal and plastic. The outside may be cleaned with mild soap and warm water; rinse and dry with a soft cloth. Do not use any type of household cleaner or abrasive cleaner.

Interior Walls:

Cleaning the Sharp Microwave Oven is very easy because no heat is generated to the interior surfaces, baking and setting spills or causing spatters. To clean the interior surfaces, bring a container of water to a boil. Let boil 2 minutes. Wipe the resulting condensation from the interior surfaces with a soft, dry cloth. Window cleaner sprayed on the oven walls will clean and polish a stainless steel interior. For heavier soil, use baking soda or a mild soap; rinse thoroughly with hot water. See the Use and Care Book for your particular oven for specific cleaning information.

Turntable:

Occasionally it will be necessary to remove the turntable for cleaning or in order to clean the floor of the oven. Wash the turntable in mild, sudsy water. Dry with a soft cloth. The turntable is dishwasher-proof.

Be cautious when cleaning the floor of the oven so as not to get water into the motor shaft.

Door:

Wipe the window on both sides with a damp cloth to remove any spills or spatter. Metal and plastic parts will be easier to maintain if wiped frequently with a damp cloth.

Condensation

Occasionally you may find that some foods will cause the Microwave Oven to "sweat"; others will not. The humidity and the moisture in the food will influence the amount of moisture you find in your oven. Generally, covered foods will not cause as much condensation as uncovered foods. Be sure that the vent of your oven is not blocked. Condensation is a normal part of microwave cooking.

The door seal on your microwave oven is designed to prevent the leakage of microwave energy from the oven during cooking. The door seal does not need to be air-tight in order to accomplish this function. Occasionally moisture may appear around the oven door. You may also be able to see some small areas of light or feel warm air movement around the oven door. None of these situations is abnormal or necessarily indicates that your oven is leaking microwave energy.

Utensils

Microwave cooking opens up many new possibilities for convenience and flexibility in the kitchen. There are many new types of utensils that can be used. Utensils change almost daily, so look for new products as they come into your stores. Manufacturers are now putting Microwave information stickers on new products.

DISH TEST

A good way to determine whether a utensil is safe for use in a Microwave Oven is to place it in the oven empty, and turn the oven on for 15 to 30 seconds on FULL POWER. If the utensil becomes very hot to the touch, it should not be used in the Microwave Oven.

Glass, ceramics, paper, and some plastics are essentially transparent to microwaves, so they allow the microwaves to pass through them freely to cook the food. This means that dishes made of these materials are the best to use. Since the microwaves pass through the dishes to the food without affecting them, only the food becomes hot.

Dishes may become warm due to the natural transfer of heat from the food to the container. Use care in removing covers or lids from microwave cooked foods. Steam builds up under the lid and can become extremely hot.

Glass, Ceramic And China Utensils

Most glass and glass-ceramic manufacturers are identifying their microwave-oven-safe dishes either by a mark right on the utensil or a note placed prominently on the product literature. Most glass, glass-ceramic and china utensils are excellent for use in Microwave Ovens. Heat-resistant glassware, unless it has metallic trim or metal portions, can almost always be used in the Microwave Oven, regardless of whether it is clear or opaque. However, you must be careful not to use delicate glassware, since it might crack from the heat of the food, but not from the microwaves.

Pyrex® and Corning® products with a (❋) or the label that reads "Good for Microwave" or "Good for Range and Microwave" are suitable for use in a Microwave Oven. Centura® cookware by Corning® without metallic trim but with a (❋) symbol is microwave-oven-safe. However, Centura® tableware is not to be used in a Microwave Oven. Several of the accessory items can be used and they are marked with the (❋) symbol.

Corelle® Livingware by Corning®, with the exception of the closed handle cups, is microwave-oven-safe.

Fire King® cookware by Anchor Hocking, without metallic trim, whether opaque or clear, is microwave-oven-safe as is stated on its product labels.

Glassbake® cookware by Jeanette Glass, without metallic trim, is also microwave-oven-safe.

Federal Glass Company's Heat Proof® cookware is labeled microwave-oven-safe and can be used as long as there is no metallic trim.

Temper-ware® by Lenox is a line of cook and serve ware acceptable for use in Microwave Ovens. Utensils with metallic trim or metal parts such as screws, bands, handles, etc., must be avoided. Dishes that are glazed with high metallic content glazes should also be avoided. Cracked or crazed glazes or chips are also indications that a dish should not be used. Delicate glassware should never be used for cooking in a Microwave Oven. Ceramic mugs or cups with glued on handles are also not recommended for use in a Microwave Oven.

Paper Goods

For low heat cooking, such as reheating or very short cooking times and for foods with low fat, sugar or water content, paper is a good utensil for Microwave Oven use. Wax paper, paper napkins, towels, plates, cups, cartons, paper freezer wrap and the paper pulp board in which meats are packed are also convenient utensils for use in the Microwave Oven. Cardboard can also be used. Paper is used in the Microwave Oven as a moisture insulator. Wax coated paper plates and cups should be avoided since the high temperatures that the foods reach may cause the wax to melt. Plastic coated dishes, however, are fine for use in the Microwave Oven.

Wax paper and paper towels provide an excellent loose cover for foods and help prevent spatters.

Plastic Utensils

"Dishwasher Safe" is usually a good indicator as to whether or not a plastic is safe for use in the Microwave Oven. Plastic dishes and containers should not be used for cooking foods with high fat or high sugar content since the heat of the food is too hot for the plastic and may cause it to melt or lose its shape.

Cooking pouches designed to withstand boiling and freezing for conventional cooking work well in the Microwave Oven. Do not close plastic cooking pouches with the metal tie wraps provided, since they get very hot and will melt the plastic wrap. Any closed pouch or cooking container should be pierced so that steam is allowed to escape. Do not attempt to cook in plastic storage bags as they will not withstand the heat of the food.

Plastic wrap may be used to cover foods during cooking. Stretch-type plastic wraps are not suitable for use in the Microwave Oven because they form too tight a seal. Whenever removing plastic wrap that has been tightly formed around the utensil, just lift the plastic away from you so that the steam can vent and there will be no danger of scalding.

Melamine® is not recommended for use in the Microwave Oven.

There are numerous new plastic cooking accessories on the market designed especially for microwave cooking. These include tube pans, bacon racks, meat roasting racks or trivets, muffin and cupcake pans and rings, molds, trays for heating leftovers or for making your own frozen dinners, omelet pans, and plastic cookie or serving trays. The design and materials from which these accessories are made vary extensively. For best results, follow individual manufacturer's instructions and use only according to directions.

Wicker, Wood And Straw

Wicker, wood and straw may be used in the oven for short periods of time, however, they should not be used for high fat or high sugar content foods since the heat of the food could possibly char the utensil. Wooden handles, scrapers, spatulas and spoons may be left in the Microwave Oven during the cooking process for short periods of time.

Browning Dishes

Browning dishes or plates made with a ferrite coating or other ferrite material, designed for use in a Microwave Oven, may be used in your Sharp Microwave Oven. The Corning® Microwave Browning Dish is a glass-ceramic dish with a special coating applied to the outside bottom of the dish. When the empty dish is preheated in the Microwave Oven, the special coating interacts with microwave energy and produces heat. Browning dishes may be used for steaks, hamburgers, chops, fried eggs, chicken, sandwiches, fish and other foods.

The empty browning dish must be preheated on FULL POWER in the Microwave Oven; when preheated, the surface temperature of the dish becomes hot enough to sear and brown meats or other foods that come into contact with the heated surface. After preheating the dish, the food is placed in the browning dish and returned to the Microwave Oven. The hot surface of the browning dish browns the food while the microwave power cooks the food. The food should be turned over halfway through the cooking time in order to brown on both sides.

Preheat time depends upon the type of food you wish to brown. Suggested preheat times are included with the browning dish. Preheat times vary from one minute for one fried egg to 5 to 6 minutes for steak. Do not preheat the dish longer than 6 minutes.

The browning dish should not be used on conventional gas or electric range surface units, in the oven or under the broiler. See the instructions provided with the browning dish and specific recommendations elsewhere in this book for additional use and care information.

Metal Utensils

1

Metal utensils and utensils with metallic trim should NOT be used in your Microwave Oven. There are two main reasons for this. Microwaves are reflected by metals; therefore, foods that are in metal containers will not cook as well as if they were in plastic, glass, china or paper. There is also a possibility of a static discharge or spark between the gap in the metal and the metal utensil. This is called ''arcing.' If you do see an arc inside the oven, do not be alarmed. Simply turn the oven off and transfer the food to a non-metallic container.

There are several cases, however, when metal may be used in the Microwave Oven.

1) Shielding with Aluminum Foil

Small amounts of aluminum foil may be used in the Microwave Oven. They are used primarily for shielding. If, for example, you are cooking a turkey, and the wings begin to overcook, you can wrap small pieces of aluminum foil around the wing tips so that the turkey will not continue to cook in this area. There should be a large volume of food whenever you are using metal. Do not allow foil to touch the sides of the oven cavity.

2) Frozen Dinners In Foil Containers

When cooking foods in foil containers, the container should be no more than ¾-inch deep. Remember that whenever you are cooking in metal, you are reflecting the waves away from the food. Therefore, you must remove any foil that is covering the top of the container. After removing the foil cover, return the metal container to the paper box or package it came in, and place this entire unit in the Microwave Oven. Frozen dinners will cook in less time and more evenly if the food is removed from the metal container and placed on a glass or paper plate.

3) Metal Skewers

Small metal skewers may be used if there is a large portion of food to the amount of metal. If arcing does begin, stop the oven, remove the food and change to a wooden skewer.

Whenever using metal foil, foil containers, or metal skewers, be sure that the metal does not touch the sides of the oven. Limit use of metal to those specific examples given above. Generally speaking, metal should not be used in the microwave oven during operation.

Thermometers

Conventional meat or candy thermometers should NEVER be used in the Microwave Oven while the oven is in operation. Only specially designed Microwave Cooking thermometers may be used in any Microwave Oven. These are the ONLY thermometers recommended for use in Sharp Microwave Ovens during operation. Other thermometers may be used FOLLOWING cooking to check internal temperature.

Suggested internal temperature readings when using a thermometer are given throughout the cookbook for appropriate foods. If you are using a conventional thermometer, use it only after cooking.

If your oven is equipped with a temperature probe, see individual use and care book for specific information.

General Cooking Hints

1. Microwave cooking times vary by volume, quantity and starting temperature of foods.
   For example, a two pound roast requires less cooking time than a three pound roast. One potato cooks much faster than four potatoes. Food that has been refrigerated will take longer to heat than the same food started from room temperature. The moisture content and density of food will also influence cooking times.
   The times stated in this cookbook are approximate and the above factors will determine the exact times. Remember, it is always better to undercook foods rather than to overcook them. If a range of times is stated in a recipe, cook the minimum suggested time, check for doneness, and then cook slightly longer if necessary. Personal preference should be the final judgement of doneness.

2. Recipes in this book were developed for 650 watt microwave ovens. If your oven has a different wattage, please refer to your individual model's Use and Care Book for information on adapting these recipes for your oven.

3. When cooking more than one item in the oven, arrange items so that there is at least one inch of space between all items. Never place food on the tray so that there is a circle of small items and one in the center. The item in the center will have a tendency to cook more slowly.

4. The arrangement of food on the plate or in the baking dish will influence how evenly the food cooks. Place thin portions of food toward the center of the dish, with thicker portions toward the outside.

5. "Standing times" following cooking times are an extremely important aspect of microwave cooking. Microwave cooked foods continue to cook somewhat after being removed from the oven. Standing times should be considered in determining doneness. Internal temperatures will increase by 10°F to 15°F during the standing time following microwave cooking. Meats and poultry should be allowed to stand 10 to 15 minutes before making a final check for doneness. Individual recipes should be consulted for recommended standing times.
   The tests for determining doneness are the same for foods cooked in the Microwave Oven as for foods cooked conventionally.

6. If you wish to retain moisture in foods, cover them with either a glass cover or plastic wrap.
   A loose cover of wax paper will prevent spatters but allow some moisture to escape. A paper towel placed over food will absorb excess moisture and prevent spatters.

7. In order to determine the best cooking time for a particular food, consult the index of the cookbook to find a recipe for the food or for another recipe most like the food you want to cook.
   For example, if you have a favorite casserole and do not find it in the cookbook, look for another "casserole type" recipe that has approximately the same type of ingredients and use that recipe as a guide.

8. Cooking hints for each food category are given at the beginning of each chapter.
   Be sure to read these as an introduction to general microwave principles. These hints will also help you in converting your own recipes to microwave cooking.

COOKING BY TEMPERATURE

Many of the recipes in this book have suggested cooking or serving temperatures in a box in the upper right-hand corner. Whether your oven is equipped with an automatic temperature probe or you wish to use a portable microwave cooking thermometer, these temperatures should serve as a guide in helping you determine when foods are cooked. The following chart gives recommended temperatures at end of cooking time for a wide assortment of foods.

TEMPERATURE CHART

Food	Internal Temperature at End of Cooking Time	Internal Temperature After 10 to 15 Minutes Standing Time
Beverages	170 – 180°F	
Breads, sandwiches	120°F	
Casseroles	150 – 160°F	
Chicken **Whole Baked** **Chicken Parts**	 180 – 185°F 180 – 185°F	 190 – 195°F 190 – 195°F
Cornish Hen	175 – 180°F	185 – 190°F
Lamb **Medium Well** **Well Done**	 155 – 160°F 165 – 170°F	 170°F 180°F
Leftovers	150 – 160°F	
Meat Loaf	160°F	165°F
Pork **Loin Roast** **Fresh Ham** **Precooked Ham**	 170 – 175°F 170 – 175°F 120°F	 180 – 185°F 180 – 185°F 130°F
Soups	160°F	
Tender Beef **Rolled Rib or** **Standing Rib Roast** **Rare** **Medium** **Well Done**	 120 – 130°F 140 – 150°F 160 – 165°F	 130 – 135°F 150 – 155°F 170 – 175°F
Tougher cuts of Beef **Rump, Chuck, Shoulder,** **Arm, Other** **Well Done**	 Cook by time, not temperature	 Until tender
Turkey **Boneless Roasts** **Whole Turkey**	 150 – 160°F 170 – 175°F	 160–170°F 180–185°F
Veal	160°F	170°F

CAUTIOUS REMINDERS FOR MICROWAVE COOKING

1. Do not operate the oven empty. Either food or water should always be in the oven during operation to absorb microwave energy.

2. Do not cook eggs in the shell. Pressure will build up inside the shell and it will explode. Do not reheat cooked eggs unless they are scrambled or chopped. Puncture the yolk before cooking eggs.

3. Avoid canning in your microwave oven.

4. Do not heat oil or fat for deep fat frying.

5. Pierce the "skin" of potatoes, whole squash, apples or any fruit or vegetable which has a skin covering, before cooking.

6. Popcorn should be cooked only in special microwave poppers carefully following manufacturer's recommendations. Do not pop popcorn in paper bags or glass utensils. Microwave popped corn produces a lower yeild than conventional popping; there will be a number of unpopped kernels. Do not use oil unless specified by the manufacturer. Do not remove the Carousel turntable while oven is in use or heat longer than recommended on instructions.

Pictured: Sweet and Sour Beef Stew

VARIABLE COOKING CONTROL

Variable Cooking Control

The Variable Cooking Control on Sharp Carousel Microwave Ovens adds a new dimension to microwave cooking. It is now possible to select the speed at which you cook foods in your Microwave Oven, just as you control the rate of cooking on your conventional range. The Variable Cooking Control lets you defrost, simmer, roast or cook at full power to give each food the proper amount of microwave energy for best results.

To understand how to use the Variable Cooking Control, you need to know how it works. The microwave energy cycles on and off at various intervals to allow you to control the rate of heating and cooking. There are four settings: FULL POWER, ROAST, SIMMER, and DEFROST.

Variable Cooking Control Setting		Approximate Percentage of Microwave Power
FULL POWER	(High)	100%
ROAST	(Medium High)	70%
SIMMER	(Medium)	50%
DEFROST	(Medium Low)	30%
WARM	(Low)	10%

14

The Variable Cooking Control is easy to use. After you have set the desired cooking or defrosting time, select the Variable Cooking Control setting you need.

In all probability the speed and convenience of microwave cooking were your major reasons for purchasing your Sharp Carousel Microwave Oven. You will find that most foods are cooked on FULL POWER or ROAST. In either case most foods can be cooked in about one-fourth their conventional times using these settings. Other foods traditionally require long, slow cooking for tenderness or to develop flavor. Even using the slower settings of SIMMER or DEFROST, foods still require much shorter times than conventionally.

The terms we have chosen to designate each power setting should serve only as a guide for choosing the appropriate power level. The recipes in this cookbook will help you learn which setting is best for a particular food. For example, we have recommended defrosting foods on DEFROST, but other foods are best defrosted on SIMMER or ROAST. Experiment, using this chapter and your own judgement and cooking experience as a guide!

If your oven is not equipped with the Variable Cooking Control, refer to your Use and Care Book for directions for adapting the recipes in this cookbook to your oven. If your oven has only a defrost cycle, many of the recipes in this chapter can be cooked on defrost.

When Should You Use The Variable Cooking Control?

FOR DEFROSTING

Most frozen foods require a standing or resting period alternated with periods of microwave energy to thaw without cooking. The Variable Cooking Control does this automatically. See the Defrosting Chapter for complete information on defrosting.

FOR COOKING LESS TENDER CUTS OF MEATS

Some less tender cuts of meat are more tender when cooked at a slower rate. It takes time to break down connective tissue in meats; longer, slower cooking may be recommended.

TO DEVELOP FLAVOR IN STEWS, SOUPS OR SAUCES

These foods benefit from prolonged cooking to develop rich, full flavor and body. By using the Variable Cooking Control, this can be achieved much faster than by conventional methods.

FOR FOODS THAT ARE ESPECIALLY SENSITIVE TO MICROWAVE ENERGY

Some food categories or ingredients such as eggs, milk, cream, cheese or sour cream are better when cooked more slowly. Soufflés and breads have better texture or volume if cooked longer.

TO PREVENT OVERCOOKING

The thin areas of some irregularly shaped foods may tend to overcook. Using a lower setting instead of cooking at FULL POWER prevents thin sections or the ends or edges of food from becoming hard or tough before the center is thoroughly cooked.

FOR FOODS THAT TEND TO OVERCOOK QUICKLY

If you see that a food is starting to cook too quickly or boil over, reset the Variable Cooking Control to a lower setting. This will slow down your Microwave Oven. You may need to reset the timer for a longer period if you lower the setting.

FOR ANY FOODS THAT YOU WOULD STEW OR SIMMER IF USING A CONVENTIONAL RECIPE

If your own recipe says to "stew" or "simmer" for several hours, the same recipe can probably be cooked much faster in the Microwave Oven on SIMMER. The volume will determine the total cooking time; use the recipes in this chapter as a guide for converting your own recipes to microwave cooking.

15

Full Power

As the term implies, FULL POWER is the highest setting and will result in the fastest cooking. FULL POWER is generally used for:

> fish
> vegetables
> fruits
> hot beverages
> some tender meats
> bacon
> preheating browning dish
> melting butter

FULL POWER		
Rolled Rib Roast (Well-done)		7 min./lb.
Rolled Rib Roast (Medium)		6 min./lb.
Rolled Rib Roast (Rare)		5 min./lb.
Meat Loaf	1 lb.	12 minutes
Snack Cake Mix	15.5 oz.	10 minutes
Fish Fillets	1 lb.	6 minutes
Preheat Browning Dish (for steaks)		5 minutes
Bacon	4 strips	4 minutes
Bacon	2 strips	2 minutes
Hot Dog	1 on bun	30 seconds

FULL POWER		
Baked Potatoes	6 medium	24 minutes
Acorn Squash	3 medium	16 minutes
Baked Potatoes	4 medium	15 minutes
Corn on the Cob	6 ears	12 minutes
Frozen Vegetables	10 oz. pkg.	7 minutes
Frozen Vegetables	10 oz. pouch	6 minutes
Baked Potato	1 large	5 minutes
Canned Vegetables	16 oz.	4 minutes
Onions, sautéed	1 cup	3 minutes
Baked Apple	1 medium	2½ minutes
Hot Beverage	1 cup	2 minutes

Roast

This setting is used primarily for baking or roasting and for reheating previously cooked foods. Foods retain more moisture on ROAST. Reducing the power to ROAST means less stirring and watching. Use ROAST:

2

to reheat leftovers
to warm pre-baked bread products
   (doughnuts, rolls, biscuits)
to roast chicken or pork
to cook some casseroles
to cook foods which contain cheese,
   cream sauce or sour cream

ROAST		
Stuffed Peppers		
	4 large	19 to 22 minutes
Pork Roast		
		12 min./lb.
Whole Chicken		
		8 min./lb.
Canned Ham		
		6 min./lb.
Casserole Reheat		
	4 cups	12 minutes
Layer Cake		
	1 layer	8 to 9 minutes
Frozen Dinner		
	11 oz.	9 minutes
Browning Ground Meat		
	1 lb.	6 minutes
Casserole Reheat		
	1 cup	4½ minutes
Egg Omelet		
	4 eggs	3¾ to 4½ minutes
Warm Rolls		
	8 oz.	1¼ minutes

Simmer

The SIMMER setting is extremely versatile as you can see from the chart below. It can be used for some defrosting and roasting, as well as for simmering. Soups and stews are cooked on this setting.

Defrost

Even the DEFROST setting is more flexible than the name implies. It can be used for cooking less tender cuts of meat, for softening cream cheese or butter, and for simmering at an even slower rate than on SIMMER.

SIMMER		
Swiss Steak	2 lbs. round	50 to 60 minutes
Rice (uncooked)	1 cup	20 minutes
Baked Pork Chops		16 min./lb.
Defrost Whole Chicken		4 min./lb.
Frozen Casserole Defrost and Reheat	2 cups	14 minutes
Chuck Steak (Boneless)		7 to 9 min./lb.
Hamburgers (4 patties)	1 lb.	7 minutes
Melt Cheese	1 lb.	5½ minutes
Baked Eggs (covered)	2 eggs	2¼ minutes
Frozen Layer Cake (Defrost)	17 oz.	1¼ minutes

DEFROST		
Roast Beef Defrost		10 min./lb.
Frozen Fish Fillets Defrost		10 min./lb.
Chicken Pieces Defrost		8 min./lb.
Ground Beef Defrost		8 min./lb.
Hamburger Patties Defrost		8 min./lb.
Chops Defrost		8 min./lb.
Frozen Fruit Defrost	12-16 oz.	5 minutes
Steak (boneless) Defrost	8 oz.	4 minutes
Soften Cream Cheese	8 oz.	1 minute
Soften Butter or Margarine	1 stick	1 minute

Pot Roasts

(Rump, Chuck, Shoulder, Arm)

These cuts of meat vary in tenderness and must be cooked slowly to the well done stage to become tender. Liquid should be used in cooking less tender cuts of meat, and they should be covered tightly with plastic wrap or a glass cover.

If less tender cuts of meat are cooked solely by temperature rather than by time, the desired temperature may be reached before the meat has cooked long enough to become tender. These cuts must be "simmered" longer, even though the thermometer may indicate they are "well done". Tougher meats require prolonged cooking to become tender, and the internal temperature must approach 200°F before the meat becomes tender. For this reason, many of the recipes in this chapter using less tender cuts do not give a suggested temperature.

Marinating less tender cuts will enhance tenderness and flavor. Tenderizers may also be used. Cutting larger roasts into several smaller pieces will decrease the density and seems to increase tenderness.

Roasting bags are ideal for cooking less tender cuts of meat. Follow manufacturer's directions, making sure to puncture the roasting bag several times to allow steam to escape. DO NOT USE the metal tie provided with the roasting bag. Secure the bag with string.

Cooking times for less tender cuts are approximate.

Less tender beef	18 min./lb. on SIMMER

Salt less tender cuts following cooking. The flavor of these cuts is improved if they are seared in a small amount of oil before being cooked in the Microwave Oven. This can be done either in a skillet on a conventional surface unit, or in a microwave browning dish.

To use a browning dish for searing, first preheat the dish in the Microwave Oven on FULL POWER for 5 minutes. Remove from oven and place roast in hot browning dish for 2 minutes. Turn roast over, add any additional ingredients, cover and cook according to time suggested above.

Large cuts of meat should be turned over after half of cooking time. Meat with a covering of fat should be started fat-side-down, turning over to fat-side-up after half of cooking time.

Standing times for meats are very important. Before checking to see if a roast is completely done, it should be allowed to stand at least 10 to 15 minutes.

Basic Pot Roast

2 tablespoons flour
¼ teaspoon pepper
2½ pound boneless beef pot roast
3 tablespoons vegetable oil
1 cup water or beef bouillon
4 to 6 potatoes, peeled and quartered
5 small carrots, peeled and cut into halves
1 medium-sized onion, thinly sliced
1 clove garlic, peeled
Flour
Water
Salt

1. Combine the 2 tablespoons of flour and pepper together in a plastic bag. Coat meat well with this mixture.

2. Heat oil in a skillet on top of a conventional surface unit. Add meat and cook until seared on all sides.

3. Place browned meat in a deep, 3-quart, heat-resistant, non-metallic casserole. Add water, potatoes, carrots, onion and garlic.

4. Heat, tightly covered, on SIMMER for 25 minutes.

5. Turn meat over and stir vegetables. Heat, tightly covered, on SIMMER for 25 additional minutes or until meat and vegetables are tender.

6. Thicken the liquid for gravy, as desired, with additional flour and water. Salt to taste.

Serves 4 to 6

Savory Pot Roast

3 to 4 pound boneless beef pot roast
1 tablespoon vegetable oil
1 (10¾-ounce) can cream
of mushroom soup
1 (1¾-ounce) envelope
dehydrated onion soup mix
1 tablespoon Worcestershire sauce
½ cup water

Serves 6 to 8

1. Sear pot roast in 1 tablespoon vegetable oil.

2. Mix soups, Worcestershire sauce and water, and pour over roast. Heat, covered, on SIMMER approximately 18 minutes per pound or until tender.

Swiss Steak

2 pounds beef round steak, cut
½-inch thick
½ cup flour
1 teaspoon salt
¼ teaspoon pepper
2 tablespoons vegetable oil
1 medium-sized onion, chopped
1 cup thinly sliced celery
1 green pepper, thinly sliced
1 (10¾-ounce) can tomato soup
1 tablespoon Worcestershire
sauce
⅔ cup water

Serves 4 to 6

1. Cut meat into serving pieces. Combine flour, salt and pepper in a plastic bag. Coat meat well with mixture. In a skillet on top of a conventional surface unit, heat vegetable oil. Brown meat in vegetable oil on both sides. Set aside.

2. In a small, heat-resistant, non-metallic mixing bowl combine onion, celery and green pepper. Heat, covered, on FULL POWER 3 to 4 minutes.

3. Place browned meat in a deep, 2½-quart, heat-resistant, non-metallic casserole. Spoon onion mixture over meat. Combine soup, Worcestershire sauce and water and pour over meat, spreading evenly.

4. Heat, covered, on SIMMER for 50 to 60 minutes or until tender.

Goulash

2 tablespoons vegetable oil
2 pounds lean beef chuck, cut
into 1-inch cubes
1 medium-sized onion, chopped
1 (8-ounce) can tomato sauce
1 cup water
2 tablespoons vinegar
2 tablespoons Worcestershire
sauce
1 tablespoon sugar
1 tablespoon paprika
1 teaspoon salt
⅛ teaspoon pepper
½ teaspoon garlic powder
2 bay leaves

Serves 5 to 6

1. Heat oil in a skillet on a conventional surface unit. Brown meat on all sides.

2. While browning the meat, heat onion, covered, in a deep, 2½-quart, heat-resistant, non-metallic casserole on FULL POWER 3 minutes or until tender.

3. Add browned beef and remaining ingredients to onions. Heat, covered, on SIMMER for 45 minutes or until beef is tender. Stir occasionally.

4. Serve over hot cooked noodles.

Baked Pork Chops

4 center cut pork chops (¾" to
1" thick) about 1½ lbs.
Thyme
Pepper
Worcestershire sauce

Serves 4

1. Place pork chops in a heat-resistant, non-metallic baking dish.

2. Sprinkle with seasonings.

3. Heat, covered, on SIMMER for 10 to 12 minutes.

4. Turn pork chops over. Sprinkle with seasonings and heat, covered, on SIMMER an additional 12 minutes.

Pork should always be cooked until well-done.

Beef Ragout

2 medium-sized onions, thinly
sliced
1 medium-sized green pepper,
thinly sliced
1 tablespoon vegetable oil
2½ pounds beef chuck, cut into
1-inch cubes
2 tablespoons vegetable oil
8 small new potatoes, peeled
and quartered
1 (17-ounce) can stewed
tomatoes, undrained
1 (6-ounce) can tomato paste
1 (10¾-ounce) can beef broth
2 tablespoons flour (optional)
¼ cup water (optional)

Serves 6 to 8

1. Heat onions, green pepper and the 1 tablespoon of oil in a deep 3-quart, heat-resistant, non-metallic casserole on FULL POWER 3 minutes or until vegetables are tender.

2. While vegetables are heating, brown the chuck in the 2 tablespoons of oil in a skillet on top of a conventional surface unit.

3. Add browned meat and potatoes to onion mixture.

4. Mash stewed tomatoes and add to meat mixture. Stir to thoroughly combine.

5. In a small bowl, mix tomato paste and beef broth until thoroughly combined. Add to other ingredients.

6. Heat, covered, on SIMMER for 25 minutes.

7. Stir casserole and continue to heat, on SIMMER for an additional 25 minutes.

8. If a thicker gravy is desired, combine flour and water in a small bowl. Add flour mixture to gravy and heat an additional 5 minutes in the Microwave Oven on FULL POWER.

Sweet And Sour Pork

6 center cut pork chops, cut
into bite-size pieces
⅔ cup Teriyaki sauce
1 (8-ounce) can pineapple
chunks in own juice,
undrained
3 to 4 tablespoons sweet and
sour sauce
1 to 2 teaspoons firmly packed
brown sugar
2 medium-sized green peppers,
cut into cubes
1 teaspoon cornstarch (optional)

Serves 4

1. Place pork and Teriyaki sauce in a deep, 2 quart, heat-resistant, non-metallic casserole dish and marinate overnight.

2. Remove meat from Teriyaki sauce, reserving any remaining sauce. Brown meat in a skillet on a conventional surface unit.

3. Add pineapple, sweet and sour sauce, brown sugar and green pepper to reserved Teriyaki sauce.

4. Add browned meat to Teriyaki sauce mixture and heat, covered, on SIMMER for 25 minutes, or until meat is tender. Stir occasionally.

5. If desired, the sauce may be thickened by making a paste of the cornstarch plus some of the liquid. Return the paste to the casserole and heat, uncovered, on FULL POWER for 2 to 3 minutes or until the sauce is thickened.

6. Serve over rice.

21

Short Ribs In Beer

3 pounds beef short ribs, cut into 3-inch sections
2 stalks celery, thinly sliced
1 medium-sized onion, thinly sliced
1 bay leaf
½ teaspoon salt
¼ teaspoon garlic salt
⅛ teaspoon pepper
1 cup beer or ale

Serves 4 to 6

1. Place all ingredients in a deep, 3-quart, heat-resistant, non-metallic casserole.

2. Heat, tightly covered, on SIMMER for 25 minutes.

3. Stir and heat an additional 25 minutes on SIMMER or until meat is tender.

Corned Beef And Cabbage

3 pounds corned beef brisket
Water
1 clove garlic, peeled
1 medium-sized onion, quartered
2 whole cloves
2 bay leaves
1 small head of cabbage, cut into wedges
2 medium-sized carrots, peeled and cut up

Serves 4 to 6

1. Place corned beef and water to cover in a deep, 3-quart, heat-resistant, non-metallic casserole.

2. Add garlic, onion, cloves and bay leaves. Heat, tightly covered, on FULL POWER for 10 minutes.

3. Add remaining ingredients. Heat, covered, on SIMMER for 75 minutes or until meat and vegetables are tender.

Beef Supreme

2 tablespoons butter or margarine
1 medium-sized onion, chopped
¼ cup flour
¾ teaspoon salt
¼ teaspoon pepper
2 pounds chuck steak, cut into 1-inch cubes
2 tablespoons butter or margarine
1 (10¾-ounce) can cream of celery soup
1 (10¾-ounce) can cream of mushroom soup
1 tablespoon Worcestershire sauce
3 medium-sized potatoes, peeled and diced
3 medium-sized carrots, thinly sliced

Serves 4 to 6

1. Heat the 2 tablespoons butter in a deep, 2½-quart, heat-resistant, non-metallic casserole on FULL POWER 30 seconds or until melted.

2. Add onion and heat, uncovered, in Microwave Oven on FULL POWER 2 to 3 minutes or until onion is tender.

3. Place flour, salt and pepper in a plastic bag. Shake steak cubes in flour mixture until well coated.

4. On a conventional surface unit, melt the additional 2 tablespoons butter. Brown steak cubes on all sides in the melted butter.

5. Transfer the browned steak cubes to the sautéed onions and add remaining ingredients.

6. Heat, covered, on SIMMER for 75 minutes or until meat and vegetables are tender. Stir occasionally during cooking.

Individual Round Steak Roasts

4 slices raw bacon, diced
1 medium-sized onion, chopped
1½ cups herb and cheese seasoned croutons
1 tablespoon dried parsley flakes
2 pounds (4 steaks) thinly sliced round steak, pounded
½ teaspoon seasoned salt
⅛ teaspoon pepper
1 cup beef bouillon
1 (8-ounce) can tomato sauce with mushroom bits

Serves 4

1. In a small, heat-resistant, non-metallic mixing bowl, heat bacon and onion on FULL POWER 4 to 5 minutes or until onion is tender and bacon is cooked. Bacon will not be crisp.

2. Add croutons and parsley flakes to bacon. Toss to combine.

3. Season round steaks with seasoned salt and pepper.

4. Spread some of bacon mixture on each of the four steaks. Roll as for jelly roll and fasten with toothpicks.

5. Arrange steak rolls in a deep, 2-quart, heat-resistant, non-metallic casserole. Pour bouillon over steak rolls and heat, covered, on SIMMER for 15 minutes.

6. Turn steak rolls over. Spoon tomato sauce on top of each roll. Heat, covered, on SIMMER for 15 minutes or until steak rolls are tender.

Beef With Peppers And Tomatoes

½ cup soy sauce
2 tablespoons water
2 teaspoons sherry
1 tablespoon cornstarch
½ teaspoon garlic powder
2 pounds flank steak
6 tablespoons vegetable oil
3 cups diced green pepper
½ teaspoon salt
⅛ teaspoon pepper
4 tomatoes, each cut into 8 wedges
Hot cooked rice

Serves 6

1. In a small bowl, combine soy sauce, water, sherry, cornstarch and garlic powder. Stir until well blended.

2. Cut steak into thin slices. Add to soy sauce mixture. Stir to coat all pieces with the sauce.

3. Place oil, green pepper, salt and pepper in a deep, 2-quart, heat-resistant, non-metallic casserole. Heat, uncovered, on FULL POWER 6 to 8 minutes or until peppers are almost tender.

4. Add meat-soy sauce mixture to green peppers and heat, tightly covered, on SIMMER for 22 minutes.

5. Add tomato wedges and heat, covered, on SIMMER for 8 minutes or until tomatoes are tender.

Sweet And Sour Beef Stew

2 tablespoons vegetable oil
1½ pounds beef stew meat, cut into 1-inch cubes
3 carrots, peeled and thinly sliced on the diagonal
1 medium-sized onion, thinly sliced
1 (8-ounce) can tomato sauce
¼ cup firmly packed dark brown sugar
¼ cup vinegar
1 tablespoon Worcestershire sauce
¼ cup water
1 teaspoon salt

Serves 4

1. Heat oil in a skillet on top of a conventional surface unit. Brown beef on all sides.

2. Place browned beef in a deep, 2½-quart, heat-resistant, non-metallic casserole. Add remaining ingredients and heat, tightly covered, on SIMMER for 60 minutes, or until meat and vegetables are tender. Stir occasionally.

3. Serve over cooked noodles if desired. May be garnished with carrot curls and parsley.

Italian Spaghetti Sauce

1 pound lean ground beef
1 large onion, chopped
2 teaspoons dried parsley flakes
½ teaspoon dried basil leaves
1 teaspoon salt
⅛ teaspoon pepper
2 teaspoons sugar
1 (2-pound, 3-ounce) can tomato bits
1 (15-ounce) can tomato sauce
1 (6-ounce) can tomato paste
2 bay leaves

Makes 2 quarts

1. Crumble ground beef into a deep, 3-quart, heat-resistant, non-metallic casserole. Add onion, parsley flakes, basil, salt, pepper and sugar.

2. Heat, uncovered, on FULL POWER 5 minutes or until browned. Stir occasionally to break up pieces.

3. Add tomato bits, tomato sauce and tomato paste to browned meat. Stir to thoroughly combine. Add bay leaves.

4. Heat meat-tomato mixture, covered, on SIMMER for 50 to 60 minutes. Stir occasionally during cooking.

5. Remove bay leaves before serving.

Macaroni And Cheese Casserole

1 cup elbow macaroni
2 tablespoons flour
1 tablespoon instant minced onion
¼ teaspoon salt
1½ cups milk
¼ cup water
1 teaspoon butter or margarine
¼ teaspoon dry mustard
Dash cayenne pepper
1 cup shredded sharp Cheddar cheese

Serves 4 (½ cup portions)

1. In a deep, 2-quart, heat-resistant, non-metallic casserole, combine all ingredients except the cheese.

2. Heat, covered, on SIMMER for 20 minutes or until macaroni is tender. Stir occasionally.

3. Stir in shredded cheese until completely melted. Allow to stand 3 to 5 minutes before serving.

Split Pea Soup

Water
1 pound green or yellow split peas
3 carrots, peeled and thinly sliced
2 medium-sized onions, thinly sliced
1 clove garlic, peeled and crushed
1 teaspoon salt
¼ teaspoon pepper

Makes 2 quarts

1. Wash and drain split peas.

2. Place split peas in a deep, 2½-quart, heat-resistant, non-metallic casserole. Add 1 cup of hot tap water and heat on FULL POWER for 3 minutes.

3. Drain water. Add 1-quart of hot tap water to peas. Add remaining ingredients. Heat, tightly covered, on SIMMER for 50 minutes or until peas are easily mashed with a fork.

4. Press peas and liquid through a food mill or sieve. Soup may also be put in a blender.

5. Adjust seasoning to taste. Serving temperature should be 160° F.

Lamb Curry

2 tablespoons flour
1 teaspoon salt
½ teaspoon garlic salt
2 pounds boneless lamb, cut into 1-inch cubes
2 tablespoons butter or margarine
2 medium-sized onions, chopped
2 medium-sized baking apples, peeled and diced
1 to 1½ tablespoons curry powder
½ to 1 tablespoon sugar
¾ cup hot tap water
Hot rice
Chutney

Serves 4 to 6

1. Combine the flour, salt and garlic salt in a plastic bag.

2. Shake lamb in flour mixture until well coated.

3. Melt the butter in a skillet on a conventional surface unit. Brown lamb on all sides.

4. While lamb is browning, place onions, apples, curry and sugar in a deep, 2½ quart, heat-resistant, non-metallic casserole. Heat, covered, on FULL POWER for 4 to 5 minutes, or until onion is almost tender. Stir once during cooking time.

5. Add the lamb and water to the onion mixture. Heat, uncovered, on SIMMER for 30 minutes or until lamb is tender. Stir once during cooking time.

6. Serve over hot rice with chutney.

Variations: Beef, chicken, or shellfish could be substituted for the lamb. It is not necessary to pre-brown the shellfish. Therefore, steps 1 through 3 should be eliminated.

Lamb And Rice Casserole

1 tablespoon olive oil
1½ pounds lamb, cut into 1-inch cubes
1 medium-sized onion, thinly sliced
½ cup chopped green pepper
1 tablespoon olive oil
1 cup uncooked long grain rice
½ teaspoon dried oregano leaves
¼ teaspoon dried basil leaves
¼ teaspoon paprika
1½ teaspoons salt
⅛ teaspoon pepper
2 beef bouillon cubes
2 cups water
1 (8-ounce) can tomato sauce

Serves 6

1. Heat the 1 tablespoon olive oil in a skillet over moderately high heat on a conventional surface unit. Add meat cubes and cook until lightly browned on all sides.

2. While meat is browning, in a deep, 2½-quart, heat-resistant, non-metallic casserole dish, heat onion slices and green pepper in the 1 tablespoon olive oil in Microwave Oven on FULL POWER for 4 to 5 minutes or until vegetables are tender. Stir once during cooking period.

3. Add browned lamb cubes, rice, oregano, basil, paprika, salt and pepper to onion mixture. Mix thoroughly.

4. In a 4-cup, heat-resistant, non-metallic measuring cup, combine the bouillon cubes and water and heat on FULL POWER for 4 to 5 minutes or until boiling. Stir to dissolve bouillon cubes.

5. Add tomato sauce to bouillon. Pour over meat mixture in casserole, cover, and heat on SIMMER for 35 minutes or until meat is tender.

6. Any excess liquid will be absorbed if casserole is allowed to stand 5 to 10 minutes before serving.

Variations: Any tender cut of beef or pork can be substituted for lamb.

Cheese Soufflé

5 egg whites
Butter or margarine
1 tablespoon grated Parmesan
** cheese**
3 tablespoons butter or
** margarine**
2 tablespoons flour
¼ teaspoon dry mustard
½ teaspoon salt
⅛ teaspoon pepper
Dash cayenne pepper
1 cup milk
1 cup shredded sharp Cheddar
** cheese**
¼ teaspoon cream of tartar
4 egg yolks
2 tablespoons shredded sharp
** Cheddar cheese**

Serves 4

1. Bring egg whites to room temperature, about one hour.

2. Butter a 1½-quart, heat-resistant, non-metallic soufflé dish or a 1½-quart, heat-resistant, non-metallic, straight-sided casserole and sprinkle with the Parmesan cheese.

3. Place the 3 tablespoons butter, flour, mustard, salt, pepper and cayenne in a large, heat-resistant, non-metallic mixing bowl and heat, uncovered, 1 minute on FULL POWER, or until butter is melted.

4. Blend flour and seasonings into melted butter. Gradually add milk, stirring until smooth. Heat sauce mixture, uncovered, on ROAST for 4 minutes or until thickened and smooth. Stir occasionally. Add the 1 cup shredded Cheddar cheese, stirring to mix. Heat on ROAST for 1 additional minute or until cheese is melted. Stir.

5. While making the sauce, beat egg whites with cream of tartar until stiff, but not dry. Set aside.

6. Beat egg yolks until thick and lemon colored. Add egg yolks gradually to sauce mixture. Beat well.

7. Mix about ¼ of the beaten egg whites with the sauce mixture. Work quickly and lightly, taking care not to break down the egg whites.

8. Fold remaining egg whites into sauce mixture.

9. Carefully spoon soufflé mixture into the prepared soufflé dish. Sprinkle the remaining 2 tablespoons of shredded cheese on top of the soufflé mixture.

10. Place the soufflé on the center of the turntable in the Microwave Oven and heat, uncovered, on DEFROST for 15 minutes or until a knife inserted in the center of the soufflé comes out clean.

11. Serve immediately. The volume of the soufflé will decrease with prolonged standing.

Variations: Swiss cheese, Monterey Jack, Tilsit or a combination of cheeses may be substituted for the Cheddar cheese.

Spinach Soufflé

4 egg whites
Butter or margarine
1 tablespoon grated Parmesan cheese
1 (10-ounce) package frozen chopped spinach
3 tablespoons butter or margarine
3 tablespoons flour
1 teaspoon salt
⅛ teaspoon pepper
⅛ teaspoon nutmeg
1 cup milk
1 teaspoon lemon juice
¼ teaspoon cream of tartar
4 egg yolks

Serves 4 to 6

1. Bring egg whites to room temperature, about one hour.

2. Butter a 1½-quart, heat-resistant, non-metallic soufflé dish or a 1½-quart, heat-resistant, non-metallic, straight-sided casserole dish and sprinkle with Parmesan cheese. Set aside.

3. Heat spinach, in store wrapping, on FULL POWER 5 minutes or until completely thawed. Press all moisture out of spinach.

4. Place the 3 tablespoons butter, the flour, salt, pepper and nutmeg in a large, heat-resistant, non-metallic mixing bowl, and heat, uncovered, on FULL POWER 1 minute or until butter is melted.

5. Blend flour and seasonings into melted butter. Gradually add milk, stirring until smooth. Heat sauce mixture, uncovered, on ROAST for 4 minutes or until thickened and smooth. Stir occasionally to blend. Add the well-drained spinach and the lemon juice.

6. While making the sauce, beat the egg whites with cream of tartar until stiff, but not dry. Set aside.

7. Beat egg yolks until thick and lemon colored. Add egg yolks gradually to sauce mixture. Beat well.

8. Mix about ¼ of the beaten egg whites with the sauce mixture. Work quickly and lightly, taking care not to break down the egg whites.

9. Fold remaining egg whites into sauce mixture.

10. Carefully spoon the soufflé mixture into the prepared soufflé dish.

11. Place the souffle on the center of the turntable in the Microwave Oven and heat, uncovered, on DEFROST for 15 minutes or until a knife inserted in the center of the soufflé comes out clean.

12. Serve immediately. The volume of the soufflé will decrease with prolonged standing.

Variations: Finely chopped broccoli or asparagus may be substituted for the spinach. The soufflé may be served with a cheese or curried sauce.

Rice

1 cup converted long grain rice
2 cups hot water
½ teaspoon salt
**1 tablespoon butter or
  margarine (optional)**

Serves 2 to 3

1. In a deep, 1½-quart, heat-resistant, non-metallic casserole, combine all ingredients. Heat, tightly covered, on SIMMER for 20 minutes or until most of the water is absorbed.

2. Allow rice to stand, at room temperature, an additional 5 to 10 minutes. Fluff with a fork before serving.

For additional servings: Use twice as much water as rice and heat according to chart below:

1½ cups rice	25 minutes on SIMMER	Serves 5 to 6
2 cups rice	30 minutes on SIMMER	Serves 7 to 8

Note: Since rice is a dehydrated product, the majority of the cooking time is for the water to be absorbed by the rice. The time saved by microwave cooking may not be as great as with some other food products. However, this method of cooking rice will produce good textured rice every time without sticking or scorching.

Defrosting

Defrosting Information

Remember the days you came home from work or shopping only to discover you had forgotten to take the roast out of the freezer to thaw for dinner? Or the times unexpected company has arrived just in time for dinner–but dinner happened to have been in the freezer? The convenience of being able to defrost frozen meats, casseroles, vegetables, desserts and other foods quickly and easily is one of the biggest advantages of your new Sharp Microwave Oven. Thawing takes a fraction of the time normally required. Foods can be packaged for the freezer in serving sizes that best suit your family's eating habits, and extra portions or leftovers can be frozen for later use.

The turnable feature of your Carousel Microwave Oven eliminates the need to rotate or reposition the dish of food during defrosting. However, it will occasionally be necessary to rearrange and/or turn the food over to obtain the most even defrosting.

When defrosting in a Microwave Oven, the microwaves first come into contact with the outer portion of the frozen surface, and the heat is then conducted to the inner portion of the food.

Alternating the use of microwave energy with standing or rest periods prevents the surface from cooking before the inner portion is thawed. The Variable Cooking Control on your Sharp Microwave Oven automatically cycles the power on and off at varying intervals to give you control over the rate of both defrosting and cooking. In general, most foods should be thawed on DEFROST. Large, dense cuts of meat, unevenly shaped foods and quantities of casseroles are defrosted at this setting to avoid any heating of the outside before the interior is thawed.

Some foods, such as poultry, frozen bread, cakes and pastries, small quantities of casseroles and foods with a substantial amount of liquid or sauce are defrosted on the SIMMER setting. Some larger, evenly shaped cuts of meat may be started on SIMMER and reduced to the DEFROST setting if the outside begins to heat.

Frozen vegetables are defrosted and heated simultaneously on the FULL POWER setting.

On the following pages you will find information and charts designed to serve as a guide for defrosting.

1. Some foods, such as vegetables and pastries, can be cooked directly from the frozen state, while others such as fish can be cooked from the partially frozen state.

2. Large dense pieces of meat and poultry should be completely thawed before beginning the actual cooking. For best results, remove from the Microwave Oven while still cool to the touch and icy in the center. Allow them to stand at room temperature for a period of time to complete thawing. By using this process you avoid cooking of thinner portions or excessive heating of the outside before the interior is defrosted.

3. Foods should be turned over (top to bottom) once during defrosting to obtain the most even results. Frozen vegetables and individual portions of casseroles can be stirred to insure the most uniform defrosting and heating.

4. Meat, fish, poultry, casseroles and vegetables should all be covered during defrosting. Rolls may be wrapped in paper towelling. Frozen cakes and pies should be left uncovered.
   Foods should be removed from their package, separated and arranged in a single layer at the earliest point possible during defrosting.

5. If foods begin to thaw unevenly or if "hot spots" develop (some areas of the food may thaw faster than others), small pieces of aluminum foil may be used to reflect the microwaves away from the part which is beginning to cook. Simply cover this area with a small piece of foil and continue defrosting.

6. A meat thermometer may be used in a large cut of meat to determine if the interior is still frozen.

Only meat thermometers designed specifically for use in your Sharp Microwave Oven may be used in the oven while it is operating. If the thermometer registers 40° F after the specified standing time, the meat is ready to cook.

Hints For Defrosting

Frozen foods can be grouped according to the ease with which they are defrosted. Defrosting times will vary according to shape of frozen food or package, density, starting temperature and total weight or volume. See Defrosting Chart for specific information.

3

Type of Food	Variable Cooking Control Setting	General Hints
Breads, Pastries, Cakes, Cookies	SIMMER	Defrost quickly and easily. Breads and pastries should be wrapped or covered with paper toweling or napkins. Smaller volumes may be defrosted and heated simultaneously on SIMMER. Whole cakes will need a standing time to equalize temperature.
Frozen Fruits	DEFROST	Quick and easy to defrost; time depends on desired serving temperature. DEFROST setting allows thawing without heating. Allow to stand at room temperature before serving.
Precooked Frozen Foods (casseroles, soups, leftovers)	SIMMER or DEFROST	Larger quantities (i.e. one quart) are thawed on the DEFROST setting. Smaller portions may be defrosted and heated simultaneously on SIMMER, or you may wish to defrost on SIMMER and then heat on ROAST. Individual portions may be thawed and heated on the ROAST setting.
Hamburger Patties, Ground Meat, Steaks, Chops, Ribs, Chicken Pieces	DEFROST	By using the DEFROST setting for these foods, you get even thawing without heating the edges. Most require about 7-8 minutes per pound, followed by a standing time to equalize temperatures and complete defrosting. Turn over once during defrosting and separate when possible.
Roasts	SIMMER or DEFROST	Larger, denser meats such as roasts require more attention and longer standing times than chops or smaller pieces. Partially defrost in the Microwave Oven and allow for standing time. Large roasts can be started on SIMMER and reduced to DEFROST if heating begins.
Whole Poultry	SIMMER or ROAST	Whole Poultry should be partially defrosted on SIMMER or ROAST. Less heating occurs at these higher settings than when DEFROST is used. If the wings and ends of drumsticks begin to cook, shield with aluminum foil. Poultry will still be icy when removed from the oven and should be allowed to stand at room temperature to completely thaw. Standing times are extremely important for whole poultry. See defrosting chart.
Fish	SIMMER or DEFROST	Fish defrosts quickly in the Microwave Oven. Whole fish fillets are thawed on DEFROST. Blocks of fish which are evenly shaped are thawed on SIMMER. Fish should be partially defrosted and allowed to stand at room temperature to complete thawing, or it may be cooked from the slightly frozen state.

Defrosting Chart

Food	Approx. Time	Variable Control	Procedure	Standing Time
Ground Beef	8 min./lb.	DEFROST	Leave wrapped in freezer wrapping. Turn over after 4 minutes. At end of 8 minutes, unwrap and break meat apart. If center is still frozen, defrost frozen portion one minute longer. If defrosting more than one pound, break defrosted portion off after 8 minutes and continue until thawed.	5 minutes
Hamburger Patties	8-9 min./lb.	DEFROST	Thaw in freezer wrapping. Turn after half of thawing time. Separate as soon as possible.	5-10 minutes
Steak ¾" thick	7-8 min./lb.	DEFROST	Thaw in freezer wrapping. Turn over after half of thawing time. Separate as soon as possible.	5 minutes
Chops	8 min./lb.	DEFROST	Thaw in freezer wrapping. Turn over after half of defrosting time. Separate as soon as possible.	5 minutes
Ribs	6 min./lb.	DEFROST	Thaw in freezer wrapping. Separate as soon as possible and turn over.	5 minutes
Roasts (Beef, Pork, Veal, Lamb)	8-10 min./lb.	DEFROST	Begin defrosting in freezer wrapping. Turn over after half of defrosting time or at the end of the first 15 minutes defrosting time. Complete defrosting covered with plastic wrap. Standing times are extremely important for larger cuts of meat such as roasts. Large roasts may be started on the SIMMER setting and reduced to DEFROST if heating begins.	45-60 minutes
Chicken Pieces	8 min./lb.	DEFROST	Defrost in freezer wrap or covered with plastic wrap. After half of defrosting time, unwrap chicken pieces and separate. Finish defrosting covered with plastic wrap.	10-15 minutes
Whole Chicken	4 min./lb.	SIMMER	Begin defrosting in freezer wrap. Unwrap and turn over after half of defrosting time. Finish defrosting covered with plastic wrap. The tips of legs or wings may need to be covered with small pieces of aluminum foil to prevent heating of thin parts. Standing times are very important for whole poultry.	30-45 minutes
Whole Turkey 12-16 lbs.		ROAST	Begin defrosting in freezer wrapping. Defrost on ROAST for 15 minutes. Allow to stand for 15 minutes. Turn over and unwrap. Cover with plastic wrap. Defrost for 10 to 15 minutes on ROAST. Allow to stand 1 to 1½ hours. If not completely defrosted, return to Microwave Oven on ROAST for 10 minutes, followed by additional standing time to equalize temperature and complete defrosting. Defrosting and standing times should be alternated to prevent excessive heating of outside of turkey.	1-2 hours

Food	Approx. Time	Variable Control	Procedure	Standing Time
Whole Turkey, continued			Remove neck and giblets as soon as possible. It may be necessary to shield the tips of legs or wings with small pieces of aluminum foil to prevent cooking of these thin parts.	
Turkey Parts	6-7 min./lb.	DEFROST	Defrost in freezer wrap. After half of defrosting time, unwrap, separate and turn over. Finish defrosting covered with clear plastic wrap. Stand.	10-15 minutes
Cornish Game Hens	8 min./lb.	DEFROST	Defrost in freezer package. Turn over after half of defrosting time. Remove neck and giblets as soon as possible. After unwrapping, cover with plastic wrap.	10-15 minutes
Turkey Breast		ROAST	Begin defrosting in freezer wrapping. Defrost on ROAST for 15 minutes, turning over after first 8 minutes. Stand 15 minutes. Unwrap. Defrost 5 additional minutes on ROAST. Allow to stand for 1 hour. If not completely thawed, defrost 5 additional minutes on ROAST. Stand.	1 hour
Fish Fillets	10 min./lb.	DEFROST	Defrost in package. Break apart as soon as possible and finish thawing covered with clear plastic wrap. Large blocks of frozen fish which are evenly shaped may be thawed on SIMMER.	5-10 minutes
Frozen Fruit 12 - 16 oz.	5 min.	DEFROST	Defrost 5 minutes or until desired serving temperature is reached. Frozen fruit packaged in a pouch will defrost in less time. Slit pouch before placing in Microwave Oven.	none
Frozen Layer Cake 17 oz.	1¼ min.	SIMMER	Defrost in freezer package for 1 minute, 15 seconds. Allow to stand for a few minutes to equalize internal temperature.	5 minutes
Frozen Fruit Pie 26 oz.	4-5 min.	DEFROST	Transfer from metal pan to glass pie plate. Defrost in Microwave Oven for 4 to 5 minutes.	5 minutes
Frozen Cream Pie 16 oz.	1¼ min.	DEFROST	Transfer from metal pan to glass pie or serving plate.	5 minutes
Frozen Casseroles **1 cup** **2 cups** **4 cups**	4 min. 6 min. 10 min.	ROAST SIMMER DEFROST	Defrost in freezer container. Stir prior to heating. Defrost in freezer container. Stir prior to heating. Defrost in freezer container. Allow to stand prior to heating.	5 minutes

Pictured: Easter Dinner: Fresh Artichokes with Mustard Sauce, Crown Roast of Lamb with Corn Bread Stuffing, Tomatoes Parmesan, Asparagus Salad, Lemon Chiffon Pie.

Dinner

Lunch

Breakfast

MEAL PLANNING HINTS

Now that you have your new Microwave Oven, you'll be amazed at how fast and simple meal planning can be. Read this chapter carefully since it will give you some important hints on how to cook an _entire_ meal in your Microwave Oven. In the beginning you may find that meals require a little more planning time; however, you'll soon find that the cooking time saved is well worth the extra planning.

When planning a meal, first read through the menu, each recipe and the directions for preparing the meal. Then prepare the ingredients and utensils needed to cook the meal.

Until you are completely at ease with your new Microwave Oven, you might want to allow yourself a little extra time in preparing the meal. Remember, with your Microwave Oven foods can be reheated without losing their fresh cooked taste. Remember, too, that it is always better to undercook foods rather than overcook them.

Your Microwave Oven should be used to compliment or supplement the other appliances in your kitchen. While entire meals can be cooked in your Microwave Oven, there may be occasions when using both your Microwave Oven and other cooking appliances will save you the most time and energy.

37

EASTER DINNER

Fresh Artichokes with Mustard Sauce*
Crown Roast of Lamb with Corn Bread Stuffing*
Tomatoes Parmesan*
Asparagus Salad*
Lemon Chiffon Pie*

Fresh Artichokes With Mustard Sauce

4 large globe artichokes
1 cup water
2 tablespoons vinegar
1 tablespoon whole pickling
**   spices**
1 cup prepared brown mustard
1 (⅝-ounce) package Italian
**   salad dressing mix**
2 tablespoons vinegar or dry
**   white wine**
Few drops Tabasco sauce
1 teaspoon Worcestershire sauce

Serves 8

1. Wash artichokes carefully and drain. Slice off upper tip of each artichoke with a sharp knife. With kitchen shears, trim off the thorny ends of the leaves. The stems should be cut off even with the base of the artichoke.

2. Combine water, vinegar and pickling spices in a deep, 3-quart, heat-resistant, non-metallic casserole.

3. Heat, uncovered, on FULL POWER 5 minutes or until mixture comes to a boil.

4. Place artichokes upright in casserole.

5. Heat, covered, on FULL POWER 12 to 15 minutes.

6. Cook until bases are tender when pierced with a fork and lower leaves pull away easily. Set aside.

7. In a small bowl combine remaining ingredients.

8. If desired, heat mustard sauce, uncovered, on FULL POWER 1½ minutes or until heated through.

9. Dip leaves into mustard sauce.

Tip: If desired, the leaves may be removed and arranged on a platter before serving. The fuzzy choke should be removed and the heart of the artichoke cut for serving.

Tomatoes Parmesan

4 large tomatoes
¼ cup butter or margarine
½ cup grated Parmesan cheese
¼ cup finely chopped parsley
1 tablespoon dried oregano
**   leaves**

1. Wash tomatoes and pat dry. Cut tomatoes in half crosswise.

   Place cut-side-up in a shallow, heat-resistant, non-metallic baking dish.

2. Dot each tomato half with about ½ tablespoon butter.

3. In a small bowl, combine remaining ingredients. Top each tomato half with some of the cheese mixture. Heat, uncovered, on FULL POWER 5 to 6 minutes, or until tomatoes are soft and topping begins to melt. Do not overcook as tomatoes will become too soft.

Variation: If desired, dry seasoned bread crumbs may be substituted for all or part of the Parmesan cheese.

□ Prepare Lemon Chiffon Pie in advance so it has time to chill before serving.
□ Prepare Asparagus Salad in advance and allow to chill before serving.
□ Prepare Artichokes up to Step 5.
□ About 1½ hours before serving time, prepare Crown Roast of Lamb with Corn Bread Stuffing.
□ While the Crown Roast is cooking, prepare Mustard Sauce and Tomatoes Parmesan up to Step 6.
□ While the Crown Roast is standing at room temperature, cook Artichokes.
□ Just before serving time, cook Tomatoes Parmesan.

Crown Roast Of Lamb With Corn Bread Stuffing

165°F

4

1 (4 to 5 pound) shaped and tied crown roast of lamb, with bone tips Frenched and trimmings ground
½ cup butter or margarine
½ cup finely chopped onion
¾ cup finely chopped celery
1 teaspoon salt
¼ teaspoon pepper
1 teaspoon sage
⅛ teaspoon garlic powder
2 cups crumbled corn bread, freshly prepared

Serves 8

1. Remove ground lamb from crown roast and crumble it into a medium-sized, heat-resistant, non-metallic bowl.

2. Heat, uncovered, on ROAST for 5 to 6 minutes, stirring frequently to break up meat. Drain fat and set meat aside.

3. In a small, heat-resistant, non-metallic bowl, melt butter on FULL POWER 1 minute.

4. Add onion and celery and heat, uncovered, on FULL POWER 5 minutes or until vegetables are tender.

5. Stir in salt, pepper, sage and garlic powder.

6. Add vegetable mixture and crumbled corn bread to cooked lamb. Toss to combine thoroughly.

7. Place roast in a shallow, heat-resistant, non-metallic baking dish. Spoon stuffing into center of crown roast.

8. Heat, uncovered, on ROAST for 40 minutes or until microwave thermometer or probe inserted in the meat between two ribs registers 165°F. DO NOT PLACE CONVENTIONAL THERMOMETER IN MICROWAVE OVEN.

9. Cover meat with aluminum foil and allow to stand at room temperature 20 to 30 minutes or until internal temperature reaches 175° to 180°F.

10. If necessary or desired, crown roast may be returned to Microwave Oven for longer cooking. DO NOT PLACE ALUMINUM FOIL OR CONVENTIONAL THERMOMETER IN MICROWAVE OVEN.

11. Place paper frills on bone tips before serving.

Asparagus Salad

3 (17-ounce) cans whole green asparagus, vertically packed
Lettuce leaves
Homemade mayonnaise, or commercial mayonnaise thinned with light cream
2 hard cooked eggs, sieved

Serves 8

1. Drain asparagus, trying to keep spears whole.

2. Place lettuce leaves on 8 salad plates and arrange asparagus on lettuce leaves, or asparagus may be placed in a vegetable bowl.

3. Place a spoonful of mayonnaise over asparagus.

4. Garnish with hard cooked egg.

5. Chill before serving.

Tip: Eggs can be baked in the Microwave Oven for use as a garnish. See page 52 for directions.

Lemon Chiffon Pie

1 envelope unflavored gelatin
½ cup sugar
½ teaspoon salt
1 (16-ounce) can sliced peaches, undrained
Water
1 (6-ounce) can frozen lemonade concentrate, undiluted
1 cup icy cold evaporated milk, whipped
1 (10-inch) graham cracker crust baked in a heat-resistant, non-metallic pie plate

Serves 8 to 10

1. In a 1½-quart, heat-resistant, non-metallic bowl, mix gelatin, sugar and salt.

2. Drain liquid from peaches into a glass measuring cup and add enough water to make ¾ cup. Add peach liquid mixture to gelatin mixture.

3. Heat gelatin mixture on ROAST for 3 minutes or until gelatin is dissolved. Stir once.

4. Add undiluted lemonade concentrate to hot gelatin mixture.

5. Chill in refrigerator until mixture mounds slightly when dropped from a spoon.

6. While lemonade mixture is chilling, whip chilled evaporated milk until stiff peaks form.

7. Fold whipped evaporated milk into chilled gelatin mixture.

8. Arrange peach slices on bottom of graham cracker crust reserving slices to garnish the top of the pie.

9. Pour mixture into pie crust.

10. Chill three hours or until firm. Garnish top of pie with peach slices just before serving.

Note: See Cakes and Pies Chapter for directions for graham cracker crust.

RECIPE NOTES

_____

_____

_____

_____

_____

_____

_____

_____

_____

_____

_____

_____

_____

_____

_____

_____

_____

_____

_____

_____

THANKSGIVING DINNER

Roast Turkey with Gravy*
Stuffin' Muffins*
Sweet Potato Casserole*
Fresh Broccoli*
Acorn Squash with Cranberry Filling*
Pumpkin Pie*

Stuffin' Muffins

½ cup butter or margarine
½ cup finely chopped onion
½ cup finely chopped celery
1 (4-ounce) can mushroom stems
  and pieces, drained
1 teaspoon sage
1 cup chicken broth
1 (8-ounce) package seasoned
  bread stuffing
Butter or margarine

Serves 8

1. In a medium-sized, heat-resistant, non-metallic bowl melt the ½ cup butter on FULL POWER 1 minute.

2. Add onion, celery and mushrooms and heat, uncovered, on FULL POWER 5 minutes or until vegetables are tender.

3. Sprinkle sage over vegetable mixture.

4. Add chicken broth and stir to combine.

5. Heat, uncovered, on FULL POWER 3 minutes.

6. Add bread stuffing and toss lightly.

7. Lightly grease 8 small, heat-resistant, non-metallic custard or coffee cups with butter.

8. Divide stuffing among cups.

9. Just before serving, heat, uncovered, on FULL POWER 8 minutes or until heated through.

Sweet Potato Casserole

150°F

2 (16-ounce) cans sweet
  potatoes
1 (14-ounce) can pineapple
  tidbits in unsweetened juice,
  undrained
4 tablespoons butter or
  margarine
4 tablespoons firmly packed
  dark brown sugar
1½ cups miniature marshmallows
Butter or margarine

Serves 8

1. Drain potatoes and discard liquid. Drain pineapple and set pineapple and juice aside.

2. In a small, heat-resistant, non-metallic bowl, melt butter on FULL POWER 30 seconds.

3. Place potatoes in medium-sized bowl and mash with a potato masher or fork.

4. Add melted butter and brown sugar. Stir until well combined.

5. Stir in pineapple juice until desired consistency is reached. Fold in pineapple tidbits and marshmallows.

6. Butter a shallow, 1½-quart, heat-resistant, non-metallic casserole and spoon potato mixture into casserole.

7. Heat, uncovered, on FULL POWER 5 to 6 minutes or until potato mixture is heated through and marshmallows begin to melt.

- Prepare Pumpkin Pie in advance and allow to cool.
- Defrost Turkey, if necessary. Begin several hours ahead of serving time if using your Microwave Oven. See Defrosting Chapter.
- While defrosting Turkey arrange ingredients for remaining recipes.
- Cook Turkey. Prepare remaining recipes up to cooking points.
- While the Turkey is standing at room temperature, cook Acorn Squash with Cranberry Filling.
- Cook Sweet Potato Casserole and keep covered until serving time.
- Cook Stuffin' Muffins and keep them covered until serving time.
- Cook Broccoli either in Microwave Oven or conventionally.
- Prepare Gravy.
- Reheat any parts of dinner that may have cooled.

4

Fresh Broccoli

1½ pounds fresh broccoli, washed and split
¼ cup water

1. Place broccoli and water in a deep, 3-quart, heat-resistant, non-metallic casserole.
2. Heat, covered, on ROAST for 15 to 16 minutes.

Acorn Squash With Cranberry Filling

4 small acorn squash
Salt
8 tablespoons butter or margarine
8 tablespoons honey
1 (16-ounce) can whole-berry cranberry sauce

Serves 8

1. Wash and dry squash. Cut small slit in skin of each squash so that steam can escape.
2. Place squash in Microwave Oven. Heat, uncovered, on FULL POWER 15 minutes or until they feel soft to the touch.
3. Let stand 5 minutes.
4. Cut in half and remove seeds.
5. Place cut-side-up in a shallow, heat-resistant, non-metallic baking dish.
6. Sprinkle with salt. Place 1 tablespoon of butter and 1 tablespoon of honey in each half.
7. Heat, uncovered, on FULL POWER 4 minutes or until butter has melted.
8. With a brush or spoon, spread honey-butter mixture over cut surfaces of squash.
9. Place a spoonful of cranberry sauce in each squash half. If warmed cranberry sauce is desired, return filled squash halves to Microwave Oven and heat on FULL POWER for 6 minutes or until cranberry sauce is hot.

THANKSGIVING DINNER

Pumpkin Pie

2 eggs
½ cup sugar
½ cup firmly packed dark
  brown sugar
1 tablespoon flour
½ teaspoon salt
1 teaspoon cinnamon
¼ teaspoon nutmeg
¼ teaspoon ginger
¼ teaspoon allspice
1 (16-ounce) can cooked
  pumpkin
1 (13-fluid ounce) can
  evaporated milk
1 baked 10-inch pastry shell
  (in a non-metallic pie plate)

Serves 8

1. In a large mixing bowl combine eggs, sugar and brown sugar. Mix well.

2. Add remaining ingredients and beat until smooth and well-blended.

3. Pour pumpkin mixture into pastry shell. Extra filling may be cooked in custard cups.

4. Heat, uncovered, on SIMMER for 5 minutes or until edges begin to set.

5. Carefully move the cooked portions toward the center.

6. Heat, uncovered, on SIMMER for 7 to 9 minutes or until a knife inserted in the center comes out clean. Cool before serving.

Variation: Heat 3 or 4 custard cups of filling, uncovered, on SIMMER for 4 to 5 minutes or until a knife inserted in the center comes out clean.

Roast Turkey With Gravy

170°F

1 (12-pound) turkey
Salt and pepper to taste
6 tablespoons flour
Salt and pepper
Chicken broth

Serves 8 to 10

1. If turkey is frozen it may be defrosted in the Microwave Oven as directed in the Defrosting Chapter, or it may be defrosted according to instructions on package. Turkey should be completely thawed before cooking.

2. Wash turkey and pat it dry. Sprinkle inside cavity with salt and pepper, to taste.

3. Tie legs together. Tie wings and legs to body.

4. Use a microwave trivet or invert a heat-resistant, non-metallic saucer or small casserole cover in a shallow, 10-inch, heat-resistant, non-metallic baking dish. A 10-inch glass pie plate is a good container.

5. Place turkey breast-side-down on the saucer or trivet.

6. Turkey should be cooked 8 minutes per pound on ROAST. Heat, uncovered, for ¾ of cooking time (about 72 minutes).

7. Turn the turkey breast-side-up. Insert temperature probe or microwave thermometer into fleshy portion of the turkey, not touching any bones. Continue cooking for the remaining ¼ of the cooking time (about 24 minutes). Small pieces of aluminum foil may be used for shielding if needed.

44

8. Internal temperature should reach 170°F.

9. If temperature is not 170°F, return turkey to Microwave Oven for an additional few minutes until correct temperature is reached.

10. Let turkey stand covered with aluminum foil at room temperature 20 to 30 minutes to finish cooking. The internal temperature of the turkey should be 180°F after standing.

11. While the turkey is standing at room temperature, prepare the gravy. The turkey should be removed from the roasting pan.

12. Pour the pan drippings into a bowl, leaving the residue in the pan.

13. Allow the fat to rise to the top. Skim off about 6 tablespoons of fat. Reserve pan drippings. (If there is not enough fat, add butter or margarine to make 6 tablespoons total. Discard any excess fat.)

14. Return fat to the baking dish.

15. Blend in flour and salt and pepper, to taste.

16. Heat, uncovered, on FULL POWER 4 minutes or until lightly browned.

17. Measure the remaining pan drippings and add enough chicken broth to make 3 cups.

18. Gradually stir liquid into flour mixture until smooth, scraping the sides of the pan to loosen any particles that stick to the pan.

19. Heat, uncovered, on FULL POWER 14 minutes or until thickened and smooth. Stir occasionally during last half of cooking.

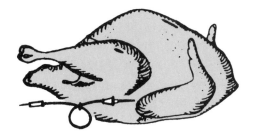

DINNER FOR THE BOSS

Creamed Scallops in Wine Sauce*
(Coquilles St. Jacques)
Shrimp de Jonghe*
Green Peas with Celery and Olives*
Duchess Potatoes*
French Bread
Strawberry Cheesecake*

Creamed Scallops In Wine Sauce (Coquilles St. Jacques)

½ pound frozen scallops
1 tablespoon butter or margarine
1 tablespoon finely chopped onion
1½ teaspoons lemon juice
¼ teaspoon salt
Few leaves dried marjoram, crushed
Dash paprika
6 tablespoons white wine
1 (4-ounce) can mushroom stems and pieces, drained
3 tablespoons butter or margarine
2 tablespoons flour
½ cup heavy cream
1 teaspoon finely chopped parsley

Serves 4

1. If scallops are frozen, partially defrost according to package directions.

2. In a deep, 1½-quart, heat-resistant, non-metallic casserole place the 1 tablespoon butter or margarine and onion. Heat, uncovered, on FULL POWER 1 minute or until onion is tender.

3. Add scallops, lemon juice, salt, marjoram, paprika and wine. Stir to combine. Heat, covered, on FULL POWER 3 minutes.

4. Add mushrooms and heat, covered, on FULL POWER 1 minute or until scallops are tender. Do not overcook scallops as they will become tough.

5. Drain liquid and reserve. Set scallops and liquid aside.

6. Melt the 3 tablespoons of butter or margarine in a small heat-resistant, non-metallic bowl on FULL POWER 30 seconds. Blend in flour.

7. Gradually stir in reserved scallop liquid and cream.

8. Heat, uncovered, on ROAST for 4 minutes or until thickened and smooth. Stir in parsley.

9. Combine reserved scallop mixture and sauce. Spoon mixture into 4 serving shells or small non-metallic ramekins.

10. Heat, uncovered, on ROAST for 5 minutes. If browning is desired, place under broiler of conventional oven several minutes or until lightly browned.

Green Peas With Celery and Ripe Olives

2 cups celery, sliced on an angle
2 tablespoons melted butter or margarine
1 (10-ounce) package frozen peas
1 (8-ounce) can pitted ripe olives, drained and thinly sliced
½ teaspoon salt
¼ teaspoon pepper
½ teaspoon monosodium glutamate (optional)

Serves 6

1. Place celery in melted butter in a deep 1½-quart, heat-resistant, non-metallic casserole and heat, covered, on FULL POWER 3 minutes.

2. Add peas, cover and heat on FULL POWER an additional 4 minutes, stirring once.

3. Stir in olives and seasonings, heat, covered, on FULL POWER 2 minutes.

□ Strawberry Cheesecake should be prepared in advance so that it has time to chill before serving.
□ Prepare Duchess Potatoes up to Step 4.
□ Prepare Creamed Scallops in Wine Sauce and set aside.
□ Prepare Shrimp de Jonghe up to Step 6.
□ Prepare Green Peas with Celery and Olives and finish cooking Duchess Potatoes.
□ Heat and serve Creamed Scallops in Wine Sauce.
□ While serving Scallops finish cooking Shrimp de Jonghe.

4

Shrimp de Jonghe

¾ cup butter or margarine
4 to 5 cloves garlic, peeled and
   sliced
¼ teaspoon tarragon
1 tablespoon chopped fresh
   parsley
Dash of nutmeg
Dash dried thyme leaves
¼ teaspoon chives or scallions,
   finely chopped
¼ teaspoon instant minced
   onion
1½ teaspoons salt
½ cup dry sherry
¾ cup fine dry bread crumbs
2 pounds raw, shelled, deveined
   shrimp

Serves 4 to 6

1. Melt ¾ cup butter in a deep, 2-quart, heat-resistant, non-metallic casserole on FULL POWER 1 minute.

2. Add sliced garlic and heat, uncovered, on FULL POWER 2½ minutes or until garlic is browned.

3. Remove garlic slices from melted butter.

4. Add tarragon, parsley, nutmeg, thyme, chives, onion, salt and sherry to butter. Stir to combine. Remove ¼ cup of seasoned butter mixture and mix with ¾ cup bread crumbs.

5. Place raw shrimp in a shallow, 2-quart, heat-resistant, non-metallic casserole with the remaining seasoned butter. Stir to coat raw shrimp with seasoned butter.

6. Sprinkle buttered bread crumbs over shrimp. Heat, uncovered, on FULL POWER 10 minutes or until crumbs are browned and shrimp are pink. Do not overcook shrimp as they will become tough.

Duchess Potatoes

160°F

6 medium-sized potatoes,
   peeled and cut into large
   cubes
Hot water
1 teaspoon salt
1 egg, slightly beaten
¼ cup milk or light cream
4 tablespoons butter or
   margarine, softened
½ teaspoon salt
⅛ teaspoon pepper
Paprika

Serves 4 to 6

1. In a deep, 2-quart, heat-resistant, non-metallic casserole place potatoes and hot water to cover. Sprinkle with the 1 teaspoon salt. Heat, uncovered, on FULL POWER 24 to 28 minutes or until potatoes are fork-tender. Drain excess water.

2. Partially mash potatoes with a potato masher.

3. Add egg, milk, butter or margarine, the ½ teaspoon salt and pepper. Beat with electric mixer until smooth.

4. Place in a heat-resistant, non-metallic serving dish and sprinkle with paprika. Heat, uncovered, on FULL POWER 7 minutes or until 160°F.

47

DINNER FOR THE BOSS

Strawberry Cheesecake

18 Zwieback crackers, crushed
3 tablespoons butter or margarine, softened
1 tablespoon sugar
2 (8-ounce) packages cream cheese, softened
½ cup sugar
2 egg yolks
1 teaspoon grated lemon rind
1 tablespoon lemon juice
2 egg whites, stiffly beaten
1 cup dairy sour cream
2 tablespoons sugar
1 teaspoon vanilla
1 (16-ounce) package frozen strawberries or 1 pint fresh strawberries, washed and hulled

Serves 8

1. Lightly grease a 9-inch, heat-resistant, non-metallic pie plate.

2. In a small bowl combine cracker crumbs, softened butter or margarine and the 1 tablespoon of sugar.   Press into the bottom of the greased pie plate.

3. Heat, uncovered, on ROAST for 3 to 4 minutes. Set aside.

4. In a large mixing bowl, beat cream cheese and the ½ cup sugar together until light and fluffy. Add egg yolks, 1 at a time, beating well after each addition.   Beat in lemon rind and juice.

5. Fold in stiffly beaten egg whites.   Pour into prepared baking dish; smooth with a spatula.

6. Heat, uncovered, on SIMMER for 10 to 12 minutes.

7. In a small bowl combine sour cream, the 2 tablespoons sugar and vanilla until well blended.   Carefully spread over top of cheesecake.

8. Heat, uncovered, on SIMMER for 2 minutes.

9. Arrange strawberries on cheesecake as desired and chill several hours before serving.

Tip: Cream cheese can be softened in the microwave oven.   Place unwrapped cream cheese in a non-metallic bowl and soften on SIMMER for 30 seconds.
The first slice of cheesecake may be difficult to remove from plate.

48

RECIPE NOTES

QUICK COMPANY DINNER

Fruit Salad
Rolled Rib Roast*
Baked Potatoes*
Orange Glazed Carrots*
Celery & Olives
Rolls
Yellow Cake with Mocha Frosting*

Rolled Rib Roast

1 (3-pound) rolled rib roast
Garlic cloves, peeled (optional)
Pepper (optional)
Salt (optional)

Serves 4

1. Use a microwave trivet or invert a heat-resistant, non-metallic saucer or small casserole cover in the bottom of a shallow, non-metallic baking dish. (This keeps the meat out of the fat as it cooks.)

2. Place roast fat-side-down on the saucer or trivet.

3. Rub meat with garlic and pepper if desired.

4. Heat, uncovered, for half of the cooking time given in the chart below. FULL POWER is used for this tender cut.

5. Drain pan juices and reserve if gravy is to be made. Turn meat over, cover loosely with wax paper or paper toweling and heat for remainder of the cooking time.

6. Let roast stand covered in aluminum foil 15 to 30 minutes or until appropriate internal temperature is reached. DO NOT PLACE CONVENTIONAL THERMOMETER OR ALUMINUM FOIL IN THE MICROWAVE OVEN.

7. If necessary, return roast to Microwave Oven for a few minutes until desired internal temperature is reached.

8. Salt meat after cooking, if desired.

	Minutes per pound	Internal Temperature at end of cooking time	Internal Temperature at end of standing time
Rare:	5 min./lb.	120°–130°F	130°–135°F
Medium:	6 min./lb.	140°–150°F	150°–155°F
Well done:	7 min./lb.	160°–165°F	170°–175°F

Baked Potatoes

4 baking potatoes

1. Scrub potatoes and pierce skins with a fork.

2. Place in Microwave Oven, leaving a 1-inch space between potatoes.

3. Heat, uncovered, on FULL POWER 13 to 15 minutes or until tender.

Note: Wrap potatoes in aluminum foil after removing from the microwave oven. During the standing time from oven to table, the potatoes will remain hot and be more uniformly cooked and more tender.

- □ Prepare Yellow Cake with Mocha Frosting in advance so it has time to cool before serving.
- □ Prepare Fruit Salad and Celery and Olives and refrigerate.
- □ Prepare and bake Baked Potatoes. Wrap in aluminum foil after cooking to keep warm.
- □ Prepare and cook Rolled Rib Roast.
- □ While Roast is standing at room temperature prepare and cook Carrots.
- □ Heat Rolls and serve.
- □ If necessary, Potatoes and Roast may be reheated in Microwave Oven just before serving.

4

Orange Glazed Carrots

**6 medium-sized carrots, peeled
  and thinly sliced
3 tablespoons firmly packed
  dark brown sugar
3 tablespoons butter or
  margarine
3 tablespoons orange juice
1 teaspoon lemon rind
¼ teaspoon salt**

Serves 4

1. Combine all ingredients in a deep, 1-quart, heat-resistant, non-metallic casserole.

2. Heat, covered, on FULL POWER 15 to 18 minutes or until carrots are tender. Stir occasionally so that carrots are well glazed.

Yellow Cake

**1 (9-ounce) package of yellow
  cake mix
Ingredients called for on package
  label
Mocha Frosting (See below)**

Serves 6

1. Mix cake according to package directions.

2. Pour batter into an 8-inch round, wax paper lined heat-resistant, non-metallic baking dish.

3. Heat, uncovered, on ROAST for 8 to 10 minutes or until a cake tester comes out clean.

4. Frost with Mocha Frosting.

Mocha Frosting

**3 tablespoons butter or
  margarine, softened
1¾ cups sifted confectioners'
  sugar
2 teaspoons instant coffee
2 teaspoons cocoa
2 tablespoons hot milk
½ teaspoon vanilla or rum extract
  or brandy flavoring**

Frosts 1 (8 or 9-inch) layer cake

1. In a mixing bowl combine butter, sugar, coffee, cocoa, 1 tablespoon of hot milk and the vanilla.

2. With portable electric mixer or wooden spoon beat mixture at medium speed until smooth and fluffy.

3. Gradually beat in a little more hot milk if mixture seems too thick to spread.

CASUAL DINNER FOR COMPANY

Melon Halves filled with Raspberries
Beef Stroganoff*
Sunshine Brussel Sprouts*
Stuffed Baked Potatoes*
Cheese n' Pumpkin Pie*

Beef Stroganoff

150°F

¼ cup vegetable oil
1 clove garlic, peeled and crushed
½ cup finely chopped onion
3 tablespoons flour
1½ teaspoons salt
¼ teaspoon pepper
1 pound boneless beef sirloin, cut into thin slices, ½-inch long
½ cup hot water
1 envelope instant beef broth
1 (3-ounce) can sliced mushrooms, drained
1 tablespoon catsup
1 tablespoon dry sherry
½ teaspoon Worcestershire sauce
Few drops Tabasco sauce
1 cup dairy sour cream

Serves 4

1. In a heat-resistant, non-metallic, 10-inch skillet place ¼ cup oil and heat on top of a conventional range.

2. Add crushed garlic and chopped onion to hot oil.

3. While onion is browning, combine flour, salt and pepper in a paper or plastic bag and coat beef slices.

4. Brown coated beef slices in hot oil with onion and garlic.

5. When beef slices are browned, add all remaining ingredients, except sour cream, to beef mixture. Stir to combine.

6. Heat, uncovered, on FULL POWER 6 minutes or until beef is tender.

7. Add sour cream to beef mixture, stirring constantly.

8. Heat, uncovered, on ROAST for an additional 4 minutes or until heated to 150°F.

Sunshine Brussel Sprouts

¼ cup dry white wine
3 tablespoons finely chopped onion
1 tablespoon lemon juice
¼ cup mayonnaise
2 hard cooked eggs, finely chopped
2 (10-ounce) packages frozen brussel sprouts
Paprika (optional)

Serves 4 to 6

1. Cook the brussel sprouts on FULL POWER for 8 to 10 minutes. Drain and set aside.

2. In a small, heat-resistant, non-metallic bowl pour wine over onion and heat, uncovered, on ROAST for 3 minutes or until onion is tender.

3. Stir in lemon juice and mayonnaise.

4. Heat, uncovered, on ROAST for 3 minutes or until mixture comes to a boil.

5. Gently stir in eggs.

6. Spoon sauce over cooked brussel sprouts.

7. If desired, sprinkle with paprika.

Tip: Eggs may be baked in your Microwave Oven. Place each egg in a glass custard cup. Pierce white and yolk. Heat, uncovered on ROAST 1 minute to 1 minute 15 seconds. Let stand to cool.

□ Melon Halves filled with Raspberries may be prepared ahead of time and refrigerated until serving.
□ Prepare Cheese n' Pumpkin Pie in advance so it has time to chill before serving.
□ Bake potatoes for Stuffed Baked Potatoes and prepare up to Step 7.
□ Prepare and cook Beef Stroganoff.
□ Prepare and cook Sunshine Brussel Sprouts and finish cooking Potatoes.
□ Reheat any parts of the meal that may have cooled, if necessary.

4

Stuffed Baked Potatoes

**4 (6-ounce) baked potatoes
(see recipe page 50)
2 tablespoons butter or
margarine
¾ cup milk
1 egg, slightly beaten
Salt and pepper, to taste
½ cup shredded Cheddar cheese
Paprika**

Serves 4

1. Allow potatoes to stand at room temperature 2 to 3 minutes after baking.
2. Cut a thin slice from the top of each potato. Caution: potato will be hot.
3. With a spoon, remove the potato pulp from each potato, leaving a thin shell.
4. Mash potato pulp with a fork or potato masher.
5. Add butter, milk, egg, salt, pepper and cheese. Whip potato mixture with a rotary beater or electric mixer until light and fluffy.
6. Spoon mixture into shells and sprinkle with paprika.
7. Heat potatoes, uncovered, on FULL POWER for 5 minutes.
8. If desired, after cooking in Microwave Oven, potatoes may be placed under the broiler unit of a conventional oven to brown for a few minutes. Be sure to use a broiler-proof dish.

Cheese n' Pumpkin Pie

**⅓ cup butter or margarine
1½ cups graham cracker crumbs
¼ cup sugar
½ teaspoon cinnamon
12 ounces cream cheese,
softened
1 cup canned pumpkin
¾ cup sugar
1½ tablespoons flour
¾ teaspoon grated lemon rind
¾ teaspoon grated orange rind
½ teaspoon vanilla
3 eggs at room temperature
1 (4-ounce) can shelled pecan
halves**

Serves 8 to 10

1. Place butter in an 8½-inch round glass cake dish. Heat on FULL POWER for 1 minute.
2. Add graham cracker crumbs, sugar and cinnamon. Stir to combine. Press cracker crumb mixture onto bottom and sides of dish.
3. Heat on ROAST for 3 minutes. Allow to stand and cool.
4. Cream cream cheese until smooth in a large, heat-resistant, non-metallic bowl.
5. Add pumpkin. and sugar. Beat until smooth and well-blended.
6. Add flour, lemon and orange rind and vanilla. Mix thoroughly.
7. Add eggs, one at a time, mixing well after each addition. Beat 2 minutes.
8. Heat, uncovered, on SIMMER for 5 minutes. Stir twice.
9. Pour filling into crust and heat on SIMMER for 8 to 9 minutes or until custard is puffed around edges and still slightly soft in the center.
10. Chill at least 4 hours before serving. Arrange pecan halves on top of pie before serving.

PLANNED LEFTOVER DINNER

Curried Pear Halves*
Watercress & Tomato Salad
Club Chicken Casserole*
Glazed Belgian Carrots*
Sautéed String Beans*
Brownies à la Mode*

Curried Pear Halves

140°F

1 (29-ounce) can pear halves, undrained
⅓ cup butter or margarine
¾ cup firmly packed dark brown sugar
1 to 2 teaspoons curry powder
Dairy sour cream (optional)

Serves 4 to 6

1. Drain pear halves and reserve ⅓ cup of the liquid. Place pear halves in shallow, 1½-quart, heat-resistant, non-metallic baking dish.

2. In a small, heat-resistant, non-metallic bowl, melt butter or margarine on FULL POWER 30 seconds. Stir in reserved pear liquid, brown sugar and curry powder to taste.

3. Spread curry mixture over pears and heat, uncovered, on FULL POWER 5 minutes or until heated through. Serve warm with dollops of sour cream, if desired.

Glazed Belgian Carrots

1 (1-pound) package frozen Belgian carrots
6 tablespoons butter or margarine
2 tablespoons honey
¼ to ½ teaspoon ginger

Serves 4 to 6

1. Place frozen carrots in a deep, 1½-quart, heat-resistant, non-metallic casserole.

2. Heat, covered, on FULL POWER for 5 minutes. Add remaining ingredients.

3. Heat, covered, on FULL POWER 8 to 10 minutes or until carrots are tender. Stir once. Let stand for 1 to 2 minutes before serving.

Club Chicken Casserole

160°F

1 tablespoon butter or margarine
¼ pound fresh mushrooms, thinly sliced
3 cups cubed cooked chicken
2 cups soft bread crumbs
1 cup milk
1 cup condensed chicken broth
¼ cup finely chopped pimiento
2 eggs, slightly beaten
2 tablespoons instant minced onion
¾ teaspoon salt
½ teaspoon pepper
⅛ teaspoon dried thyme leaves
1 cup Chicken Gravy with Mushrooms (recipe page 110)

Serves 6

1. In a deep, 2-quart, heat-resistant, non-metallic casserole melt butter on FULL POWER 30 seconds.

2. Add mushrooms and heat, uncovered, on FULL POWER 1½ minutes or until mushrooms are tender.

3. Add remainder of ingredients to mushrooms and stir to blend well.

4. Heat, uncovered, on FULL POWER 10 to 12 minutes stirring occasionally.

5. Serve topped with Chicken Mushroom Gravy.

- Brownies may be prepared in advance and reheated at serving time.
- Prepare Club Chicken Casserole to Step 4.
- Prepare Glazed Belgian Carrots and Sautéed String Beans and cover.
- Prepare Curried Pear Halves.
- Finish cooking Club Chicken Casserole.
- While serving Curried Pear Halves, reheat Glazed Belgian Carrots and Sautéed String Beans in Microwave Oven.
- While dishes are being cleared, reheat brownies for serving. If ice cream is too hard to be scooped, it may be softened on DEFROST.

Sautéed String Beans

4 tablespoons butter or margarine
2 (17-ounce) cans whole string beans, drained
¼ teaspoon dried savory leaves, crushed
⅛ teaspoon dried oregano leaves, crushed
½ teaspoon salt
⅛ teaspoon pepper

Serves 4 to 6

1. In a shallow, 1-quart, heat-resistant, non-metallic baking dish, melt butter or margarine on FULL POWER 30 seconds.
2. Add string beans and heat, uncovered, on FULL POWER 5 minutes or until heated through.
3. Add remaining ingredients and toss lightly to coat all beans with butter sauce. Heat, uncovered, on FULL POWER 2 minutes.

Brownies à la Mode

¾ cup flour
1 cup sugar
7 tablespoons cocoa
¾ teaspoon salt
½ teaspoon baking powder
⅔ cup butter or margarine, softened
2 eggs
1 tablespoon corn syrup
1 teaspoon vanilla
Vanilla ice cream

Serves 8

1. Grease an 8-inch square, heat-resistant, non-metallic baking dish and set aside.
2. Sift together flour, sugar, cocoa, salt and baking powder into the large bowl of an electric mixer. Add remaining ingredients and beat until smooth.
3. Pour batter into the prepared baking dish. Heat, uncovered, on ROAST for 8 to 9 minutes.
4. Test for doneness with a wooden pick; if not done return to Microwave Oven for an additional 1 minute.
5. Allow to cool slightly and cut into squares for serving.
6. Place a scoop of vanilla ice cream on each serving.

Tip: To retain moistness, keep covered with clear plastic wrap.

Brownies can be warmed on ROAST:
1 brownie (1-inch square) — 45 seconds
2 brownies — 1 minute, 15 seconds
4 brownies — 2 minutes

ITALIAN DINNER

Italian Antipasto
Lasagne*
Italian Style Zucchini*
Garlic Bread*
Rum Cake*

Lasagne

140°F

1 pound lean ground beef
2 links sweet Italian sausage
2 links hot Italian sausage
1 (1 pound, 12-ounce) can peeled Italian tomatoes
1 (6-ounce) can tomato paste
1 teaspoon salt
¼ teaspoon pepper
2 cloves garlic, peeled and crushed
1 (16-ounce) container ricotta or creamed cottage cheese
2 tablespoons dried parsley flakes
2 eggs, well beaten
½ teaspoon dried oregano leaves
¼ teaspoon dried sweet basil leaves
Dash salt and pepper
½ cup grated Parmesan cheese
15 cooked lasagne noodles
1 (8-ounce) package shredded mozzarella cheese

Serves 6

1. In a heat-resistant, non-metallic, 10-inch skillet, brown beef and sausage on ROAST for 8 minutes. Drain off excess fat. Slice sausage to ¼-inch slices.

2. Add tomatoes, tomato paste, 1 teaspoon salt, ¼ teaspoon pepper, and 2 cloves garlic to browned meat.

3. Heat meat mixture, uncovered, on ROAST for 20 minutes or until sauce thickens. Stir occasionally.

4. In a large bowl, combine ricotta cheese, parsley flakes, eggs, oregano, sweet basil, dash of salt and pepper and Parmesan cheese. Blend until all ingredients are thoroughly combined.

5. Pour enough of the meat sauce into a deep, 4-quart, heat-resistant, non-metallic casserole to just cover the bottom.

6. Add layers of ⅓ of the cooked noodles, ⅓ of the ricotta cheese mixture, ⅓ of the mozzarella cheese and ⅓ of the remaining meat sauce.

7. Repeat layers, twice more, ending with tomato sauce.

8. Heat, uncovered, on ROAST for 40 to 50 minutes.

9. Let stand for 5 minutes before serving.

Tip: Lasagne noodles may be cooked in the Microwave Oven. See Cereals and Grains chapter for directions for cooking pasta.

Italian Style Zucchini

6 large zucchini
¼ cup water
3 tablespoons butter or margarine
3 tablespoons olive oil
1 teaspoon salt
2 teaspoons chopped parsley
½ teaspoon dried basil leaves
½ teaspoon dried oregano leaves

Serves 6

1. Wash zucchini but do not peel. Cut zucchini into ¼-inch slices. Place zucchini and water in a deep, 1½-quart, heat-resistant, non-metallic casserole. Heat, covered, on FULL POWER 7 minutes or until zucchini is crisp-tender.

2. Drain water. Add butter or margarine and olive oil to zucchini. Heat, uncovered, on FULL POWER 1 minute.

3. Add remaining ingredients and toss gently to combine. Heat, uncovered, on FULL POWER 2 to 3 minutes or until zucchini has reached desired degree of doneness.

- Prepare Rum Cake in advance so it has time to chill.
- Arrange Italian Antipasto and refrigerate until serving time.
- Prepare Lasagne up to Step 8.
- Prepare Italian Style Zucchini.
- While Italian Style Zucchini is cooking, prepare Garlic Bread up to Step 4.
- Finish cooking Lasagne while eating Antipasto.
- While clearing Antipasto dishes reheat Zucchini, if necessary.
- Finish cooking Garlic Bread.

Garlic Bread

120° F

1 loaf French or Vienna bread
⅓ cup melted butter or margarine
½ teaspoon garlic salt
½ teaspoon grated Parmesan cheese

1. Slice bread in ½-inch slices, but do not cut all the way through to crust.
2. In a small bowl combine remaining ingredients and heat on ROAST for 1½ minutes.
3. Spread mixture between each slice and on the top of bread.
4. Wrap in paper toweling and, if desired, place in bread basket.
5. Heat on ROAST for 1¼ to 1½ minutes. Serving temperature for bread products is 120° F.

Rum Cake

1 (18½-ounce) package devil's food cake mix
Ingredients as called for on package label
3 egg whites, at room temperature
¼ teaspoon salt
6 tablespoons sugar
1 cup plus 2 tablespoons light corn syrup
2 teaspoons vanilla
Rum
Apricot preserves

Serves 8

Tip: Frosting will be neater if you place strips of wax paper under the bottom edges of the cake before frosting the sides. Remember to gently remove wax paper before serving cake. Any leftover frosting can be used on cupcakes or stored in refrigerator for later use. Extra cake batter may be used for cupcakes.

1. Grease two 8-inch round, heat-resistant, non-metallic cake dishes. Set aside.
2. Prepare cake mix according to package directions.
3. Pour 2⅔ cups of the batter into each prepared dish.
4. Place one dish on the center of the turntable. Bake on ROAST for 9 to 10 minutes.
5. Repeat Step 4 for second dish.
6. Allow cakes to cool for 5 minutes before inverting onto cooling rack.
7. While cakes are cooling, prepare frosting. In a small mixing bowl, beat egg whites with salt until foamy. Add sugar, 1 tablespoon at a time, beating until stiff peaks form.
8. Pour corn syrup into a 2-cup, heat-resistant, non-metallic measuring cup.
9. Heat corn syrup, uncovered, on FULL POWER 2 minutes or until corn syrup comes to a boil.
10. Gradually pour boiling syrup over egg whites, beating constantly until frosting is cool and very stiff. Beat in vanilla.
11. Pour rum over the tops of both cake layers.
12. Spread apricot preserves over one of the cooled layers. Then spread some of the frosting on it.
13. Place second layer on top of first layer and spread entire cake with frosting.

New England Clam Chowder*
Lettuce & Tomato Salad
Baked Stuffed Fish*
Creamed Spinach*
Corn*
Crème de Menthe Pie*

New England Clam Chowder

150°F

3 slices raw bacon
1 (8-ounce) can minced clams, undrained
1½ cups peeled and cubed potatoes
½ cup finely chopped onion
1 medium carrot, diced
2 tablespoons flour
1½ cups milk
1 cup light cream
1 tablespoon salt
⅛ teaspoon pepper
¼ teaspoon dried thyme leaves

Serves 6

1. Place bacon in a deep, 2-quart, heat-resistant, non-metallic casserole.

2. Heat, covered with a paper towel, on FULL POWER for 3 to 4 minutes or until bacon is crisp.

3. Remove cooked bacon with a slotted spoon. Crumble bacon and set aside. Reserve drippings in casserole.

4. Drain liquid from clams and add liquid to bacon drippings. Set clams aside.

5. Add potatoes, onion and carrots to casserole.

6. Heat, covered, on ROAST for 12 minutes or until vegetables are tender; stir occasionally.

7. In a small bowl, gradually stir milk into flour.

8. Blend flour and milk into vegetable mixture.

9. Heat, uncovered, on ROAST for 6 minutes or until thickened and smooth.

10. Stir in cream, salt, pepper, thyme and reserved clams.

11. Heat, uncovered, on ROAST for 6 minutes or until heated to 150°F.

12. Garnish with crumbled bacon before serving.

Note: We recommend ROAST for blending of flavors and thickening. If your time is limited, soup may be prepared on FULL POWER. Shorten heating times to 8 minutes in Step 6, 4 minutes in Step 9 and 4 minutes in Step 11.
For more flavor, use 2 (6½-ounce) cans of clams. Use all of broth and decrease milk to one cup.
Fresh clams may be used. Steam 1 to 2 pounds of steamers following directions in Fish Chapter. Use 1 cup of broth and 1 cup of milk in soup. (Clams should be removed from shells and added to soup in Step 10.)

□ Prepare Crème de Menthe Pie and allow to chill before serving.
□ Prepare ingredients for Baked Stuffed Fish and New England Clam Chowder.
□ Prepare Lettuce and Tomato Salad and keep refrigerated.
□ Prepare Baked Stuffed Fish. Wrap Baked Stuffed Fish in aluminum foil following cooking.
□ Prepare New England Clam Chowder to Step 9.
□ Prepare Creamed Spinach to Step 4.
□ Prepare Corn either conventionally or in Microwave Oven.
□ Finish preparing New England Clam Chowder.
□ While eating New England Clam Chowder, finish preparing Creamed Spinach.
□ If necessary, reheat Baked Stuffed Fish. Remove aluminum foil before reheating. DO NOT PLACE ALUMINUM FOIL IN MICROWAVE OVEN.

4

Baked Stuffed Fish

2 tablespoons butter or margarine
1 medium-sized onion, finely chopped
¼ cup finely chopped green pepper
1 (3-ounce) can sliced mushrooms broiled-in-butter, undrained
1 cup herb seasoned dressing
1 (6-ounce) package frozen king crab meat, defrosted
¾ cup chicken broth or clam juice
4 (8-ounce) whole trout

Serves 4

1. Lightly grease a shallow, heat-resistant, non-metallic baking dish and set aside.

2. In a medium-sized, heat-resistant, non-metallic bowl heat butter on FULL POWER 30 seconds or until melted. Add chopped onion and green pepper. Heat, uncovered, on FULL POWER 3 minutes or until onion and pepper are tender.

3. Add mushrooms, seasoned dressing and crab meat. Toss to gently combine.

4. Add chicken broth or clam juice and stir to combine. Stuff each fish with some of the mixture.

5. Secure openings with string, wooden picks or small metal skewers.

6. Place stuffed fish in prepared baking dish. Heat, covered with clear plastic wrap, on FULL POWER 10 minutes or until fish flakes easily with a fork. Let fish stand, covered, at room temperature 2 minutes to finish cooking.

Creamed Spinach

¼ cup butter or margarine
½ cup finely chopped onion
2 (10-ounce) packages frozen chopped spinach
½ teaspoon salt
⅛ teaspoon pepper
¼ teaspoon nutmeg
2 (3-ounce) packages cream cheese
Milk (optional)

Serves 6

1. In a small heat-resistant, non-metallic bowl melt butter on FULL POWER for 30 seconds.

2. Add onions and heat, uncovered, on FULL POWER for 4 minutes or until onion is lightly browned. Stir occasionally.

3. Cook spinach on FULL POWER 9 to 10 minutes. Drain well.

4. Set Variable Cooking Control on SIMMER. Soften cream cheese for 30 seconds.

5. Combine browned onion, spinach, salt, pepper, nutmeg and softened cream cheese in a shallow, 1½-quart, heat-resistant, non-metallic casserole. If desired, add milk to make a thinner mixture.

6. Heat, uncovered, on ROAST for 7 to 8 minutes or until heated to 150°F.

Corn

Times for heating corn in your Microwave Oven are:

10 oz. package	— FULL POWER —	5 to 7 minutes
10 oz. pouch	— FULL POWER —	6 minutes
16 oz. can	— FULL POWER —	4 minutes
12 oz. can	— FULL POWER —	3 minutes

Crème de Menthe Pie

⅓ cup butter or margarine

1½ cups chocolate cookie crumbs (about 24 cookies yield 1½ cups)

½ cup sugar

3 cups miniature marshmallows

½ cup milk or light cream

3 tablespoons white crème de cocoa

3 tablespoons green crème de menthe

1 cup chilled heavy cream, whipped

Chocolate curls

Serves 8

1. In a 9-inch, heat resistant, non-metallic pie plate, melt butter on FULL POWER 1 minute.

2. Combine cookie crumbs and sugar in a small bowl until well blended.

3. Stir cookie mixture into butter.

4. Press mixture onto bottom and sides of pie plate.

5. Heat, uncovered, on ROAST for 3 to 4 minutes or until crust has a crunchy texture. Allow to cool while preparing filling.

6. In a large, heat-resistant, non-metallic bowl, combine marshmallows and milk.

7. Heat, uncovered, on ROAST for 3 minutes or until marshmallows begin to puff. Stir to blend. If not completely melted, return to Microwave Oven and heat on ROAST an additional 30 seconds.

8. Stir in crème de cocoa and crème de menthe.

9. Chill until thickened but not set, about 20 minutes.

10. Fold in whipped cream.

11. Pour mixture into crust.

12. Refrigerate at least 4 hours.

13. Serve garnished with chocolate curls.

Pictured: New England Dinner: New England Clam Chowder, Lettuce and Tomato Salad, Baked Stuffed Fish, Corn, Creamed Spinach, Crème de Menthe Pie

SPRING CHICKEN DINNER

Vichyssoise*
Lemon Chicken*
Minted Fresh Peas*
Zesty Stewed Tomatoes*
Herb Bread*
Cocoa Frosting*
Golden Cake*

Vichyssoise

160°F

2 tablespoons butter or
   margarine
3 medium leeks, washed
   and minced
1 medium onion, minced
2 cups potatoes, finely diced
   (about 2 large potatoes)
4 cups chicken broth
1 cup half and half
Salt, to taste
White pepper, to taste

Serves 4 to 6

1. In a deep, 2½–quart to 3-quart, heat-resistant, non-metallic casserole, melt butter on FULL POWER 30 seconds. Add leeks and onions. Heat, uncovered, on FULL POWER an additional 3 minutes.

2. Add diced potatoes and chicken broth to butter-leek mixture. Heat, covered, on FULL POWER 15 to 18 minutes or until potatoes are very tender.

3. Press mixture through a sieve or electric blender until smooth.

4. Return mixture to heat-resistant, non-metallic casserole and gradually stir in cream. Add salt and pepper to taste.

5. Heat, covered, on ROAST for 6 minutes or until soup is very hot.

Chilled Vichyssoise: Soup may be thoroughly chilled for cold Vichyssoise. Sprinkle with chopped chives to serve.

Minted Fresh Peas

8 large lettuce leaves
3 pounds green peas, shelled
¾ teaspoon sugar
⅛ teaspoon pepper
1½ teaspoons finely chopped
   fresh mint or ¼ teaspoon
   dried mint leaves
3 tablespoons butter or
   margarine
¾ teaspoon salt

Serves 6 to 8

1. Wash lettuce leaves and line a deep, 1½-quart, heat-resistant, non-metallic casserole with half of the moist lettuce leaves. Top with peas.

2. Sprinkle peas with sugar, pepper, and mint and dot with butter. Cover peas with remaining lettuce leaves. Heat, covered tightly, on FULL POWER 7 minutes or until peas are tender.

3. Carefully tilt cover to allow steam to escape. Then remove cover.

4. Remove lettuce leaves, salt and toss peas well before serving.

Variations: ¼ teaspoon dried chervil or savory may be substituted for dried mint leaves.

- Prepare Golden Cake with Cocoa Frosting in advance so it has time to chill.
- Prepare Herb Bread up to Step 4 and set aside.
- Prepare Vichyssoise up to Step 4 and set aside if it is to be served hot. If it is to be served chilled, complete preparation and chill.
- Prepare and cook Lemon Chicken.
- While Chicken is cooking prepare ingredients for Minted Fresh Peas and Zesty Stewed Tomatoes.
- While Chicken is standing at room temperature, cook Minted Fresh Peas and Zesty Stewed Tomatoes.
- Heat Vichyssoise and serve.
- While serving Vichyssoise finish Herb Bread.

4

Lemon Chicken

180°F

1 (2½ to 3-pound) broiler-fryer chicken, cut into 8 pieces
½ cup lemon juice, divided
1½ teaspoons salt
Garlic powder, to taste
Pepper, to taste

Serves 4

1. In a 10-inch square, heat-resistant, non-metallic baking dish, place chicken, skin side down. Pour ¼ cup lemon juice over chicken.

2. Heat, covered, on ROAST for 10 minutes.

3. Turn chicken over and add remaining lemon juice and seasonings to chicken.

4. Heat, covered, on ROAST for 9 to 11 minutes or until chicken is tender.

Note: Chicken pieces are cooked 8 minutes per pound on ROAST. The time on this recipe may be adjusted for any weight chicken. Add an additional ½ cup of lemon juice if using more than 3 pounds of chicken.
Garnish with lemon slices and sprigs of parsley.

Zesty Stewed Tomatoes

3 tablespoons butter or margarine
¼ cup finely chopped onion
¼ cup finely chopped green pepper
6 large tomatoes, peeled and quartered
½ teaspoon sugar
½ teaspoon dried oregano leaves
⅛ teaspoon garlic salt
⅛ teaspoon pepper
¾ teaspoon salt

Serves 6

1. In a deep, 2-quart, heat-resistant, non-metallic casserole melt butter or margarine on FULL POWER 30 seconds. Add onion and green pepper, and heat, uncovered, on FULL POWER 3 minutes or until lightly browned.

2. Add remaining ingredients and stir to combine.

3. Heat, covered, on FULL POWER 5 to 6 minutes or until tomatoes are very tender. Stir occasionally. Add salt after heating. Serve hot or cold.

SPRING CHICKEN DINNER

Herb Bread

½ cup butter or margarine
½ teaspoon salt
½ teaspoon garlic salt
¼ teaspoon paprika
2 teaspoons chopped parsley
¼ teaspoon dried thyme leaves
1 medium-sized loaf French or
Vienna Bread

1. Place butter and spices in a glass custard cup and heat on FULL POWER 1 minute. Mix thoroughly.
2. Slice bread crosswise in ½ inch slices, being careful not to slice through bottom crust.
3. Brush herb spread on slices. Wrap in paper toweling and place in bread basket.
4. Heat herb bread on ROAST for 1¼ to 1½ minutes. Serving temperature for bread products is 120°F.

Golden Cake

2 cups cake flour, sifted
2 teaspoons baking powder
½ teaspoon salt
½ cup vegetable shortening
½ cup sugar
1 teaspoon vanilla
2 eggs
¾ cup milk

Serves 8 to 10

1. Sift together flour, baking powder and salt; set aside.
2. Cream shortening until light and fluffy. Add sugar gradually to shortening and continue to beat until mixture is light and fluffy.
3. Add vanilla and eggs to sugar mixture. Beat until thoroughly combined.
4. Add dry ingredients alternately with milk.
5. Allow batter to stand 10 to 15 minutes.
6. Lightly grease two 8-inch round glass baking dishes.
7. Pour ½ of the batter into each baking dish.
8. Heat one layer at a time, centered on turntable, on ROAST for 6½ to 7½ minutes or until wooden pick inserted in center comes out clean.
9. Allow to cool 5 minutes. Remove from dish and place on cooling rack.
10. Frost with Cocoa Frosting. (See recipe below.)

Cocoa Frosting

2 tablespoons cocoa
3 tablespoons milk
2 tablespoons butter or
margarine
3 cups confectioners' sugar,
sifted
1 teaspoon vanilla

1. Combine cocoa, milk and butter in a medium-sized, heat-resistant, non-metallic bowl.
2. Heat, uncovered, on ROAST for 1½ minutes or until butter is melted.
3. Gradually add confectioners' sugar and beat with electric mixer until smooth. Stir in vanilla.

Fills and frosts two 8-inch layers.

Note: If consistency is too thick, add 1 to 2 tablespoons more milk as you are beating in confectioners' sugar.

RECIPE NOTES

SUNDAY DINNER

Stuffed Mushrooms*
Tossed Salad
Glazed Baked Ham*
Green Beans Deluxe*
Boiled Parsley Potatoes*
Blueberry Buckle*

Stuffed Mushrooms

12 large fresh mushrooms
Salt and pepper
¼ cup butter or margarine
⅓ cup finely chopped onion
1 tablespoon flour
½ cup heavy cream
¼ cup chopped parsley
¼ cup shredded Swiss cheese
(optional)

Serves 4 to 6

1. Wipe mushrooms with damp cloth. Carefully remove stems and set aside.
2. Place mushrooms hollow-side-up, in a shallow, heat-resistant, non-metallic baking dish. Sprinkle mushroom caps with salt and pepper to taste. Heat, uncovered on FULL POWER for 3 minutes; drain.
3. Finely chop reserved mushroom stems. In a medium-sized, heat-resistant, non-metallic bowl, melt butter on FULL POWER 30 seconds. Add onions and chopped mushroom stems; stir to combine.
4. Heat, uncovered, on FULL POWER 3 minutes or until onions and mushrooms are tender. Blend in flour until smooth. Gradually stir in heavy cream until smooth.
5. Heat, uncovered, on ROAST for 3 to 4 minutes or until thickened and smooth. Stir in chopped parsley.
6. Fill each mushroom cap with some of mushroom mixture. If desired, sprinkle a little shredded Swiss cheese over each mushroom (refrigerate if not going to serve them at this time).
7. Heat, uncovered, in a heat-resistant, non-metallic pie plate on ROAST for 2 minutes just before serving. (If refrigerated, heating will take an additional 1 minute.)

Green Beans Deluxe

2 (16-ounce) cans cut green beans
1 (10½-ounce) can cream of mushroom soup
1 (8-ounce) can French fried onion rings
Serves 6

1. In a deep, 1½-quart, heat-resistant, non-metallic casserole, combine cut green beans and soup. Blend well.
2. Heat, uncovered, on ROAST for 9 to 11 minutes.
3. Sprinkle top of bean mixture with onion rings and heat, uncovered, on ROAST for 5 minutes or until onions are heated through.

Boiled Parsley Potatoes

6 medium potatoes, peeled and quartered
Water
½ teaspoon salt
⅓ cup butter or margarine
¼ cup finely chopped parsley

Serves 6

1. Place potatoes in water to cover in a deep, 2-quart, heat-resistant, non-metallic casserole.
2. Add salt and heat, covered, on FULL POWER 20 minutes or until fork-tender. Drain.
3. Add butter and parsley.
4. Heat, uncovered, on FULL POWER 2 minutes. Toss to combine thoroughly.

66

□ Tossed Salad may be prepared in advance so that there is less to do at mealtime. Do not put dressing on salad until just before serving.
□ The Stuffed Mushrooms may also be prepared in advance and heated just before mealtime.
□ In advance of dinner time, prepare Potatoes up to Step 4. Reheat at serving time. Potatoes may be boiled conventionally and finished in Microwave Oven at serving time.
□ Prepare Blueberry Buckle up to Step 8.
□ Prepare and begin to cook Baked Ham.
□ While Ham is cooking, prepare glaze and finish baking Ham.
□ While Ham is standing at room temperature, prepare Green Beans Deluxe and finish cooking Potatoes.
□ Just before serving time heat Stuffed Mushrooms.
□ While serving Stuffed Mushrooms and Tossed Salad, cook Blueberry Buckle.

Blueberry Buckle

¾ cup sugar
¼ cup vegetable shortening
1 egg
½ cup milk
1½ cups flour, sifted
2 teaspoons baking powder
½ teaspoon salt
2 cups blueberries, drained
1 cup firmly packed dark brown sugar
1 teaspoon cinnamon
½ cup softened butter or margarine

Serves 8 to 10

1. In a large mixing bowl, mix sugar, shortening and egg thoroughly.
2. Stir in milk.
3. Blend in dry ingredients.
4. Fold in blueberries.
5. Allow batter to stand 15 minutes.
6. Lightly grease an 8-inch square glass baking dish. Pour batter into baking dish.
7. In a small bowl combine remaining ingredients until well blended. Sprinkle topping mixture on top of batter.
8. Heat, uncovered, on ROAST for 15 to 17 minutes or until wooden pick inserted in center comes out clean.

Glazed Baked Ham

120°F

1 (3-pound) precooked canned ham
1 (8-ounce) can pineapple slices in unsweetened juice, undrained
½ cup firmly packed dark brown sugar
2 teaspoons dry mustard
Whole cloves

Serves 6 to 8

1. Remove ham from wrapping and place in a shallow heat-resistant, non-metallic baking dish. Heat, uncovered, on ROAST for 8 minutes.
2. Drain pineapple slices and reserve juice. In a small heat-resistant, non-metallic bowl combine brown sugar, dry mustard and 3 tablespoons of the reserved pineapple juice.
3. Heat sugar mixture, uncovered, on ROAST for 2 minutes.
4. Score the top and sides of the ham, making diagonal cuts with a sharp knife.
5. Brush liberally with brown sugar mixture. Arrange pineapple slices on top and brush again with sugar mixture.
6. Place whole cloves in pineapple as desired.
7. Heat, uncovered, on ROAST for 10 minutes, brushing twice with brown sugar mixture.
8. Allow to stand covered with aluminum foil 15 minutes before serving.

Note: Precooked canned hams should be cooked 6 minutes per pound using the ROAST setting or until an internal temperature of 120°F is reached.

Onion Soup

½ cup butter or margarine
6-8 medium onions
1 bay leaf
¼ teaspoon pepper
1 envelope onion soup mix
2 envelopes instant beef broth
   or beef bouillon cubes,
   crumbled
6 cups hot water
1 teaspoon Worcestershire sauce
6 (2-inch) rounds toasted
   French bread
Grated Parmesan cheese

Serves 6

1. Place butter and onions in a 4-quart, heat-resistant, non-metallic casserole.

2. Heat, uncovered, on ROAST for 10 minutes, stirring occasionally.

3. Add soup mixes, water and Worcestershire.

4. Heat, covered, on FULL POWER for 30 minutes, stirring occasionally.

5. Pour into heat-resistant, non-metallic soup bowls and float a round of French bread in each bowl. Sprinkle liberally with Parmesan cheese.

6. Heat, uncovered, on FULL POWER 3 to 4 minutes, or until cheese has melted.

Note: For added flavor, soup can be heated on the SIMMER setting. Increase total heating time to 1 hour.

Veal Roast

160°F

1 (3-pound) rolled veal roast
Garlic cloves, peeled (optional)
Pepper (optional)
Salt (optional)

Serves 6

1. Use a microwave trivet or invert a heat-resistant, non-metallic saucer or small casserole cover in the bottom of a shallow non-metallic baking dish. (This keeps the meat out of the fat as it cooks.)

2. Place roast fat-side-down on the saucer or trivet.

3. Rub meat with garlic and pepper if desired.

4. Well done veal requires 8 minutes per pound total cooking time. Heat, uncovered, on FULL POWER for half of total cooking time.

5. Drain pan juices and reserve if gravy is to be made. Turn meat over, cover loosely with wax paper and heat for remainder of the cooking time on FULL POWER until internal temperature reaches 160°F.

6. Let roast stand covered in aluminum foil 15 to 30 minutes or until internal temperature reaches 170°F. DO NOT PLACE CONVENTIONAL THERMOMETER OR ALUMINUM FOIL IN THE MICROWAVE OVEN.

7. If necessary, return roast to Microwave Oven for a few minutes until desired internal temperature is reached.

8. Salt meat after cooking, if desired.

- In advance, prepare Boston Cream Pie so that it can chill before serving.
- Tossed Salad may also be prepared in advance and kept in the refrigerator.
- Prepare Onion Soup up to Step 6 and set aside.
- Prepare and cook Veal Roast.
- While Veal Roast is standing, cook Baked Sweet Potatoes and Harvard Beets.
- Finish cooking Onion Soup and serve.

Harvard Beets

1 (16-ounce) can sliced beets, undrained
Water
1 tablespoon cornstarch
1 tablespoon plus 1 teaspoon sugar
¾ teaspoon salt
¼ cup vinegar

Serves 4

1. Drain liquid from beets into measuring cup. Add enough water so that beet liquid measures ⅔ of a cup. Set aside.

2. Mix together cornstarch, sugar and salt in a deep, 1½-quart, heat-resistant, non-metallic casserole.

3. Gradually add beet liquid and vinegar to cornstarch mixture. Stir until smooth.

4. Heat, covered, on FULL POWER 1½ minutes or until beet liquid comes to a boil. Stir.

5. Boil beet liquid for an additional 1 minute. Stir after 30 seconds.

6. Add beets and heat, uncovered, on FULL POWER 3 minutes or until beets are heated through.

Baked Sweet Potatoes

Medium-sized sweet potatoes

1. Select sweet potatoes for uniform shape and size. Scrub potatoes well and pierce each potato with tines of fork.

2. Arrange on paper toweling, leaving at least 1 inch between potatoes.

3. Bake according to cooking chart below.

4. Check for doneness as cooking times vary according to variety and shape of potatoes.

1 potato	4 minutes	FULL POWER
2 potatoes	7 minutes	FULL POWER
4 potatoes	15 minutes	FULL POWER
6 potatoes	25 minutes	FULL POWER

Tip: Potatoes should be arranged in a circle with as much space as possible between them. Never place one potato in the center of the circle, as it may cook more slowly.
After cooking, wrap each potato in aluminum foil and allow to stand for a few minutes before serving. The potatoes will remain hot and will be more uniformly tender.

69

Boston Cream Pie

⅓ cup granulated sugar
2 tablespoons flour
1 egg, well-beaten
¾ cup milk
1 tablespoon rum
½ cup light corn syrup
1 (6-ounce) package semi-sweet
   chocolate pieces
1 tablespoon butter or
   margarine
¼ cup half and half or milk
¼ teaspoon vanilla
1 (18½-ounce) package yellow
   cake mix
Ingredients as called for on
   package label

Serves 8

1. Sift together sugar and flour into a medium-sized, heat-resistant, non-metallic bowl.

2. Add well-beaten egg, ¾ cup milk and rum. Mix thoroughly using an egg beater or hand mixer.

3. Heat, uncovered, on ROAST for 3 minutes. Stir. You will notice sauce is thickening.

4. Heat on ROAST an additional 1 minute, stirring once.

5. Place in refrigerator to chill.

6. In a 1-quart, heat-resistant, non-metallic measuring cup, combine corn syrup, chocolate pieces and butter.

7. Heat, uncovered, on ROAST for 2 minutes. Stir. If chocolate is not completely melted, heat on ROAST an additional 30 seconds.

8. Gradually stir in half and half and vanilla. Blend well.

9. Heat, uncovered, on ROAST for 2 minutes. Chill in refrigerator.

10. While custard and topping are cooling, prepare cake mix according to package directions.

11. Lightly grease two 8-inch round glass cake dishes. Pour 2⅔ cups batter into each prepared cake dish.

12. Bake one layer at a time on ROAST for 8 to 10 minutes or until wooden pick inserted in center comes out clean.

13. Allow cake to cool for 5 minutes then invert onto cooling rack.

14. When cake has cooled, place one layer on serving plate. Spread chilled custard on top.

15. Place other layer on top of custard and spread chilled chocolate sauce over top and let drizzle down sides.

16. Chill in refrigerator for 1 hour before serving.

RECIPE NOTES

A SIMPLE LUNCHEON

Tomato Soup*
Tuna Burgers*
Molded Vegetable Surprise*
Assorted Pickles
Black Bottom Pie*

Tomato Soup

160°F

3 (10½-ounce) cans
   tomato soup
3 soup cans water
Grated Parmesan cheese

Serves 8

1. In a heat-resistant, non-metallic soup tureen or a deep, 3-quart, heat-resistant non-metallic casserole, combine soup and water.

2. Heat, covered, on FULL POWER 8 to 10 minutes or until heated to 160°F.

3. Soup can also be prepared in individual mugs. Divide soup and water evenly among mugs.

4. Heat, uncovered, on FULL POWER according to the following:

Quantity	Total Cooking Time
2 to 3 mugs	3 to 4 minutes
4 to 6 mugs	6 to 8 minutes

5. Garnish soup with a sprinkling of grated Parmesan cheese.

Tip: By heating soup in mugs, you can heat only the amount of soup needed at one time.

Tuna Burgers

4 slices American cheese, cut
   into eighths
2 hard-cooked eggs, chopped
2 medium-sized sweet pickles,
   diced
1 (6½-ounce) can tuna, drained
   and flaked
1 tablespoon finely chopped
   green pepper
2 tablespoons finely chopped
   onion
1 tablespoon finely chopped
   celery
1 tablespoon finely chopped
   pimiento
½ cup mayonnaise
6 hamburger buns, split and
   buttered

Serves 6

1. Combine all ingredients except buns in a large mixing bowl. Blend thoroughly.

2. Place bottom of hamburger buns in a shallow, 10-inch round, heat-resistant, non-metallic baking dish. Spoon tuna mixture onto bun halves.

3. Place top half of hamburger bun on tuna mixture.

4. Heat, uncovered, on ROAST for 3 minutes or until cheese melts.

Note: Egg may be baked in your Microwave Oven and used in this recipe. See page 52 for directions. When heating sandwiches, using a layer of paper toweling beneath the sandwiches to absorb moisture will prevent the bun from becoming soggy.

- Several hours or the day before the luncheon, prepare the Molded Vegetable Salad and allow to chill and set.
- Prepare the Black Bottom Pie at the same time and allow to chill thoroughly.
- On the day of the luncheon, prepare Tuna Burgers to Step 3.
- Prepare and heat Tomato Soup.
- While clearing the dishes from Tomato Soup, heat Tuna Burgers.

4

Molded Vegetable Surprise

1 (3-ounce) package lime gelatin
¾ cup water
Ice cubes
1 medium cucumber, washed and sliced thinly
1 tablespoon unflavored gelatin
½ cup water
1 (6-ounce) can frozen cranberry juice
¾ cup water
½ teaspoon salt
1 cup shredded green cabbage

Serves 8

1. Place lime gelatin and ¾ cup water in a 1-quart, heat-resistant, non-metallic measuring cup.

2. Heat, uncovered, on FULL POWER 2 minutes or until mixture boils.

3. Add enough ice cubes to bring liquid level up to 2 cups. Stir until most of the ice cubes are melted and mixture is consistency of unbeaten egg whites (level of lime mixture should be 1½ cups; add enough water, if necessary, to get that measurement).

4. Pour lime gelatin into 3 cup mold. Place sliced cucumbers in gelatin.

5. Chill until almost set.

6. Soften unflavored gelatin in ½ cup water.

7. Place frozen cranberry juice and ¾ cup water into a 1-quart, heat-resistant, non-metallic measuring cup. Heat, uncovered, on FULL POWER 1 minute or until juice has melted.

8. Stir in unflavored gelatin mixture, salt and cabbage.

9. Chill in refrigerator until consistency of unbeaten egg whites.

10. Pour cranberry mixture on top of lime mixture.

1. Chill 3 hours or overnight until set.

Black Bottom Pie

⅓ cup butter or margarine
1½ cups chocolate cookie crumbs
(about 24 cookies yield 1½
cups)
½ cup sugar
1 (3-ounce) package vanilla
pudding and pie filling (not
instant)
1½ cups milk
1 cup heavy cream, chilled
3 tablespoons crème de cocoa
2 tablespoons chocolate
sprinkles

Serves 8

1. In a 9-inch, heat-resistant, non-metallic pie plate melt butter on FULL POWER 1 minute.
2. Combine cookie crumbs and sugar in a small bowl until well blended.
3. Stir cookie mixture into butter.
4. Press mixture onto bottom and sides of pie plate.
5. Heat, uncovered, on ROAST for 3 to 4 minutes or until crust has a crunchy texture. Allow to cool while preparing filling.
6. In a medium-sized, heat-resistant, non-metallic bowl empty package of pudding mix.
7. Gradually stir in milk until smooth.
8. Heat, uncovered, on ROAST for 4 minutes.
9. Stir and heat on ROAST for 4 minutes or until mixture boils. Stir occasionally.
10. Place wax paper on top of pudding so that a skin does not form and chill in refrigerator.
11. While pudding is chilling, whip cream.
12. Stir 3 tablespoons crème de cocoa into pudding.
13. Fold whipped cream into chilled pudding.
14. Pour into prepared crust and chill 3 to 4 hours or until set.
15. Garnish top with chocolate sprinkles.

RECIPE NOTES

FRENCH LUNCHEON

Oysters in Blankets*
Creamed Flounder Tarragon*
Asparagus Almondine*
Relish Tray
Chocolate Mousse*

Oysters in Blankets

1 (8-ounce) can oysters, drained
½ pound raw bacon, cut in half

25 appetizers

1. Wrap individual oysters with ½ strip bacon and fasten with a wooden pick.

2. Line a heat-resistant, non-metallic baking dish with a double thickness of paper toweling. Place 25 bacon-wrapped oysters on paper toweling in a circle.

3. Heat, covered with paper toweling, on FULL POWER 12 to 15 minutes.

4. Remove wooden pick and serve on toast or crackers.

Creamed Flounder Tarragon

2 tablespoons butter or margarine
½ cup chopped onion
½ teaspoon dried tarragon leaves
1 (8-ounce) can sliced mushrooms
1 cup dairy sour cream
⅔ cup light cream
1 tablespoon flour
1½ teaspoons paprika
1 teaspoon salt
1½ pounds flounder fillets
½ tablespoon dried parsley flakes

Serves 6

1. In a medium-sized, heat-resistant, non-metallic skillet, melt butter on FULL POWER 30 seconds. Add chopped onion and heat, uncovered, on FULL POWER 3 minutes, or until onion is soft.

2. Add tarragon leaves and mushrooms to onions and heat, covered, on FULL POWER 3 minutes.

3. In a small bowl, combine sour cream, light cream, flour, paprika and salt. Add to onion-mushroom mixture. Heat, uncovered, on ROAST for 2 minutes. Stir. Heat, uncovered, on ROAST an additional 2 minutes.

4. In a buttered, 3-quart, heat-resistant, non-metallic baking dish, pour half of the mushroom sauce. Arrange fillets on top. Spoon remaining mushroom sauce over fish. Sprinkle with parsley flakes.

5. Heat, uncovered, on ROAST for 9 minutes, or until fish flakes easily with a fork.

76

- Prepare Chocolate Mousse the day before the luncheon and allow to chill.
- On the day of the luncheon prepare relish tray and refrigerate.
- Prepare Creamed Flounder Tarragon.
- While Creamed Flounder Tarragon is cooking, prepare Oysters in Blankets to Step 2.
- Prepare ingredients for Asparagus Almondine.
- Cook Oysters in Blankets.
- While eating Oysters in Blankets, cook asparagus for Asparagus Almondine.
- While clearing appetizer dishes, reheat Asparagus Almondine and Creamed Flounder Tarragon, if necessary.

4

Asparagus Almondine

¼ **cup finely chopped almonds**
½ **cup butter or margarine**
1 **teaspoon tarragon vinegar**
2 **(10-ounce) packages frozen asparagus spears, cooked and drained**

Serves 6

1. In a small, heat-resistant, non-metallic bowl, place almonds and butter.
2. Heat, uncovered, on FULL POWER 1½ minutes or until nuts are lightly browned.
3. Stir in vinegar.
4. Pour sauce over hot or cooled asparagus.

Note: 2 (10-ounce) packages of frozen asparagus may be cooked in the Microwave Oven on FULL POWER for 10 minutes.

Chocolate Mousse

1 **(4-ounce) package chocolate pudding mix (not instant)**
2 **cups milk**
¼ **cup crème de cocoa**
1 **teaspoon orange extract**
2 **(2-ounce) packages whipped topping mix**
Ingredients called for on package
¼ **cup shredded coconut**

Serves 6

1. Place chocolate pudding in large, heat-resistant, non-metallic bowl. Gradually stir in milk and heat, uncovered, on ROAST for 10 minutes, or until pudding has thickened.
2. Stir in crème de cocoa and orange extract. Chill in refrigerator.
3. While chocolate pudding is cooling, prepare whipped topping mix.
4. Wrap a double thickness of waxed paper (6-inches wide) around a 6-cup soufflé dish or any straight-sided 6-cup dish. Tie a string or cellophane tape wax paper to hold in place.
5. Fold whipped topping into chocolate pudding mixture.
6. Pour mixture into prepared dish and chill overnight.
7. At serving time, garnish top with ¼ cup coconut.

LADIES' LUNCHEON

Potage Mongol*
Crab Meat Custard*
Tossed Salad
Pickled Beets and Cucumbers*
Sesame Rolls
Glazed Orange Cake*

Potage Mongol

160° F

1 (10½-ounce) can
 tomato soup
1 (10½-ounce) can
 green pea soup
2 soup cans water
¼ cup dry sherry

Serves 6

1. In a deep, 2½-quart, heat-resistant, non-metallic casserole or heat-resistant, non-metallic soup tureen, combine the tomato soup, pea soup and water; stir until smooth.

2. Heat, covered, on FULL POWER 10 minutes or until soup bubbles. Stir several times during heating.

3. Before serving, stir in sherry.

Crab Meat Custard

4 slices crustless bread
1 (6- ounce) package frozen
 snow crab meat, defrosted
 and drained
1 cup shredded sharp
 Cheddar cheese
Salt and pepper
4 eggs
3 cups milk
½ teaspoon salt
Dash cayenne pepper

Serves 8

1. Place bread slices in the bottom of a lightly greased, shallow, 2-quart, heat-resistant, non-metallic casserole.

2. In a small bowl, combine crab meat, ½ cup of the cheese and salt and pepper to taste. Spread on top of bread slices.

3. In a large mixing bowl beat together eggs, milk, ½ teaspoon salt and cayenne.

4. Pour egg-milk mixture over crab meat and top with remaining ½ cup cheese.

5. Heat, covered, on ROAST for 22 to 25 minutes or until custard is set.

Pickled Beets and Cucumbers

2 (17-ounce) cans sliced beets,
 undrained
2 teaspoons whole pickling
 spices
1 large cucumber, cut into
 ¼-inch slices
1 medium onion, thinly sliced
⅔ cup sugar
⅔ cup white vinegar

Serves 8

1. Drain beets and reserve ⅔ cup liquid.

2. Tie pickling spices in a piece of cheesecloth.

3. Combine beets, sliced cucumber, onion, reserved liquid, sugar, vinegar and cheesecloth bag in a deep, 2-quart, heat-resistant, non-metallic casserole.

4. Heat, covered, on FULL POWER 12 minutes or until mixture boils. Stir occasionally.

5. Chill to marinate.

6. Remove pickling spices before serving.

78

4

Glazed Orange Cake

2 egg whites, at room temperature
½ cup sugar
2¼ cups unsifted cake flour
1 cup sugar
1 tablespoon baking powder
1 teaspoon salt
⅓ cup vegetable oil
1 cup orange juice
2 egg yolks
Orange glaze

Serves 8 to 10

1. In the small bowl of an electric mixer, beat egg whites until foamy. Beat in the ½ cup sugar, 1 tablespoon at a time, beating until stiff and glossy. Set meringue aside.

2. Place flour, the 1 cup sugar, baking powder, salt, oil, and half of the orange juice into a large, heat-resistant, non-metallic bowl; beat 1 minute at high speed, scraping sides of bowl constantly.

3. Add remaining orange juice and egg yolks; beat an additional 1 minute at high speed, scraping sides of bowl constantly.

4. Gently fold in meringue.

5. Lightly grease two 8-inch round glass cake dishes.

6. Pour half of batter into each prepared cake dish.

7. Bake one layer at a time, centered on turntable, on ROAST for 8 to 9 minutes, or until wooden pick inserted in center comes out clean.

8. Let cool in dish for 5 minutes. Invert layers onto rack to cool.

9. Place one layer on serving plate; spread with Orange Glaze. Allow glaze to drizzle off sides of layer. Top with second layer and remaining glaze.

10. Chill cake to allow glaze to set.

Orange Cake Glaze

1 cup confectioners' sugar, sifted
2 tablespoons water
1 teaspoon orange juice
½ teaspoon grated orange ring
2 drops yellow food coloring
1 drop red food coloring

1. Combine all ingredients and beat until smooth.

FALL LUNCH

Quick Corn Chowder*
Texas Hot Hash*
Assorted Pickles & Relishes
Tossed Salad
Chocolate Chip Date Nut Bars*

Quick Corn Chowder

160°F

3 slices raw bacon, diced
¼ cup finely chopped onion
1 (16-ounce) can cream-style
corn
1 cup milk
¼ cup hot water
½ teaspoon salt
¼ teaspoon pepper
Finely chopped fresh parsley

Serves 4 to 5

1. Place bacon and onion in a deep, 2-quart, heat-resistant, non-metallic casserole.

2. Heat, covered with paper toweling, on FULL POWER 3 minutes.

3. Add remaining ingredients, except parsley. Stir to combine.

4. Heat, uncovered, on ROAST for 7 minutes or until soup is heated to 160°F. Stir occasionally.

5. Allow soup to stand 2 to 3 minutes before serving.

6. Garnish with parsley.

Texas Hot Hash

160°F

1 pound lean ground beef
1 large onion, thinly sliced
1 large green pepper, finely
chopped
1 clove garlic, peeled and
crushed
1 (16-ounce) can stewed
tomatoes
1 (8-ounce) can tomato sauce
¾ cup instant rice
2½ teaspoons chili powder
1½ teaspoons salt
⅛ teaspoon pepper
¼ cup shredded sharp Cheddar
cheese (optional)

Serves 4

1. In a deep, 2-quart, heat-resistant, non-metallic casserole crumble the ground beef. Add the onion, green pepper and crushed garlic.

2. Heat, uncovered, on ROAST for 8 minutes or until meat is browned. Stir occasionally to break up the meat.

3. Add the remaining ingredients except the Cheddar cheese. Mix thoroughly to combine.

4. Heat, covered, on ROAST for 8 minutes.

5. If desired, sprinkle Cheddar cheese over the top of the meat mixture.

6. Heat, uncovered, on ROAST for 3 minutes or until cheese melts.

□ Tossed Salad may be prepared in advance and chilled until serving.
□ Prepare Chocolate Chip Date Nut Bars.
□ Prepare Texas Hot Hash to Step 5.
□ While Texas Hot Hash is heating, prepare ingredients for Quick Corn Chowder.
□ Prepare Quick Corn Chowder.
□ While eating Quick Corn Chowder, finish cooking Texas Hot Hash.
□ Reheat Texas Hot Hash, if necessary, just before serving.

4

Chocolate Chip Date Nut Bars

¼ cup boiling water
½ cup chopped dates
½ cup sugar
⅓ cup butter or margarine, softened
1 egg
1 cup flour, sifted
2 teaspoons cocoa
½ teaspoon baking powder
¼ teaspoon salt
¾ cup semi-sweet chocolate pieces
¼ cup nuts
¼ cup sugar

Serves 8

1. In a small bowl pour boiling water over chopped dates. Let cool.

2. Lightly grease an 8-inch square, heat-resistant, nonmetallic baking dish. Set aside.

3. Cream ½ cup sugar and ⅓ cup butter until light and fluffy.

4. Add egg to creamed sugar mixture. Blend well.

5. Sift together flour, cocoa, baking powder and salt.

6. Add date and flour mixture alternately to creamed butter and sugar mixture.

7. Pour batter into prepared dish. Smooth top of batter with spatula.

8. In small bowl combine, semi-sweet chocolate pieces, nuts and ¼ cup sugar. Sprinkle topping mixture on top of batter and press topping into batter lightly.

9. Heat, on ROAST for 7 to 8 minutes or until a wooden pick inserted in center comes out clean. Let cool in pan 5 minutes.

Baked Grapefruit*
Poached Eggs for Four*
Canadian Bacon*
Toast and Butter*
Coffee*

Baked Grapefruit

2 medium grapefruit
4 teaspoons firmly packed
   dark brown sugar
2 teaspoons butter or margarine
4 maraschino cherries

Serves 4

1. Cut each grapefruit in half crosswise. Remove any pits and cut around each section with a sharp knife.

2. Sprinkle each grapefruit with 1 teaspoon sugar.

3. Dot each half with ½ teaspoon of butter. Place grapefruit halves on a paper plate.

4. Heat, uncovered, on FULL POWER 4 minutes.

5. Garnish each half with a maraschino cherry.

6. Serve hot.

Poached Eggs For Four

2 quarts hot water
2 teaspoons salt
½ teaspoon white vinegar
8 eggs

Serves 4

1. Heat water, salt and vinegar on FULL POWER in a deep, heat-resistant, non-metallic casserole until boiling (about 10 to 12 minutes).

2. Carefully break eggs into boiling water, one at a time. Heat, covered, on FULL POWER 3 minutes or until almost done.

3. Allow eggs to stand at room temperature in the water 3 to 4 minutes to finish cooking; lift eggs out of water using a slotted spoon.

4. If necessary, return to Microwave Oven 30 seconds to 1 minute or until desired degree of doneness is reached.

Canadian Bacon

8 slices Canadian bacon, cut
   ¼ inch thick

Serves 4

1. Arrange bacon slices in a single layer on a paper-towel-lined double paper plate.

2. Heat, covered loosely with wax paper or paper toweling on FULL POWER 6 minutes or until the edge of the meat begins to sizzle and bacon is well heated.

3. Pork products should always be heated to well-done.

□ Prepare Toast and Coffee conventionally. If necessary, they can both be reheated in the Microwave Oven with no loss of their fresh cooked flavor.
□ Prepare Baked Grapefruit to Step 4.
□ Prepare Poached Eggs for Four to Step 1.
□ While water is coming to a boil, arrange Canadian Bacon on a paper-towel-lined paper plate.
□ Finish cooking Poached Eggs for Four.
□ While the Poached Eggs are standing at room temperature, heat Canadian Bacon.
□ Cook Baked Grapefruit.
□ Reheat Toast and Coffee if necessary.

4

To Reheat Coffee

170°F

1. Place coffee in individual heat-resistant, non-metallic mugs or cups or a heat-resistant, non-metallic carafe and heat on FULL POWER until hot. Do not boil. If coffee is allowed to boil, it may become strong and bitter.

1 cup	1½ to 2 minutes
2 cups	2½ to 3½ minutes
4 cups	4 to 5 minutes

To Reheat Buttered Toast

1. Place conventionally toasted bread in Microwave Oven in a single layer on a paper towel or cloth-lined paper plate and heat, uncovered, on FULL POWER according to the chart below. The times are approximate, as they are dependent upon the temperature of the toast when placed in the Microwave Oven. Do not overheat the toast, as it will become tough and dehydrated. It is better to heat for the minimum amount of time, rather than risk overheating toast.

1 slice	15 seconds to 30 seconds
2 slices	30 seconds to 45 seconds
4 slices	1 minute to 1¼ minutes

A SIMPLE BREAKFAST

Orange & Pineapple Ambrosia
Farina with Brown Sugar and Raisins*
Cooked Ham*
Coffee Cake*
Hot Cocoa*

Farina With Brown Sugar And Raisins

3 cups water or milk
8 tablespoons quick-cooking Farina
4 tablespoons raisins
Dash salt
8 tablespoons firmly packed dark brown sugar

Serves 4

1. In each of 4 heat-resistant, non-metallic cereal bowls combine ¾ cup milk, 2 tablespoons cream of wheat, salt and 2 tablespoons raisins.

2. Heat, uncovered, on FULL POWER 4½ minutes or until mixture boils, stirring twice.

3. Sprinkle brown sugar on top of cereal in each bowl.

4. Let stand 1 to 2 minutes before serving.

Cooked Ham

4 slices ham (¼-inch thick and 4x5-inches)

Serves 4

1. Place ham slices in a single layer on a heat-resistant, non-metallic serving platter.

2. Heat, covered with a paper towel, on FULL POWER 4 minutes or until edges begin to sizzle.

Coffee Cake

¼ cup butter or margarine
¾ cup sugar
1 egg, slightly beaten
1½ cups sifted flour
2 teaspoons baking powder
½ teaspoon salt
½ cup milk
¾ cup firmly packed dark brown sugar
1 teaspoon cinnamon

Serves 8

1. Lightly grease an 8-inch, heat-resistant, non-metallic cake dish.

2. Preheat a conventional broiler.

3. Cream butter and the ¾ cup sugar together in a large bowl until fluffy. Beat in egg.

4. Sift the flour, baking powder and salt together.

5. Add flour mixture and milk to the sugar mixture alternately, beginning and ending with flour mixture.

6. Pour into prepared cake dish. Spread evenly. Combine the ¾ cup dark brown sugar and cinnamon in a small bowl and sprinkle over the batter.

7. Heat, uncovered, on ROAST for 8 to 9 minutes.

8. Insert a wooden pick to test for doneness.

9. Place cake in a conventional oven 4 inches away from broiler element for a few minutes or until topping is browned.

Hot Cocoa

170°F

3 **tablespoons cocoa**
¼ **cup sugar**
¼ **cup cold water**
3 **cups milk**

Serves 4

1. Combine cocoa, sugar and water in a heat-resistant, non-metallic pitcher or in individual serving mugs or cups.

2. Heat, uncovered, on FULL POWER 2 minutes.

3. Stir in milk and heat, uncovered, on FULL POWER 4¼ to 5½ minutes or until hot. Do not allow milk to boil.

BRUNCH

Bananas Ambrosia*
Ham & Eggs Bravo*
Bran Muffins*
Quick Apple Coffee Cake*
Coffee

Bananas Ambrosia

3 tablespoons butter or margarine
6 large ripe bananas, peeled and quartered lengthwise
Juice of 1 orange
1 orange peeled, pitted and diced
3 tablespoons firmly packed brown sugar
½ cup shredded coconut

Serves 6

1. Melt butter or margarine in a shallow, heat-resistant, non-metallic baking dish on FULL POWER 30 seconds.
2. Place bananas in baking dish and coat well with butter or margarine.
3. In a small bowl, combine the orange juice, orange pieces and brown sugar until well blended. Spoon over bananas.
4. Heat, uncovered, on FULL POWER 4 minutes or until bananas are soft and glazed.
5. Just before serving, sprinkle with coconut. Serve either hot or cold.

Quick Apple Coffee Cake

¾ cup sugar
¼ cup butter or margarine, softened
1 egg
½ cup milk
1½ cups flour, sifted
2 teaspoons baking powder
½ teaspoon salt
1 cup uncooked apple slices
2 tablespoons sugar
1 teaspoon cinnamon

Serves 8

1. In a large mixing bowl, blend together sugar, butter and egg. Beat until thoroughly blended.
2. Sift flour, baking powder and salt together.
3. Stir milk into sugar-butter-egg mixture.
4. Add dry ingredients to milk mixture and stir until thoroughly blended.
5. Spread batter into an 8-inch square, heat resistant, non-metallic baking dish.
6. Arrange apple slices in a design on top, pressing them slightly into the batter.
7. Combine sugar and cinnamon in a small bowl and sprinkle on top of apple slices.
8. Heat, covered with clear plastic wrap, on ROAST for 8 minutes. Uncover and heat on ROAST for 6 to 7 minutes or until apples are tender and wooden pick inserted in center comes out clean.
9. Allow to stand 10 minutes before serving.

Tip: Butter may be softened in your Microwave Oven.
Place butter in a non-metallic container and soften on DEFROST for 30 seconds.

4

Ham And Eggs Bravo   140°F

¼ cup flour
¼ teaspoon salt
 Dash of pepper
½ cup mayonnaise
2 cups milk
¼ pound American cheese,
   cubed
¼ cup sliced green onion
¼ cup chopped pimiento
1½ cups cubed cooked ham
4 hard-cooked eggs, sliced
4 English muffins, split, toasted
   conventionally

Serves 6 to 8

1. Blend flour, salt and pepper into mayonnaise; gradually add milk.

2. Heat, uncovered, on ROAST for 3 to 4 minutes or until thickened. Stir occasionally.

3. Add cheese and heat, uncovered, on ROAST approximately 1½ minutes, or until cheese has melted.

4. Add onion, pimiento, ham and eggs. Heat, uncovered, on ROAST for 3 to 5 minutes or until heated to 140°F. Serve on muffins.

Bran Muffins

2¼ cups whole bran
1 cup buttermilk
⅓ cup dark molasses
¼ cup firmly packed dark brown
   sugar
1 cup sifted flour
1 teaspoon baking powder
1 teaspoon baking soda
1 teaspoon salt
½ cup dark seedless raisins
   (optional)
1 egg, slightly beaten
¼ cup vegetable shortening,
   melted

Makes 18 muffins.

1. Mix bran, buttermilk, molasses and brown sugar in a small bowl, let stand until all liquid is absorbed.

2. Sift flour, baking powder, baking soda and salt into large bowl. Stir in raisins, if desired.

3. Stir egg and melted shortening into bran mixture. Add bran-egg mixture to flour mixture. Stir lightly with a fork until evenly moist.

4. Spoon batter into heat-resistant plastic coffee cup holders that have been lined with paper muffin liners. Fill muffin cups ½ full.

5. Place 6 muffins at a time around the outside edge of the turn-table, leaving the center of the turntable empty. Heat, uncovered, on ROAST for 3 to 4 minutes, or until muffins test done with a wooden pick.

6. Repeat with remaining muffin batter.

Pictured: Cocktail Meatballs, Crab and Clam Dip

Cooking Hints

With your Microwave Oven, you can now serve piping hot appetizers, snacks and hors d'oeuvres as needed. You can save time by preparing these recipes in advance and just heating them in the Microwave Oven when your guests arrive.

Heat-resistant, non-metallic platters can go directly from your Microwave Oven to your table in just minutes. The recipes in this chapter are simple enough to be prepared ahead of time or to be whipped up when unexpected company arrives. Many of these recipes can be frozen successfully, enabling you to combine the advantages of your freezer and Microwave Oven.

When preparing appetizers for baking, arrange in a single layer on a glass or paper plate. Appetizers may be covered with paper toweling to prevent spatters.

Breads and bread-based foods may be more crisp by placing them on paper towels to absorb excess moisture.

Hot Cheese Dip

140°F

1 (16-ounce) package of
  processed sharp Cheddar
  cheese, cubed
1 (7-ounce) can minced clams,
  drained
¼ cup green pepper, finely
  chopped
4 scallions, finely chopped
2 drops Tabasco sauce

Makes 1½ cups

1. Combine all ingredients in a deep, 1½-quart, heat-resistant, non-metallic casserole.

2. Heat, uncovered, on SIMMER for 5½ minutes or until cheese melts. Stir once. Heat an additional 4½ minutes on SIMMER.

3. Serve very hot with crisp corn chips for dipping.

5

Hot Roquefort Canapes

1 (3-ounce) package cream
  cheese
¼ cup Roquefort cheese,
  crumbled
¼ cup finely chopped walnuts
½ teaspoon Worcestershire sauce
¼ teaspoon dry mustard
Crackers or melba toast
Chopped walnuts

1. Place cream cheese in a small, heat-resistant, non-metallic bowl and heat, uncovered, on DEFROST for 30 seconds or until cheese is soft.

2. Add Roquefort cheese, chopped walnuts, Worcestershire sauce, mustard and stir to blend.

3. Spread cheese mixture on crackers. Arrange a maximum of 10 canapes on a large paper plate or heat-resistant, non-metallic serving platter lined with a paper or cloth napkin.

4. Heat, uncovered, on ROAST for 1 minute or until cheese begins to melt.

5. Top with a piece of walnut and serve hot.

Variation: Blue cheese, sharp Cheddar cheese or any strong-flavored cheese may be substituted for the Roquefort cheese.

Miniature Pizzas

English muffins
Tomato sauce
Mozzarella cheese slices, diced
Dried oregano leaves
Grated Romano or Parmesan
  cheese
Garnishes (anchovy fillets,
  pepperoni slices, sausage slices
  or mushroom slices)

1. Split and toast English muffins conventionally.

2. Spread a heaping teaspoon of tomato sauce on each toasted English muffin half. Arrange mozzarella cheese pieces on muffin halves.

3. Place 6 muffin halves at a time on a heat-resistant, non-metallic serving platter that has been covered with a paper or cloth napkin.

4. Heat, uncovered, on ROAST for 3 minutes or until cheese begins to melt and becomes bubbly.

5. Spread a little additional tomato sauce on each muffin half. Sprinkle with oregano and grated cheese.

6. Arrange garnish on tops of pizzas as desired and heat, uncovered, on ROAST for 45 seconds to 1 minute or until cheese is completely melted and garnishes are hot.

7. Cut each pizza into individual hors d'oeuvres as desired.

8. Serve hot.

Cheese Toasties

1 cup shredded Cheddar cheese
1 tablespoon mayonnaise
1 teaspoon milk
1 teaspoon finely chopped
  onion
½ teaspoon dry mustard
4 drops Worcestershire sauce
Dash garlic powder
Dash paprika
2 English muffins
4 slices of bacon

Makes 16 toasties

1. In a small bowl, combine cheese, mayonnaise, milk, onion, mustard, Worcestershire sauce, garlic powder and paprika. Mix thoroughly.

2. Break English muffins in half and toast in a conventional toaster. It may be necessary to toast them twice on light setting to obtain desired degree of crispness.

3. Place bacon on a paper plate lined with paper toweling. Cover with a sheet of paper toweling. Heat on FULL POWER 4½ minutes.

4. Spread about 2 tablespoons of cheese mixture on each half slice of English muffin. Cut each slice into 4 wedges. Place ¼ piece of bacon on top of each wedge.

5. Place 12 toasties around outside edge of turntable. Place remaining 4 toasties inside outside circle of toasties, leaving center of turntable empty.

6. Heat on ROAST for 2 minutes, or until cheese melts.

Rumaki

1 pound extra thin sliced bacon,
  cut in half
2 (5-ounce) cans water
  chestnuts, drained and cut in
  half
1 pound chicken livers, cut in
  half
1 cup soy sauce
½ cup firmly packed dark brown
  sugar
⅛ teaspoon ginger

Makes 50

1. Wrap a piece of bacon around water chestnut and chicken liver. Fasten with wooden pick.

2. Combine soy sauce, brown sugar and ginger in a shallow 2-quart baking dish. Mix well.

3. Marinate bacon wrapped chicken livers for 2 hours. Drain excess liquid.

4. Place 17 Rumaki on a double layer of paper toweling in a shallow, heat-resistant, non-metallic baking dish.

5. Heat on ROAST for 15 to 16 minutes, covered with a paper towel.

Marinated Chicken Wings

1 cup dry sherry
½ cup soy sauce
1 teaspoon ginger
¼ teaspoon garlic powder
48 chicken wings

Serves 12

1. In a large bowl combine sherry, soy sauce, ginger and garlic powder; set aside.

2. Disjoint chicken wings into 3 parts each. Discard the tip end or save to use for soup stock at a later time.

3. Marinate chicken pieces in sherry mixture in the refrigerator at least three hours, but not longer than 24 hours.

4. Arrange 24 pieces at a time in a single layer on a heat-resistant, non-metallic serving platter.

5. Heat, uncovered, on ROAST for 18 to 22 minutes or until chicken is well cooked. Turn chicken over after half of cooking time.

6. Repeat with remaining pieces as needed.

Tip: Uncooked chicken pieces can either be stored in refrigerator for 2 to 3 days or may be frozen for 3 months. Cooked pieces may be reheated.

Chicken Kabobs

2 pounds boned chicken breasts
⅓ cup soy sauce
1 tablespoon sugar
1 teaspoon salt
¼ teaspoon garlic powder
¼ teaspoon ginger
⅛ teaspoon pepper
2 green peppers, cut into
  ½-inch cubes
1 (8-ounce) can mushroom caps,
  drained
3 tablespoons honey

Serves 4 to 5

1. Remove skin from chicken breasts and cut chicken into 1-inch cubes.

2. In a large bowl combine soy sauce, salt, pepper, garlic powder, sugar and ginger; stir to combine.

3. Add chicken pieces and toss lightly to coat pieces well.

4. Alternate chicken pieces, green peppers and mushroom caps on wooden skewers. Reserve soy sauce mixture.

5. Combine honey with reserved liquid.

6. Brush each kabob liberally with the mixture.

7. Place kabobs in a single layer in a shallow, heat-resistant, non-metallic baking dish.

8. Heat, uncovered, on FULL POWER 5 to 9 minutes turning kabobs occasionally until chicken is cooked and green peppers are tender.

9. Kabobs may be served either hot or cold.

Ham Roll-Ups

1 pound thinly sliced boiled
  ham
2 tablespoons prepared brown
  mustard
1 pound thinly sliced American
  cheese

1. Spread each slice of ham with a little mustard.

2. Place a slice of cheese on each slice of ham and roll from the short end so that the cheese is completely enclosed in the ham.

3. Cut roll-ups in quarters crosswise and secure loose ends of ham with wooden picks.

4. Arrange 20 roll-ups in a single layer on a heat-resistant, non-metallic serving platter.

5. Heat, uncovered, on FULL POWER 3 to 4 minutes until cheese begins to melt and ham is hot.

6. Heat remaining roll-ups.

Variation: Any cheese slices may be substituted for American cheese.

Crab And Clam Dip

1 (8-ounce) package cream
  cheese
5 tablespoons soft butter or
  margarine
5 tablespoons French dressing
1 (8-ounce) can minced clams,
  drained
1 (6-ounce) package frozen crab
  meat, thawed and drained
Few drops Tabasco sauce
Melba toast rounds

Makes 2 cups dip

1. In a medium-sized mixing bowl, blend together cream cheese, butter or margarine and French dressing with an electric mixer, until smooth.

2. Add drained clams and crab meat. Stir to combine.

3. Add Tabasco sauce, to taste. Mix well.

4. Spread on Melba toast rounds. Place on a heat-resistant, non-metallic serving plate and heat, uncovered, on ROAST for 45 seconds. Serve immediately.

Hot Crab Meat Canapes

1 (6½-ounce) can crab meat
½ cup mayonnaise
1 teaspoon lemon juice
Dash cayenne pepper
Crackers or Melba toast
Paprika

1. Rinse and drain crab meat and remove any ligament, cartilage or shell. Shred crab meat with a fork.

2. Combine crab meat, mayonnaise, lemon juice and cayenne pepper, to taste, in a bowl. Stir to blend.

3. Spread about 1 teaspoon of crab mixture on each cracker and sprinkle with paprika.

4. Arrange 24 canapes on a large, heat-resistant, non-metallic serving platter.

5. Heat, uncovered, on ROAST for 4 to 5 minutes or until heated through.

6. Serve hot.

Tip: If desired, 12 canapes may be heated at a time on ROAST for 2 minutes.

Baked Clams

1 dozen cherrystone clams
2 tablespoons butter or margarine
¼ cup finely chopped onion
1 clove garlic, peeled and crushed
1 egg, slightly beaten
¼ cup seasoned bread crumbs
⅛ teaspoon dried oregano leaves
⅓ cup seasoned bread crumbs
2 tablespoons butter or margarine, melted

Serves 4

1. Remove clams from half shell and chop coarsely. Set clams and shells aside.

2. In a medium-sized, heat-resistant, non-metallic mixing bowl place 2 tablespoons butter. Heat on FULL POWER for 30 seconds or until melted.

3. Add onion and garlic. Heat, uncovered, on FULL POWER 3 minutes or until onion is tender. Add egg, the ¼ cup bread crumbs, chopped clams and oregano to onion mixture.

4. Spoon mixture into reserved shells. Place shells on a heat-resistant, non-metallic serving platter.

5. In a small bowl, heat the 2 tablespoons butter on FULL POWER for 30 seconds. Stir in the ⅓ cup bread crumbs. Sprinkle buttered bread crumbs on top of clam mixture.

6. Heat, uncovered, on FULL POWER for 5 minutes or until heated through.

Cocktail Meatballs

1½ pounds lean ground beef
1 egg
½ cup fine dry bread crumbs
½ cup water
1 (12-ounce) bottle chili sauce
6 ounces grape jelly
2 tablespoons lemon juice

Serves 10 to 12

1. In a large mixing bowl combine ground beef, egg, bread crumbs and water. Mix until thoroughly blended.

2. In a deep, 3-quart, heat-resistant, non-metallic casserole combine chili sauce, grape jelly and lemon juice.

3. Shape meat mixture into balls the size of a walnut. Place in chili sauce mixture.

4. Heat, covered, on FULL POWER 12 minutes.

5. Skim off any fat. Stir.

6. Heat, covered, on FULL POWER an additional 8 minutes or until sauce bubbles and meatballs are cooked.

Pictured: Hot Mulled Cider, Irish Coffee, Hot Buttered Rum

BEVERAGES

Cooking Hints

Beverages may be mixed, heated and served all in the same container. Heat items that tend to boil over in uncovered containers. If a boil-over does occur, opening the oven door will stop it instantly. Use a container which is somewhat larger than usual when preparing beverages containing milk, since milk does boil over rather quickly.

This chapter includes recipes for everyday beverages such as tea and coffee, as well as festive drinks like Irish Coffee and Hot Buttered Rum. The chart below lists heating times for a number of servings. Beverages are heated on FULL POWER.

Mugs or Cups	Total Cooking Time
1	1½ to 2½ minutes
2	3 to 3½ minutes
3	4 to 4½ minutes
4	5 to 5½ minutes
5	6½ to 7 minutes
6	7½ to 8½ minutes
7	9 to 9½ minutes
8	10 to 11 minutes
9	12 to 13 minutes
10	13 to 14 minutes

*   Suggested serving temperature for beverages is 170° to 180°F.
*   If beverages containing milk tend to boil, you may wish to use the ROAST setting.

Instant Coffee

170°F

1 cup water
Instant coffee

Serves 1

1. Pour water into a heat-resistant, non-metallic mug or cup.
2. Add desired amount of instant coffee. Stir.
3. Heat, uncovered, on FULL POWER 1½ to 2 minutes.

Tea

170°F

1 cup cold water
1 tea bag or 1 teaspoon loose tea in tea ball

Serves 1

1. Pour water into a heat-resistant, non-metallic mug or cup.
2. Heat, uncovered, on FULL POWER 1½ to 2½ minutes.
3. Submerge tea bag in water.
4. Allow to steep 1 to 2 minutes or until desired strength is reached.

Hot Chocolate Milk

170°F

1 to 2 tablespoons chocolate syrup
½ teaspoon vanilla
¾ cup milk

Serves 1

1. Combine chocolate syrup and vanilla in a heat-resistant, non-metallic mug or cup.
2. Stir in milk and heat, uncovered, on FULL POWER 1½ to 2½ minutes or until hot. Do not allow milk to boil.

Hot Mocha Milk

170°F

1 to 2 tablespoons chocolate syrup
½ teaspoon instant coffee
⅛ teaspoon cinnamon
¾ cup milk
Whipped cream

Serves 1

1. Combine chocolate syrup, instant coffee and cinnamon in a heat-resistant, non-metallic mug or cup.
2. Stir in milk and heat, uncovered, on FULL POWER 1½ to 2½ minutes or until hot. Do not allow milk to boil.
3. Garnish with a dollop of whipped cream.

Hot Spiced Drink

170°F

1 quart milk
¼ cup molasses
4 (3-inch) cinnamon sticks
Whipped cream
Nutmeg

Serves 4 to 6

1. In a 2-quart, heat-resistant, non-metallic pitcher or casserole, combine milk and molasses. Add cinnamon sticks.
2. Heat, uncovered, on FULL POWER 6 minutes or until hot. Remove cinnamon sticks.
3. Serve in mugs, garnished with whipped cream and a sprinkling of nutmeg.

Hot Mulled Cider

170°F

¾ cup apple cider or juice
1 to 2 whole cloves
1 1-inch piece cinnamon stick
Whipped cream
Nutmeg

Serves 1

1. Combine apple cider, whole cloves and cinnamon stick in a heat-resistant, non-metallic mug, cup or glass.
2. Heat, uncovered, on FULL POWER 2 to 3 minutes.
3. Garnish with a dollop of whipped cream and a sprinkling of nutmeg.

Irish Coffee

1 teaspoon sugar
¾ to 1 cup strong black coffee
1 jigger (1½-ounces) Irish
    Whiskey
Whipped cream

Serves 1

1. Dissolve sugar in black coffee in an Irish coffee glass or a heat-resistant, non-metallic glass, cup or mug.
(DO NOT USE A GLASS WITH METALLIC TRIM.)

2. Heat, uncovered, on FULL POWER 1½ to 2 minutes or until hot.

3. Stir in Irish Whiskey.

4. Carefully float a spoonful of whipped cream on top.

Tom And Jerrys

¾ cup milk or water
2 tablespoons butter or
    margarine
2 egg whites
1 tablespoon sugar
2 egg yolks, slightly beaten
¼ teaspoon vanilla
3 ounces brandy
3 ounces dark rum
Nutmeg

Serves 3

1. Combine the milk and butter in a 2-cup, heat-resistant, non-metallic measuring cup.

2. Heat, uncovered, on FULL POWER 1½ minutes or until butter melts and milk is hot.

3. Beat egg whites until soft peaks form. Beat in sugar until stiff and glossy.

4. Beat egg yolks and vanilla into egg whites.

5. Slowly pour milk mixture into egg mixture, beating constantly. Add brandy and rum, beating constantly.

6. Heat, uncovered, on FULL POWER 1 minute or until heated through.

7. Beat mixture until frothy.

8. Serve hot with a sprinkling of nutmeg.

Hot Buttered Rum

1 tablespoon firmly packed
    brown sugar
⅔ cup apple cider, milk or water
1 tablespoon water
1 1-inch piece cinnamon stick
1 jigger (1½-ounces) rum
1 teaspoon butter or margarine
Nutmeg

Serves 1

1. Dissolve sugar in apple cider and water in a heat-resistant, non-metallic mug or cup. Add cinnamon stick.

2. Heat, uncovered, on FULL POWER 1½ to 2 minutes or until it comes to a boil.

3. Stir in rum.

4. Top with butter and a sprinkling of nutmeg.

Pictured: Hot Gazpacho

SOUPS

Cooking Hints

An individual serving or a whole recipe can be made quickly and easily in your new Sharp Microwave Oven. Soups can be made and served in the same container so there are fewer dishes to wash. There are recipes in this section that all members of the family will enjoy and they are so easy to make that any family member can become the chef. Try a hot soup on a cold winter's evening or an unusual cold soup on a warm summer's day—all of these recipes are included in the following pages.

Hearty homemade soups containing beef should be cooked slowly to develop flavor and tenderize the meat, while many other soups are quick and do not require such long cooking times. The Variable Cooking Control makes it possible to cook all types of soups. Your own favorite soups containing meats should be cooked on SIMMER. See the Variable Cooking Control Chapter for more information.

Milk-based soups or sauces should be prepared in a dish twice as deep as your ingredients because of overboiling.

Soups are generally heated uncovered. Serving temperature should be 150° to 160° F.

Reheating Soups

Serves 1 to 5

1. Place soup in a deep, heat-resistant, non-metallic casserole large enough to prevent any boil-over.

2. Heat, uncovered, on FULL POWER according to the chart below or until soup bubbles. Stir several times during heating.

1 cup — 3 minutes
2 cups — 6½ minutes
3 cups — 8½ minutes
4 cups — 13 minutes

Tip: The type and amount of soup will determine the heating time.

Individual Servings Of Dehydrated Soup

180°F

7

¾ **cup water**
1 **envelope dehydrated soup mix, for 1 serving**

Serves 1

1. Pour water in a heat-resistant, non-metallic mug, cup or bowl.

2. Stir in soup mix.

3. Heat, uncovered, on FULL POWER 2½ minutes or until water reaches a full rolling boil. Stir.

Canned Condensed Soups

160°F

1 **(10 to 12-ounce) can condensed soup**
Water or milk

Serves 2 to 3

1. Place soup in a deep, 1½-quart, heat-resistant, non-metallic casserole.

2. Add water or milk as label directs, stirring until smooth.

3. Heat, uncovered, on FULL POWER 8 minutes or until soup bubbles. Stir several times during heating.

Old-Fashioned Chicken Soup

1 **(3-pound) broiler-fryer, with neck and gizzard**
1 **large onion**
1 **stalk celery, quartered with leaves**
1 **large carrot, peeled and cut in half**
6 **cups hot water**
1½ **teaspoons salt**
½ **teaspoon pepper**
1 **sprig of dill**
2 **envelopes instant chicken broth**
Cooked noodles

Serves 6 to 8

1. Place all ingredients in a deep, 3-quart, heat-resistant, non-metallic casserole. Heat, covered, 15 minutes on FULL POWER.

2. Skim any foam from top. Cover and heat on FULL POWER an additional 10 to 12 minutes or until chicken is tender. Remove chicken, onion, celery and carrots. Strain soup through cheesecloth or strainer. Skim excess fat off surface and add 2 envelopes instant chicken broth. If desired, add cooked noodles before serving.

3. Chicken may be removed from the bone, diced and added to soup before serving. Soup may be quickly reheated if it has cooled.

Vegetable Soup

3 slices raw bacon, diced
¼ cup finely chopped onion
1 cup finely chopped celery
1 cup thinly sliced carrots
2 cups potatoes, cut into
    ¼-inch cubes
2¼ cups water, divided
3 tablespoons flour
3 cups vegetable juice cocktail
    or tomato juice
½ teaspoon dried thyme leaves
1 cube beef bouillon, crumbled
    or 1 envelope instant beef
    broth
Salt and pepper
1 (8½-ounce) can peas, drained

Serves 6 to 8

1. Place bacon and onion in a deep, 2½-quart, heat-resistant, non-metallic casserole.

2. Heat, covered with paper toweling, on FULL POWER 3 minutes. Stir mixture occasionally.

3. Add celery, carrots, potatoes, and ¼ cup water. Heat, covered, on FULL POWER 10 minutes or until vegetables are tender. Stir mixture occasionally.

4. Blend in flour.

5. Gradually stir in the remaining water, vegetable juice cocktail, thyme, bouillon cube and salt and pepper to taste.

6. Heat, covered, on FULL POWER 10 minutes, stirring occasionally.

7. Add peas and heat, uncovered, on FULL POWER an additional 5 minutes or until soup bubbles and peas are hot.

8. Allow soup to stand 2 to 3 minutes before serving.

> **Note:** This soup may be prepared on SIMMER for added flavor.
> Increase the heating time in step 6 to 20 minutes and step 7 to 10 minutes.

Hot Gazpacho

3 cups tomato juice or
    vegetable juice cocktail
2 beef bouillon cubes,
    crumbled or 2 envelopes
    instant beef broth
2 medium ripe tomatoes,
    peeled and chopped
¼ cup chopped green pepper
¼ cup chopped onion
¼ cup wine vinegar or cider
    vinegar
2 tablespoons olive oil
1 teaspoon salt
1 teaspoon Worcestershire sauce
Few drops Tabasco sauce, to
    taste
1 clove garlic, peeled and
    crushed
Flavored croutons
Chopped tomato
Chopped cucumber
Chopped onion
Chopped green pepper

Serves 8

1. Place tomato juice in a non-metallic soup tureen or deep, 2½-quart, heat-resistant, non-metallic casserole and heat, uncovered, on FULL POWER 6 minutes or until boiling.

2. Stir in bouillon cubes until dissolved. Add the 2 chopped tomatoes, the ¼ cup green pepper, the ¼ cup onion, vinegar, oil, salt, Worcestershire sauce, Tabasco sauce and garlic.

3. Heat, uncovered, on FULL POWER 2 minutes.

4. Serve accompanied by croutons and chopped tomato, cucumber, onion and green pepper.

5. Serve either hot or cold.

Borscht (Beet Soup)

1 to 1½ pounds beets
1 quart water
2 tablespoons sugar
1½ teaspoons salt
¼ teaspoon pepper
⅓ cup lemon juice
Dairy sour cream

Serves 8 to 10

1. Wash, scrape and coarsely grate beets.

2. Place beets, water, sugar, salt, pepper and lemon juice in a deep, 2-quart, heat-resistant, non-metallic casserole.

3. Heat, covered, on FULL POWER 19 to 21 minutes or until beets are tender.

4. Chill soup several hours or overnight.

5. Serve cold, garnished with dollops of sour cream.

Manhattan Clam Chowder
170°F

2 strips bacon, finely diced
1 small onion, finely chopped
1 cup finely chopped celery
3 tablespoons flour
2 cups vegetable juice cocktail or tomato juice
1 (8-ounce) bottle clam juice
1 (8-ounce) can minced clams, undrained
¼ teaspoon ground thyme leaves
Salt and pepper, to taste

Serves 4

1. In a deep, 2½-quart, heat-resistant, non-metallic casserole place diced bacon. Heat, uncovered, on FULL POWER 2 minutes or until bacon is crisp.

2. Add chopped onion and celery and heat, uncovered, on FULL POWER 2 minutes or until vegetables are tender.

3. Blend flour into vegetable mixture and stir until smooth. Add vegetable cocktail gradually, stirring until smooth. Add remaining ingredients.

4. Heat, covered, on FULL POWER 5 minutes. Stir.

5. Heat, covered, on FULL POWER an additional 10 minutes.

6. Adjust seasonings if necessary.

Note: For more flavor, use 2 (8-ounce) cans of minced clams. Fresh clams may be used. Steam clams following directions in the Fish Chapter. Use 1 cup of broth in the soup. (Clams should be removed from the shell and added to the soup in step 5.)

Cream Of Pea Soup
160°F

2 tablespoons butter or margarine
2 tablespoons finely chopped onion
2 cups cooked or canned peas
1 teaspoon sugar
½ teaspoon salt
2 cups water
1 cup light cream or milk
¼ teaspoon garlic salt
¼ teaspoon pepper

Serves 4 to 6

1. Place butter and onion in a deep, 2½-quart, heat-resistant, non-metallic casserole. Heat, uncovered, on FULL POWER 3 minutes or until onion is tender. Stir mixture occasionally.

2. Add peas, sugar, salt and water. Heat, uncovered, on FULL POWER 3 minutes. Puree mixture in a blender until smooth.

3. Add light cream and heat, uncovered, on ROAST for 5 to 7 minutes or until heated through. Stir occasionally.

4. Stir in remaining ingredients and heat, uncovered, on ROAST 2 minutes longer or until soup bubbles.

5. Allow soup to stand 2 to 3 minutes before serving.

Note: Cubed, precooked ham is a flavorful addition to Cream of Pea Soup. Serve with seasoned croutons.

Egg Drop Soup

6 cups hot water
1 (3½-ounce) package chicken noodle soup mix (2 envelopes)
2 eggs, well beaten
1 tablespoon soy sauce (optional)
Chinese fried noodles

Serves 6

1. Pour water into a deep, 2-quart, heat-resistant, non-metallic casserole and heat, covered, on FULL POWER 10 minutes or until boiling.

2. Add noodle soup mix and heat on FULL POWER, covered, 4 minutes. Allow to stand 4 to 5 minutes or until noodles and chicken are tender.

3. Pour beaten eggs into soup mixture gradually, stirring with a fork and heat on ROAST, uncovered, 4 to 5 minutes or until eggs are cooked. Stir frequently with a fork to make eggs form thin strings.

4. If desired, stir in soy sauce. Garnish with fried noodles.

Greek Lemon Soup

160°F

2 (10½-ounce) cans chicken rice soup
2 soup cans water
1 egg, well beaten
2 medium lemons

Serves 6

1. In a medium-sized, heat-resistant, non-metallic bowl, combine the chicken rice soup and water. Heat, covered, on FULL POWER for 6 to 8 minutes or until soup is very hot.

2. Gradually, add some of the hot soup mixture to the well-beaten egg; stir until completely combined. Return the egg-soup mixture to the hot soup; stir to combine.

3. Heat, uncovered, on FULL POWER 2 minutes or until soup thickens slightly. While the soup is heating, slice one of the two lemons into thin circles. Squeeze the juice from the other lemon.

4. Just before serving, add the lemon slices and juice to the soup. Heat, uncovered, on FULL POWER 2 minutes.

Autumn Soup

1 tablespoon vegetable oil
1 cup finely chopped onion
1 pound lean ground beef
4 cups hot water
2 cups potatoes, diced into ½-inch cubes (4 medium)
1 cup thinly sliced carrot (3 large)
1 cup celery, diced
2 teaspoons salt
½ teaspoon pepper
1 bay leaf, crumbled
Few leaves dried basil
6 whole fresh tomatoes, stems removed and cut into eighths

Serves 6 to 8

1. Place oil and onion in a deep, 4-quart, heat resistant, non-metallic casserole. Heat, uncovered, on FULL POWER for 3 minutes.

2. Add meat and heat, uncovered, on ROAST for 6 minutes. Drain excess fat.

3. Add hot water, potatoes, carrot, celery and seasonings. Mix thoroughly.

4. Heat, covered, on FULL POWER for 20 minutes.

5. Add tomatoes to soup and heat, covered, on FULL POWER for 10 minutes or until vegetables are tender.

Canadian Cheese Soup

1 cup water
1 large potato, finely chopped
1 large onion, finely chopped
¼ cup carrots, thinly sliced
¼ cup finely chopped celery
2 cups chicken consommé or
   chicken broth
1 cup shredded sharp Cheddar
   cheese
½ cup half and half
2 tablespoons chopped parsley

Serves 4 to 6

1. In a deep, 3-quart, heat-resistant, non-metallic casserole place 1 cup water, potatoes, onion, carrots and celery. Heat, covered, on FULL POWER for 10 minutes or until vegetables are tender.

2. Add remaining ingredients, except parsley, and heat on ROAST, covered, 9 minutes or until soup bubbles and cheese has melted. Stir occasionally.

3. Serve garnished with chopped parsley.

Cherry Soup

3 (20-ounce) cans bing cherries,
   undrained or 4 (16-ounce)
   cans bing cherries, undrained
1 cup claret wine
4 (1-inch) cinnamon sticks
Juice of 1 lemon
2 tablespoons cornstarch
¼ cup water
1 egg yolk, well beaten

Serves 8 to 10

1. In a deep, 3-quart, heat-resistant, non-metallic casserole, combine cherries, cherry liquid, wine, cinnamon sticks and lemon juice.

2. Heat, covered, on FULL POWER 15 minutes or until liquid comes to a boil.

3. In a small bowl, combine cornstarch and the ¼ cup water. Stir into hot cherry mixture.

4. Heat, uncovered, on FULL POWER 6 minutes or until thickened and smooth.

5. Pour soup very gradually over egg yolk, stirring constantly.

6. Refrigerate 6 hours or overnight. Serve cold.

Fruit Soup

2 (10-ounce) packages frozen
   raspberries, in pouches
2 chicken bouillon cubes or
   2 envelopes instant chicken
   broth
1¼ cups boiling water
½ cup pineapple juice
2 tablespoons sugar
½ cup dairy sour cream

Serves 4 to 6

1. To thaw raspberries, slit pouches and place in Microwave Oven on DEFROST for 4 to 5 minutes or until completely defrosted.

2. Pour thawed berries and juice into the container of a blender and blend until smooth. Berries may also be pressed through a sieve or food mill.

3. In a large, heat-resistant, non-metallic bowl, combine chicken bouillon, water, pineapple juice and sugar; stir until dissolved.

4. Heat, uncovered, on FULL POWER 2 minutes. Stir in raspberries.

5. Chill several hours or overnight.

6. Serve garnished with a dollop of sour cream.

Sauces

SAUCES

Cooking Hints

Sauces are more easily prepared in your Microwave Oven. The fear of overcooking, scorching and sticking is no longer a problem. Stirring and watching the sauce is important since cooking times will vary depending upon the type of cookware and the temperature of the ingredients used, but sauces do not require constant stirring as with conventional cooking. The Variable Cooking Control allows you to adjust the speed of microwave cooking just as you adjust your conventional surface units. If a sauce seems to be cooking too fast, adjust the control to a lower setting.

Serving temperature for sauces is 140° to 150° F.

Medium White Sauce

2 tablespoons butter or
  margarine
2 tablespoons flour
½ teaspoon salt
1 cup milk

Makes 1 cup

1. In a deep, 1-quart, heat-resistant, non-metallic casserole melt butter on FULL POWER for 30 seconds.

2. Blend in flour and salt until smooth.

3. Gradually, stirring constantly, add milk.

4. Heat, uncovered, on ROAST for 3 to 4 minutes or until thickened and smooth. Stir occasionally.

Variations: Thin White Sauce: Follow recipe for Medium White Sauce reducing butter and flour to 1 tablespoon each.
Thick White Sauce: Follow recipe for Medium White Sauce increasing butter and flour to 3 to 4 tablespoons each depending upon desired thickness.

Cheese Sauce

1 cup Medium White Sauce
  (recipe above)
¾ to 1 cup shredded sharp
  Cheddar cheese
Dash cayenne pepper

Makes 1½ cups

1. Prepare Medium White Sauce according to recipe.

2. Add cheese and cayenne during the last 1½ minutes of heating.

8

Creamed Mushroom Sauce

1 cup Medium White Sauce
  (recipe above)
1 (4-ounce) can sliced
  mushrooms, drained

Makes 1¼ cups

1. Prepare Medium White Sauce according to recipe.

2. Add mushrooms during the last 1½ minutes of heating.

Brown Gravy

2 tablespoons fat
1 cup pan drippings or beef
  broth
1 tablespoon flour
Salt and pepper
Brown bouquet sauce (optional)

Makes 1 cup

1. After roasting meat in Microwave Oven remove meat from baking dish and set aside. Pour pan drippings into a bowl, leaving residue in baking dish. Allow fat to rise to the top. Skim off 2 tablespoons fat and return it to the baking dish. Discard any remaining fat.

2. Reserve pan drippings and pour into a 1 cup measuring cup. Add beef broth, if necessary to make 1 cup. Set aside.

3. Blend flour, salt and pepper, to taste, into fat in baking dish.

4. Heat, uncovered, on FULL POWER 5 to 7 minutes or until lightly browned.

5. Gradually add reserved pan drippings. Heat, uncovered, on FULL POWER 2 minutes or until slightly thickened and smooth. Stir gravy several times during cooking.

6. If desired, brown bouquet sauce may be added to gravy for color.

Chicken Gravy With Mushrooms

2 tablespoons butter, margarine
or chicken fat
2 tablespoons flour
Salt and pepper
1 cup chicken stock or broth
1 (4-ounce) can sliced
mushrooms, drained

Makes 1 cup

1. Melt butter in a deep, 1-quart, heat-resistant, non-metallic casserole on FULL POWER 30 seconds.

2. Blend in flour, salt and pepper, to taste. Stir until smooth Heat, uncovered, on FULL POWER 1 to 2 minutes or until lightly browned.

3. Gradually stir in chicken stock. Add mushroom slices; stir to combine.

4. Heat, uncovered, on ROAST for 6 minutes or until gravy is thickened and smooth. Stir occasionally during cooking.

Meat Sauce

190°F

1 pound lean ground beef
1 clove garlic, peeled and
crushed
1 teaspoon salt
½ teaspoon dried oregano leaves
½ teaspoon dried basil leaves
½ teaspoon sugar
¼ teaspoon pepper
1 (15-ounce) can tomato sauce

Serves 4

1. In a medium-sized, heat-resistant, non-metallic bowl crumble beef.

2. Heat, uncovered, on ROAST for 6 to 7 minutes, stirring frequently until meat is browned. Drain off excess fat.

3. Add remaining ingredients and stir to blend well.

4. Heat, uncovered, on ROAST for 7 to 8 minutes, stirring occasionally.

5. Serve over spaghetti.

Note: If time allows, Meat Sauce may be heated on SIMMER for 25 to 35 minutes to develop flavor and thicken.

White Clam Sauce

½ cup olive oil
1 to 3 cloves garlic, peeled and
quartered
2 (8-ounce) cans chopped
clams, undrained
¼ cup chopped parsley
1 teaspoon dried oregano leaves

Serves 4

1. Place oil and garlic, to taste, in a small, heat-resistant, non-metallic bowl and heat, uncovered, on FULL POWER 3 minutes.

2. Remove garlic pieces.

3. Add remaining ingredients and heat, uncovered, on FULL POWER 4 minutes or until heated through. Stir occasionally.

4. Serve over spaghetti.

Mornay Sauce

2 tablespoons butter or
margarine
2 tablespoons flour
1 cup chicken stock or broth
¼ cup light cream
¼ cup Romano cheese
¼ cup shredded Swiss cheese
2 tablespoons dried parsley
flakes

Makes 1½ cups

1. In a 2-cup, heat-resistant, non-metallic measuring cup melt butter on FULL POWER 30 seconds.

2. Blend in flour.

3. Gradually stir in chicken stock and light cream.

4. Heat, uncovered, on ROAST for 4 to 5 minutes or until thickened and smooth. Stir frequently.

5. Add cheese and parsley flakes and heat, uncovered, on ROAST for 1 minute, or until cheese is melted and sauce is smooth. Allow sauce to stand until cheese has completely melted.

Italian Tomato Sauce

180°F

2 tablespoons olive oil
1 medium-sized onion, finely chopped
1 clove garlic, peeled and crushed
1 (15-ounce) can tomato sauce
1 teaspoon sugar
1 teaspoon salt
¼ teaspoon pepper
½ teaspoon dried oregano leaves
½ teaspoon dried basil leaves

Makes 2½ cups

1. Place olive oil, onion and garlic in a deep, 1½-quart, heat-resistant, non-metallic casserole. Heat, uncovered, on FULL POWER 3 minutes or until onion is tender; stir occasionally.

2. Add remaining ingredients and stir to combine.

3. Heat, covered, on FULL POWER 5 to 7 minutes or until sauce bubbles. For more flavor, sauce may be heated on SIMMER for 25 to 35 minutes.

Barbecue Sauce

2 tablespooons butter or margarine
1 medium onion, finely chopped
1 clove garlic, peeled and crushed
2 tablespoons finely chopped green pepper
¾ cup catsup
¼ cup firmly packed dark brown sugar
¼ cup water
¼ cup cider vinegar
¼ teaspoon dry mustard
¼ teaspoon salt
Few drops Tabasco sauce, to taste

Makes 2¼ cups

1. Place butter, onion, garlic and green pepper in a deep, 1½-quart, heat-resistant, non-metallic casserole and heat on FULL POWER 3 minutes or until tender. Stir occasionally.

2. Add remaining ingredients; stir well to combine.

3. Heat, uncovered, on FULL POWER 2 minutes or until sauce bubbles. Serve over meat or poultry.

Applesauce Barbecue Sauce

1 cup thinly sliced onion
3 tablespoons butter or margarine
2 cups applesauce
1 cup catsup
2 tablespoons lemon juice
1 tablespoon Worcestershire sauce
1 teaspoon salt

Makes 3 cups

1. Place onions and butter in a deep, 1½-quart, heat-resistant, non-metallic casserole.

2. Heat, uncovered, on FULL POWER 2 to 3 minutes or until onion is tender.

3. Add applesauce, catsup, lemon juice, Worcestershire sauce and salt.

4. Heat, uncovered, on FULL POWER 7 minutes or until sauce is bubbly.

Spicy Pineapple Sauce

2 tablespoons sugar
1 tablespoon cornstarch
1 (8-ounce) can pineapple chunks in unsweetened juice, undrained
2 tablespoons butter or margarine
¼ teaspoon cinnamon

Makes ¾ cup

1. Combine sugar and cornstarch in a deep, 1-quart, heat-resistant, non-metallic casserole.
2. Gradually add juice from pineapple, stirring constantly.
3. Add pineapple, butter and cinnamon.
4. Heat, uncovered, on FULL POWER 3 minutes. Stir and heat on FULL POWER an additional 4 minutes or until sauce has thickened. Stir occasionally. Serve with meat or as a dessert sauce.

Orange Glaze

½ cup orange marmalade
4 tablespoons honey

Makes ½ cup

1. Combine marmalade and honey in a small, heat-resistant, non-metallic bowl.
2. Heat, uncovered, on FULL POWER for 1 minute. Use as a glaze on poultry.

Cherry Sauce

1 (17-ounce) can dark sweet cherries, undrained (pitted or unpitted)
1 tablespoon cornstarch
1½ teaspoons lemon juice
1 teaspoon grated lemon rind

Makes 2 cups

1. Drain cherry juice into a deep, 1-quart, heat-resistant, non-metallic casserole. Set cherries aside. Blend cornstarch into cherry juice until smooth.
2. Heat, uncovered, on FULL POWER 4 minutes or until thickened and clear. Stir occasionally.
3. Add cherries, lemon juice and lemon rind to thickened cherry juice. Stir to combine.
4. Heat, uncovered, on FULL POWER 1 minute or until sauce bubbles and cherries are hot.
5. Spoon over ice cream or cake.

Variation: If desired, sauce may be made from canned blueberries, stawberries, raspberries, pineapple or diced peaches.
Cherries Jubilee: Heat ¼ cup brandy on FULL POWER in a heat-resistant, non-metallic long-handled dish or spoon for 30 seconds. Ignite brandy and pour over cherry sauce. Spoon over ice cream.
Tip: If a heat-resistant, non-metallic spoon is not available, brandy may be heated in any heat-resistant, non-metallic vessel and transferred to a long-handled ladle before igniting.

Strawberry Sauce

1½ pounds strawberries, washed and hulled
1½ cups sugar
1 teaspoon lemon juice

Makes 2½ cups

1. Place stawberries in a medium-sized, heat-resistant, non-metallic bowl. Pour sugar on top and stir to mix thoroughly.
2. Heat, uncovered, on FULL POWER 5 minutes. Stir.
3. Heat, uncovered, an additional 5 minutes on FULL POWER.
4. Add lemon juice and stir to mix thoroughly.
5. Cool before serving.

Lemon Sauce

½ cup sugar
1 tablespoon cornstarch
1 cup water, at room temperature
2 tablespoons butter or margarine
1½ teaspoons lemon juice
½ teaspoon grated lemon rind
Dash salt

Makes 1 cup

1. In a deep, 1-quart, heat-resistant, non-metallic casserole combine sugar and cornstarch.
2. Gradually stir in water.
3. Heat, uncovered, on FULL POWER 3 to 4 minutes or until sauce has thickened and is smooth. Stir occasionally.
4. Add butter, lemon juice, lemon rind and salt.
5. Serve warm or cold.

Hot Vanilla Sauce

1 cup sugar
2 tablespoons cornstarch
2 cups water
¼ cup butter or margarine
2 teaspoons vanilla

Makes 2 cups

1. Combine sugar and cornstarch in a deep, 1-quart, heat-resistant, non-metallic casserole.
2. Gradually add water, stirring constantly
3. Add butter and heat, uncovered, on FULL POWER for 5 minutes. Stir occasionally.
4. Heat, uncovered, on FULL POWER an additional 3 minutes or until sauce is thickened and clear.

Chocolate Mint Sauce

3 (1-ounce) squares unsweetened chocolate
¼ cup water
1 cup sugar
½ cup light corn syrup
⅛ teaspoon salt
⅔ cup light cream or undiluted evaporated milk
⅛ teaspoon peppermint extract

Makes 2 cups

1. Place chocolate and water in a deep, 1½-quart, heat-resistant, non-metallic casserole.
2. Heat, uncovered, on FULL POWER 45 seconds or until chocolate is melted. Stir to blend chocolate and water.
3. Add sugar, corn syrup and salt. Heat, uncovered, on ROAST for 11 minutes or until a candy thermometer reaches 240°F. (If a candy thermometer is not available, drop a small amount of the mixture into very cold water. The mixture should form a soft ball which flattens when removed from the water. DO NOT PLACE CONVENTIONAL THERMOMETER IN MICROWAVE OVEN OR USE TEMPERATURE PROBE). Stir occasionally.
4. Gradually blend in cream and extract.

Pictured: Roast Loin of Pork with Apricot Glaze, Rolled Rib Roast

Cooking Hints

The cooking times of meats may vary slightly when cooked in your Microwave Oven, depending upon the shape and size of the meat, the amount of fat present, the degree of aging, and the type of cut. Because it is often difficult to judge the doneness of meat by external appearance, you will find that using a microwave thermometer or the temperature probe is a tremendous help in cooking meats.

Meat should be roasted in a shallow, heat-resistant, non-metallic baking dish. Place the meat on an inverted saucer in the center of the dish so that it does not sit in the drippings. Plastic trivets or racks designed for microwave cooking may be used in your Sharp Microwave Oven. Start meat fat-side-down, turning over to fat-side-up after half of cooking time.

Wax paper or paper toweling may be placed loosely over the top of the meat to control spattering and help in basting. Meats may be cooked in roasting bags, provided that string is used instead of the metal tie to secure bag. Follow package directions, making sure to slit the bag.

When cooking meat in your Microwave Oven, we suggest that you do not salt the meat before cooking. Salt draws the moisture out of meat and toughens the outer layer. Add salt after the meat is cooked. Pepper and other seasonings may be added prior to cooking.

Microwave cooked foods continue to cook somewhat even after being removed from the oven. Meats should be allowed to stand, covered in aluminum foil, at room temperature 10 to 15 minutes before making a final temperature reading to determine doneness. The internal temperature of meats will increase by 10° to 15°F during this standing time following microwave cooking.

Small portions of meat may not be as brown as you desire when cooked by microwaves. Larger roasts and other meats, cooked longer than 10 minutes, will become acceptably brown. The amount of browning varies with the amount of fat on the surface of the meat. To add to the brown appearance of smaller portions, try basting the meat with a diluted brown gravy mix such as Kitchen Bouquet®.

A browning dish may be used to brown meats in your Microwave Oven. See information in this chapter for directions and individual recipes.

Best results are achieved when meats, particularly roasts and larger cuts, are completely defrosted before cooking.

Thinner sections of meats may be shielded with aluminum foil to prevent overcooking before thicker portions are done. For example, corners or thinner areas of meat can be covered with small, smooth pieces of foil before cooking, or the wing and leg tips of a turkey may be wrapped in a small amount of foil to reflect microwaves away from these thin areas. Foil should be removed during part of the cooking time in order to cook covered portions.

For tips on cooking less tender cuts of meat, refer to the Variable Cooking Control Chapter.

Meat Thermometers

Conventional meat thermometers should not be used in the Microwave Oven during operation. Specially designed Microwave Cooking Thermometers may be used in your Sharp Microwave Oven during operation, but these are the only thermometers which should be used during cooking.

If using a conventional meat thermometer, insert into meat at the end of the suggested cooking time, after removing meat from oven. Insert thermometer in the center and fleshy portion of the meat, away from boney or fatty sections. For poultry, insert between the inner thigh and body of the bird.

If your oven has a temperature probe, see your use and care book for more information.

Steak

There are several ways to prepare brown, moist steaks in your Microwave Oven. Tenderness will depend on the type of cut, but less tender cuts may be slowed down by adjusting the Variable Cooking Control to a lower setting. Tender cuts may be cooked on FULL POWER.

Steaks may be quickly seared on both sides in a hot electric skillet or in a skillet on a conventional surface unit. They may then be finished in your Microwave Oven, cooking each steak to individual preference.

Steaks may be grilled outdoors and finished by microwaves. The grill gives that good charcoal flavor and browness, and microwave cooking retains the moisture and flavor. Extra steaks may be precooked, frozen, and then defrosted and heated by microwaves as needed. This is an excellent example of combining your Microwave Oven with other appliances.

Steaks cooked in your Microwave Oven without searing or grilling will be similar to baked steak. Kitchen Bouquet® or other browning agents may be used to give a browner appearance, but there will not be a crisp, brown crust as when cooked under a broiler.

Browning dishes give excellent results for steaks. The browning dish should be preheated empty for 5-6 minutes for an average steak. The steak is then placed in the hot dish and cooked by microwaves, turning over halfway during cooking. When cooking consecutively, the browning dish should be re-preheated a shorter period of time after removing food, before adding additional food.

Browning Dish Chart*

Food	Quantity	Preheat Time	Cooking Time
Steak	(1) 7 oz. 3/4-inch thick	5 to 6 minutes FULL POWER	FULL POWER, uncovered 1 minute, 45 seconds Turn over after half of cooking time
Hamburgers	(1 or 2 patties) 3/4-inch thick	5 to 6 minutes FULL POWER	FULL POWER, uncovered 2½ minutes Turn over after half of cooking time
Hamburgers	2 patties (1/2 lb. meat) 1/2-inch thick	5 to 6 minutes FULL POWER	FULL POWER, uncovered 2 minutes Turn over after half of cooking time
Pork Chops	3 chops (1 lb.)	4 to 5 minutes FULL POWER	FULL POWER, uncovered 5 minutes Turn over after half of cooking time

*This chart should be used only as a guide for preheat times and cooking times. Information packed with your browning dish gives more complete instructions and additional foods.

Meat Roasting Chart

BEEF

CUT	Variable Cooking Control Setting	Approx. Cooking Time	Internal Temp. At End Of Cooking Time	Internal Temp. At End Of Standing Time
Rib Roast, rolled or standing **Rare** **Medium** **Well-Done**	FULL POWER FULL POWER FULL POWER	5 min./lb. 6 min./lb. 7 min./lb.	120°–130°F 140°–150°F 160°–165°F	130°–135°F 150°–155°F 170°–175°F
Chuck Roast (Cook in liquid, covered)	SIMMER	18 min./lb.	Cook by time, not temperature	Until tender.
Rump Roast (Cook in liquid, covered) **Well-Done**	SIMMER	18 min./lb.	Cook by time, not temperature	Until tender.
Chuck Steak (Boneless) 1 pound	SIMMER	7-9 min./lb.	160°–165°F	170°–175°F
Hamburgers (4 patties) 1 pound	SIMMER	5-7 min./lb.		
Ground Meat (to brown for casserole) 1 pound	ROAST	6 minutes		
Meat Loaf 1 pound hamburger (see individual recipes)	FULL POWER	12 minutes	160°F	165°F
Swiss Steak 2 pounds, round	SIMMER	50-60 min.		
Hot Dog (1 on a bun)	FULL POWER	30 seconds		

PORK

CUT	Variable Cooking Control Setting	Approx. Cooking Time	Internal Temp. At End Of Cooking Time	Internal Temp. At End Of Standing Time
Fresh Ham	ROAST	12 min./lb.	170°–175°F	180°–185°F
Pork Loin Roast	ROAST	12 min./lb.	170°–175°F	180°–185°F
Canned Ham (precooked)	ROAST	6 min./lb.	120°F	130°F
Pork Chops, baked	SIMMER	16 min./lb.	170°–175°F	180°–185°F
Bacon	FULL POWER	Approx. 1 min./strip		

LAMB

CUT	Variable Cooking Control Setting	Approx. Cooking Time	Internal Temp. At End Of Cooking Time	Internal Temp. At End Of Standing Time
Medium-Well	ROAST	10 min./lb.	155°–160°F	170°F
Well-Done	ROAST	11 min./lb.	165°–170°F	180°F

VEAL

CUT	Variable Cooking Control Setting	Approx. Cooking Time	Internal Temp. At End Of Cooking Time	Internal Temp. At End Of Standing Time
Well-Done	FULL POWER	8 min./lb.	160°F	170°F

9

Silver Tip Roast Beef

1 (3-pound) silver tip roast beef
Garlic cloves, peeled (optional)
Pepper (optional)
Salt (optional)

Serves 6

1. Invert a heat-resistant, non-metallic saucer or small casserole cover in the bottom of a shallow, non-metallic baking dish, or use a microwave trivet to keep the meat out of the fat as it cooks.

2. Place roast, fat-side-down on the saucer or trivet.

3. Rub meat with garlic and pepper, if desired.

4. Heat, uncovered, on ROAST. Cook 6 min./lb. for rare, 7 min./lb. for medium, or 8 min./lb. for well done. Cook half of total time.

5. Drain pan juices and reserve if gravy is to be made. Turn meat over, cover loosely with wax paper. Heat remainder of total cooking time.

6. Let roast stand covered in aluminum foil 15 to 30 minutes or until appropriate internal temperature is reached. DO NOT PLACE CONVENTIONAL THERMOMETER OR ALUMINUM FOIL IN THE MICROWAVE OVEN.

7. If necessary, return roast to Microwave Oven for a few minutes until desired internal temperature is reached.

8. Salt meat after cooking, if desired.

Bacon

To cook 2 or 3 slices, place bacon on 1 or 2 layers of paper towels on a paper plate or on a heat-resistant, non-metallic baking dish. Cover with a paper towel to prevent spattering.

For more than 3 slices of bacon, place bacon on several layers of paper towels in an oblong heat-resistant, non-metallic utility dish. There is too much grease to use a paper plate for larger volumes of bacon.

Cook bacon on FULL POWER.

1 slice	1–1½ minutes
2 slices	2–2½ minutes
3 slices	3–3½ minutes
4 slices	4–4½ minutes
6 slices	5½–6 minutes
8 slices	6–7 minutes

Bacon generally cooks 1 minute per strip.

Bacon will become crisper during the standing time following cooking. Crispness depends on the brand, thickness, curing process, starting temperature, and degree of doneness desired.

Microwave trivets or roasting racks are ideal for cooking bacon. The fat will drain away and can easily be reserved.

Beef Stew

4 tablespoons vegetable oil
¼ cup flour
Salt and pepper
2 pounds boneless lean beef chuck, cut into 1-inch cubes
2½ cups water
2 bay leaves
2 teaspoons salt
¼ teaspoon pepper
1 clove garlic, peeled and crushed
3 medium carrots, peeled and thinly sliced
6 medium potatoes, peeled and cubed
2 stalks celery, cut in ½-inch slices
½ cup catsup
3 to 6 tablespoons flour
¾ cup cold water
½ to 1 teaspoon brown bouquet sauce (optional)
1 (10-ounce) package frozen peas, partially thawed

Serves 6 to 8

1. Heat 2 tablespoons of oil in a large skillet over moderate heat on a conventional range.

2. Combine flour, salt and pepper to taste in a plastic or paper bag. Shake meat cubes in seasoned flour to coat.

3. Brown beef cubes, a few at a time, on all sides in hot oil. Add the remaining 2 tablespoons of oil as needed.

4. Transfer browned beef cubes into a deep, 3-quart, heat-resistant, non-metallic casserole. Add the 2½ cups of water, bay leaves, the 2 teaspoons of salt, the ¼ teaspoon pepper and the garlic. Heat, uncovered, on SIMMER for 15 minutes. Stir once. Skim any foam that may form.

5. Add carrots, potatoes, celery and catsup. Stir to combine. Heat, covered, on SIMMER for 1 hour or until meat and vegetables are tender.

6. While beef and vegetables are cooking, combine the 6 tablespoons flour and the ¾ cup of water in a small bowl.

7. Remove bay leaves from stew.

8. Gradually stir the flour mixture into the stew. If desired, add brown bouquet sauce, a little at a time until desired color is reached. Color will deepen as stew cooks.

9. Add peas and heat, covered, on SIMMER for 10 to 15 minutes or until sauce is thickened and peas are hot.

Sicilian Supper

165°F

2 cups noodles, uncooked
1¼ cups hot water
1 teaspoon salt
1 pound lean ground beef
½ cup finely chopped onion
1 (6-ounce) can tomato paste
¾ cup water
½ teaspoon garlic salt
¼ teaspoon pepper
¾ cup milk
1 (8-ounce) package cream cheese, softened and cubed
½ cup grated Parmesan cheese
½ cup chopped green pepper

Serves 4

1. In a deep, 2-quart, heat-resistant, non-metallic casserole place noodles, the 1¼ cups hot water and the 1 teaspoon salt. Heat, covered, on FULL POWER 11 minutes or until noodles are tender. Drain noodles and set aside.

2. Place ground beef into a deep, heat-resistant, non-metallic 2-quart casserole and heat, uncovered, on ROAST for 6 minutes. Stir occasionally to break up meat pieces.

3. Add onions and heat, uncovered, on ROAST 4 minutes or until onion is tender. Drain excess fat.

4. Add tomato paste, the ¾ cup water, the garlic salt and the pepper to the beef-onion mixture. Stir to combine. Heat, covered, on ROAST for 5 minutes or until mixture bubbles.

5. Add cooked noodles, milk, cream cheese, Parmesan cheese and chopped green pepper. Heat, covered, on ROAST for 20 minutes or until mixture is heated through.

Note: If desired, noodles may be cooked conventionally while meat portion of recipe is being prepared in the Microwave Oven.

Stroganoff Superb

170°F

3 tablespoons butter or
  margarine
1 pound round steak, cut into
  thin strips
½ cup chopped onion
1 (4-ounce) can sliced
  mushrooms, drained
¼ teaspoon dry mustard
½ teaspoon salt
¼ teaspoon pepper
1 (8-ounce) package cream
  cheese, cubed
⅔ cup milk
Hot parsleyed noodles

Serves 4

1. Place 3 tablespoons butter in a deep, 2-quart, heat-resistant, non-metallic casserole. Melt on FULL POWER 30 seconds.

2. Add steak strips to butter and heat, uncovered, on FULL POWER for 10 minutes or until meat is browned.

3. Add onion, mushrooms and seasonings to meat. Heat, uncovered, on FULL POWER for 4 minutes.

4. Add cubed cream cheese and milk to meat mixture and heat, uncovered, on ROAST for 6 minutes or until cheese melts. Stir occasionally. Serve over hot parsleyed noodles.

Oriental Beef And Tomato Casserole

1 pound tender beef, thinly
  sliced
1 clove garlic, peeled and
  crushed
2 tablespoons soy sauce
1 tablespoon sugar
1 teaspoon ginger
1 cup thinly sliced celery
1 cup thinly sliced onion
1 green pepper, thinly sliced
4 small tomatoes, peeled and
  cut into wedges
1 tablespoon cornstarch
1 tablespoon water

Serves 4

1. In a deep, 2-quart, heat-resistant, non-metallic casserole place thinly sliced beef and heat on FULL POWER 5 minutes or until meat is no longer red. Drain excess liquid.

2. Add garlic, soy sauce, sugar, ginger, celery, onion, green pepper and tomatoes and heat on FULL POWER 5 minutes or until vegetables are tender. In a small custard cup combine cornstarch and water until a smooth paste is formed. Add cornstarch mixture to liquid in casserole and heat on FULL POWER 2 minutes until mixture is thickened and smooth.

Oriental Hamburger Casserole

180°F

1 pound lean ground beef
2 medium onions, finely
  chopped
1 cup chopped celery
1 (10½-ounce) can cream of
  mushroom soup
1 (10½-ounce) can cream of
  chicken soup
1 cup water
½ cup uncooked rice
1 tablespoon soy sauce
¼ teaspoon pepper
1 can chow mein noodles
½ teaspoon monosodium
  glutamate (optional)

Serves 4

1. Crumble meat into a deep, 3-quart, heat-resistant, non-metallic casserole and heat, uncovered, on ROAST for 6 minutes or until meat is browned. Stir after half of cooking time.

2. Add remaining ingredients to meat mixture.

3. Cover and heat on ROAST for 25 minutes or until mixture is hot. Uncover, stir and heat for an additional 5 minutes.

Stuffed Green Peppers

160°F

4 medium green peppers, washed
1 pound lean ground beef
½ cup quick-cooking rice, uncooked
1 teaspoon salt
¼ teaspoon pepper
½ teaspoon dried oregano leaves
⅛ teaspoon garlic powder
⅓ cup water, milk or tomato juice
1 egg slightly beaten
1 (8-ounce) can tomato sauce with onion bits

Serves 4

1. Cut green peppers in half lengthwise; remove core and seeds.

2. Place peppers, hollow-side-up, in a shallow, heat-resistant, non-metallic baking dish.

3. In a medium-sized bowl, crumble beef. Add rice, salt, pepper, oregano, garlic powder, water, egg and ½ cup of tomato sauce. Mix until thoroughly combined.

4. Spoon mixture into pepper halves.

5. Spoon remaining tomato sauce over peppers.

6. Heat, covered loosely with wax paper, on ROAST for 19 to 22 minutes or until meat is cooked and peppers are as tender as desired.

7. Allow to stand 4 minutes, covered, before serving.

Sloppy Joes

165°F

2 tablespoons vegetable oil
2 pounds lean ground beef
2 teaspoons salt
¼ teaspoon pepper
6 to 8 teaspoons chili powder
1 (15-ounce) can tomato sauce
1 pound frankfurters, cut into ¼-inch rounds
Hamburger buns

Serves 8

1. In a deep, 3-quart, heat-resistant, non-metallic casserole heat oil on FULL POWER 2 minutes.

2. Crumble meat into hot oil and heat, uncovered, on ROAST for 10 minutes, breaking up meat pieces occasionally.

3. Drain off excess fat.

4. Stir in salt, pepper, chili powder and tomato sauce.

5. Heat, uncovered, on FULL POWER 4 minutes or until heated through.

6. Add frankfurter rounds and heat, uncovered, on FULL POWER an additional 4 minutes or until frankfurters are hot.

7. Spoon Sloppy Joe mixture over hamburger buns. (Buns may be toasted conventionally, if desired.)

Note: Recipe may be cut in half thus cutting cooking times in half, or extra meat mixture may be frozen for later use.

Swedish Meatballs

¼ cup butter or margarine
1 cup finely chopped onion
3 eggs
1⅓ cups milk
1½ teaspoons allspice
½ teaspoon nutmeg
1 tablespoon salt
2 cups soft bread crumbs
2 pounds lean ground beef
1 pound lean ground lamb
1 envelope instant beef broth
 or 1 cube beef bouillon,
 crumbled
1 cup boiling water
4 tablespoons flour
2 cups light cream or milk

Serves 12

1. Melt butter in a large, heat-resistant, non-metallic bowl on FULL POWER 30 seconds.

2. Add onions and heat, uncovered, on FULL POWER 3 minutes or until onions are lightly browned. Set aside.

3. In a small bowl, mix eggs and milk until well blended.

4. Add egg mixture, allspice, nutmeg, salt and bread crumbs to cooked onions. Stir to combine.

5. Crumble meat into mixture.

6. Mix with hands or fork until thoroughly combined.

7. Form meat mixture into 1-inch balls.

8. Heat half of the meatballs in a single layer in a shallow, 1-quart, heat-resistant, non-metallic casserole on ROAST for 7 to 8 minutes or until almost done. Turn meatballs occasionally during cooking.

9. While meatballs are cooking, combine beef bouillon and water in a small bowl and set aside.

10. Repeat the cooking process with the remaining meatballs.

11. Reserve any meat juices that collect in the bottom of the baking dish. Skim off excess fat and discard. Pour meat juices into a deep, 2½-quart, heat resistant, non-metallic casserole and stir in flour. Stir in reserved beef broth.

12. Heat, uncovered, on FULL POWER 2 minutes or until slightly thickened.

13. Gradually stir in cream.

14. Heat, uncovered, on ROAST for 8 minutes or until thickened and smooth. Stir occasionally.

15. Place meatballs in sauce. If necessary, meatballs and sauce may be reheated on ROAST to bring them to a serving temperature of 160°F.

Variation: Any ground meat or combination of meats may be substituted for all or a portion of the ground beef.

Saucy Franks

1 (15-ounce) can whole-berry
 cranberry sauce
1 (12-ounce) bottle chili sauce
2 pounds frankfurters

Serves 6 to 8

1. Combine whole-berry cranberry sauce and chili sauce in a deep, 2-quart, heat-resistant, non-metallic casserole. Add frankfurters.

2. Heat, covered, on ROAST for 6 minutes. Stir.

3. Heat, covered, on ROAST for 12 minutes or until franks are heated through. Stir occasionally.

Basic Meat Loaf

160°F

3 slices bread
Water
1 small onion, finely chopped
1 clove garlic, peeled and
   crushed
¼ cup finely chopped celery
½ teaspoon salt
⅛ teaspoon pepper
1 egg, slightly beaten
⅓ cup milk
1 pound lean ground beef
¼ cup catsup

Serves 4

1. In a small bowl soak bread in water to cover 5 minutes. Squeeze out excess water.

2. In a large bowl combine bread, onion, garlic, celery, salt, pepper, egg and milk. Stir until well blended. Crumble ground beef into bread mixture and stir to combine thoroughly.

3. Shape meat mixture into a loaf and place in a shallow heat-resistant, non-metallic baking dish.

4. Heat, uncovered, on FULL POWER 6½ minutes.

5. Spread catsup over top of meat loaf and heat, uncovered, on FULL POWER 5½ minutes.

6. Allow meat loaf to stand covered 3 to 5 minutes before serving.

Tip: Meat loaf may be shaped in a ring like a donut with a hole in the center. This shape is attractive and cooks very evenly.

9

Gourmet Meat Loaf

160°F

1½ cups soft bread crumbs
¾ cup Rosé wine
1 package instant beef broth
¼ cup water
2 tablespoons instant minced
   onion
2 tablespoons bell pepper flakes
½ teaspoon salt
½ teaspoon dry mustard
1 egg, slightly beaten
1½ pounds lean ground meat

Serves 6

1. Combine soft bread crumbs, wine, the package of instant beef broth, onion, pepper and water in a large, heat-resistant, non-metallic bowl. Heat, uncovered, on FULL POWER 4 minutes.

2. Stir in salt, dry mustard, egg and ground meat.

3. Press firmly into an 8½-inch, heat-resistant, non-metallic round baking dish with custard cup in the center (right side of cup facing down).

4. The ring shape will bake very evenly and the excess fat will be collected under the inverted cup. Heat, loosely covered with paper towel, on FULL POWER 12 minutes.

Note: Any combination of beef, veal, lamb or pork may be used.

Hot Dogs In Beer

1 (12-ounce) can or bottle beer
   or ale
1 pound frankfurters
Hot dog buns, warmed
Sauerkraut, warmed

Serves 4

1. In a deep, 2½-quart, heat-resistant, non-metallic casserole combine beer and frankfurters.

2. Heat, covered, on FULL POWER 6 to 8 minutes or until heated through.

3. Serve on hot buns with warmed sauerkraut.

Stuffed Meat Loaf

160°F

1 cup soft bread crumbs
⅓ cup finely chopped onion
1 teaspoon salt
⅛ teaspoon pepper
¼ cup milk
1 egg, slightly beaten
½ pound lean ground beef
½ pound lean ground pork
½ cup shredded Cheddar cheese
1 (4-ounce) can mushroom
   stems and pieces, drained
1½ cups seasoned mashed
   potatoes; leftover, made
   freshly or from packaged
   instant potatoes
Paprika (optional)

Serves 4

1. In a large mixing bowl combine bread crumbs, onion, salt, pepper, milk and egg; mix thoroughly using a rubber spatula.

2. Crumble the ground meats into the bread crumb mixture and gently mix until thoroughly combined.

3. In a shallow, heat-resistant, non-metallic baking dish shape about one-third of meat mixture into a 4x6-inch rectangle.

4. Sprinkle meat with half of shredded cheese. Arrange mushroom pieces over cheese, leaving about ½-inch border around edges. Sprinkle with remaining cheese.

5. Carefully shape the remaining meat mixture over cheese and mushrooms, carefully sealing the edges.

6. Heat, uncovered, on FULL POWER 9 minutes or until almost done.

7. With a spatula frost the meat loaf with mashed potatoes, completely covering the top and sides. If desired sprinkle with paprika.

8. Heat, uncovered, on ROAST for 4 to 5 minutes or until potatoes are hot and meat is completely cooked.

9. Allow to stand at room temperature 4 minutes before slicing.

Variation: Peas, hard-cooked eggs, artichoke hearts, olives, pimientos or many other foods may be used in place of the mushrooms.
Swiss, Muenster, Monterey Jack, Tilsit, mozzarella or any other cheese may be substituted for the Cheddar cheese.

Ground Beef Casserole

160°F

1½ pounds lean ground beef
1 teaspoon salt
Dash pepper
¼ teaspoon garlic salt
1 (8-ounce) can tomato sauce
1 cup creamed cottage cheese
1 cup dairy sour cream
6 green onions, finely chopped
3 cups cooked egg noodles
¾ cup shredded sharp cheese

Serves 4 to 5

1. Place meat in a medium-sized, heat-resistant, non-metallic mixing bowl. Heat, uncovered, on ROAST for 8 minutes or until meat is browned. Stir occasionally.

2. Drain excess fat.

3. Add salt, pepper, garlic salt and tomato sauce to the meat. Stir to combine.

4. Heat, uncovered, on ROAST for 3 minutes.

5. In a medium-sized bowl, combine cottage cheese, sour cream, onion and cooked noodles.

6. In a 3-quart, heat-resistant, non-metallic casserole alternate layers of noodle mixture and meat mixture, starting with the noodles. Heat, uncovered, on ROAST for 13 minutes.

7. Sprinkle cheese over top of casserole. Heat, uncovered, on ROAST for 5 minutes or until cheese has melted.

Cheeseburgers

1½ pounds lean ground beef
Salt
Brown bouquet sauce (optional)
Water (optional)
6 hamburger buns
6 cheese slices

Serves 6

1. Form beef into 6 patties about ½-inch thick.
2. Sprinkle with salt and brush patties with a 1-to-1 mixture of brown bouquet sauce and water, if a deep brown color is desired.
3. Arrange patties in a circle in a paper-towel-lined, shallow, heat-resistant, non-metallic baking dish. Do not place any patties in the center of the circle. Heat, covered with paper toweling, on ROAST for 7 minutes. Turn patties over.
4. Brush again with brown bouquet mixture, if desired.
5. Heat, uncovered, on ROAST for 1 minute. Burgers will be rare. Heat an additional 1 to 2 minutes for medium or well-done.
6. Place 1 patty on each hamburger bun and top each hamburger with a slice of cheese. Arrange hamburgers on a heat-resistant, non-metallic serving platter and heat, uncovered, on ROAST for 3 minutes or until cheese is melted.

9

Fiesta Tamale Pie   140°F

1 tablespoon vegetable oil
1 small onion, minced
1 clove garlic, peeled and crushed
1 pound lean ground beef
¼ pound bulk pork sausage
1 (16-ounce) can stewed tomatoes, undrained
1 (17-ounce) can whole kernel corn, drained
1½ teaspoons salt
1½ teaspoons chili powder
2 eggs, well beaten
1 cup corn meal
1 cup milk
18 pitted ripe olives
1 cup shredded Cheddar cheese

Serves 6

1. Combine vegetable oil, onion and garlic in a large, heat-resistant, non-metallic mixing bowl; heat, uncovered, on FULL POWER 2 minutes or until onion is tender.
2. Add ground beef and sausage to onion and garlic. Heat, uncovered, on ROAST for 7 minutes or until meat is browned. Stir occasionally.
3. Drain excess fat.
4. Add tomatoes, corn, salt and chili powder to meat mixture. Heat, uncovered, on ROAST for 6 minutes.
5. While meat mixture is cooking, combine eggs, corn meal and milk in a medium-sized bowl. Blend thoroughly. Set aside.
6. Pour meat mixture into an 8-inch square, heat-resistant, non-metallic baking dish.
7. Press olives into meat mixture.
8. Pour corn meal mixture over meat mixture.
9. Sprinkle cheese on top. Heat, uncovered, on ROAST for 12 minutes or until cheese melts.

Roast Loin Of Pork With Apricot Glaze

170°F

1 (12-ounce) package dried
  apricots
1 (3-inch) stick cinnamon
½ lemon, seeds removed
½ cup water
1 cup apricot nectar
2 tablespoons orange juice
3 tablespoons honey
1 (6-pound) loin of pork roast
  with bone tips Frenched

Serves 6 to 8

1. Remove twice as many dried apricot halves from the package as there are bones on the roast and set aside. Place remaining dried apricots, cinnamon, the juice from the lemon half, the remainder of the lemon half cut into quarters, and the water in a medium-sized heat-resistant, non-metallic bowl.

2. Heat mixture, uncovered, on ROAST for 10 minutes or until apricots are tender. Remove cinnamon stick and lemon rind chunks.

3. Add apricot nectar, orange juice and honey. Heat, uncovered, on ROAST for 3 minutes.

4. Spread glaze over pork loin and heat, uncovered, in a shallow, heat-resistant, non-metallic baking dish in Microwave Oven on ROAST for 12 minutes per pound, or until meat thermometer inserted in the thickest part of the meat registers 170° to 175°F.

5. While roast cooks, baste meat with glaze. Place thickest section of roast to outside edge of turntable.

6. Allow roast to stand wrapped in aluminum foil 15 minutes. DO NOT PLACE CONVENTIONAL THERMOMETER OR ALUMINUM FOIL IN MICROWAVE OVEN.

7. Before serving, place two of the reserved apricot halves on each bone tip. Press apricot halves firmly together so they stay in place. Pork should be cooked to well-done. After standing time, pork should register 180° to 185°F.

Pork Chops And Sauerkraut

170°F

2 tablespoons vegetable oil
4 pork chops, cut 1-inch thick
  (about 2 pounds)
Salt and pepper
½ cup thinly sliced onion
1 (16-ounce) can sauerkraut,
  undrained
½ teaspoon caraway seeds
1 tart apple, peeled, cored and
  thinly sliced
½ cup water

Serves 3 to 4

1. In a heat-resistant, non-metallic skillet, heat oil on a conventional surface unit until hot.

2. Sear pork chops on both sides until browned.

3. Sprinkle chops lightly with salt and pepper, to taste. Drain any excess fat.

4. Arrange onion and sauerkraut over pork chops.

5. Heat, covered, on SIMMER for 10 minutes.

6. Sprinkle caraway seeds over sauerkraut and arrange apple slices on top.

7. Add water and heat, covered, on SIMMER for 10 minutes. Heat, uncovered, on SIMMER for 10 minutes or until pork chops are fork-tender. Pork should always be cooked to well-done.

Tip: If a heat-resistant, non-metallic skillet is not available, any skillet may be used for browning, and the seared chops may be transferred to a shallow, 1½-quart or 2-quart, heat-resistant, non-metallic casserole after Step 3.

Stuffed Pork Chops

170°F

4 double pork chops, with pockets cut (1½ to 2 pounds)
2 cups bread stuffing

1. Fill pockets of pork chops with your favorite bread stuffing and secure with wooden picks.
2. Brown pork chops in a skillet on top of a conventional surface unit.
3. Place chops in a shallow, 3-quart, heat-resistant, non-metallic baking dish. Heat, covered, on SIMMER for 25 to 30 minutes. Pork should always be cooked until well-done.

Pork Chop Casserole

170°F

4 pork chops, (about 1½ pounds)
2 tablespoons Worcestershire sauce
2 tablespoons butter or margarine
1 (10½-ounce) can cream of celery soup
1 medium onion, finely chopped
¼ teaspoon pepper
1½ teaspoons dried parsley flakes

Serves 4

1. Brush pork chops with Worcestershire sauce and brown in the 2 tablespoons butter in a large skillet on a conventional surface unit.
2. In a small bowl combine celery soup, onion, pepper and parsley flakes.
3. Pour half the celery soup mixture in a 3-quart, heat-resistant, non-metallic baking dish. Place pork chops on top and pour remaining sauce over pork chops.
4. Heat, uncovered, on SIMMER for 22 to 24 minutes. Pork should always be cooked to well-done.
5. Serve with noodles or mashed potatoes.

Barbecued Spareribs

3 pounds pork or lamb spareribs, cut into serving pieces
2 teaspoons chili power
2 cups barbecue sauce (see recipe pape 111)
2 tablespoons lemon juice (optional)

Serves 4 to 5

1. Place spareribs in a large, shallow, heat-resistant, non-metallic baking dish.
2. Heat, uncovered, on SIMMER for 14 minutes.
3. Turn spareribs over and heat on SIMMER for 14 minutes.
4. Drain off excess fat.
5. Combine chili powder and barbecue sauce.
6. Pour half of sauce over ribs.
7. Heat, uncovered, on SIMMER for 8 minutes.
8. Turn spareribs again. Sprinkle with lemon juice if desired.
9. Pour on remaining sauce and heat, uncovered, for 16 minutes or until fork-tender. Pork should always be cooked until well-done.

Cinnamon Spareribs

3 pounds spareribs, cut into ribs
Cinnamon
Ground cloves
½ cup soy sauce
2 tablespoons sugar

1. Place spareribs on turntable or on large, heat-resistant, non-metallic platter. Sprinkle with cinnamon and cloves. Baste with mixture of soy sauce and sugar.
2. Heat, uncovered, on SIMMER for 50 to 55 minutes. Turn over occasionally and drain fat as needed. Baste with soy sauce mixture occasionally.

German Style Barbecued Spareribs

2 tablespoons butter
¼ cup finely chopped onion
2 tablespoons firmly packed dark brown sugar
½ teaspoon salt
⅛ teaspoon pepper
2 tablespoons prepared mustard
½ cup catsup
3 cups sauerkraut, drained
1 large apple, pared, cored and chopped
2 teaspoons caraway seeds
3 pounds spareribs, cut into ribs

Serves 6

1. In a medium-sized, heat-resistant, non-metallic bowl, heat butter on FULL POWER 30 seconds.

2. Add onion, brown sugar, pepper, salt, mustard and catsup.

3. Heat, uncovered, on FULL POWER 3 minutes.

4. In a 3-quart, heat-resistant, non-metallic casserole, place sauerkraut, apple and caraway seeds. Stir to combine thoroughly.

5. Dip each sparerib into sauce and place on top of sauerkraut. Pour remaining barbecue sauce over the top. Heat, covered, on SIMMER for 40 to 50 minutes. Pork should always be cooked to well-done.

Lamb Stew

3½ pounds lean lamb neck meat, cut in large cubes
2 bay leaves
10 whole black peppercorns
1 teaspoon dried thyme leaves
1 tablespoon salt
1 clove garlic, peeled and crushed
3 cups water
3 medium carrots, peeled and thinly sliced
3 cups potatoes, cut into ½-inch cubes
6 tablespoons flour
¾ cup cold water

Serves 6

1. Place lamb, bay leaves, peppercorns, thyme, salt, garlic and the 3 cups water in a deep, 3-quart, heat-resistant, non-metallic casserole.

2. Heat, covered, on FULL POWER 5 minutes.

3. Skim any foam that may form.

4. Heat, covered, on FULL POWER for an additional 25 minutes or until lamb is almost tender. Stir occasionally.

5. Add carrots and potatoes, and heat, covered, on FULL POWER 20 minutes or until lamb and vegetables are tender. Stir occasionally.

6. While lamb and vegetables are cooking, combine the 6 tablespoons flour and ¾ cup water in small bowl.

7. Remove bay leaves and peppercorns from stew.

8. Gradually stir flour mixture into stew and heat on FULL POWER 3 minutes or until sauce is thickened and smooth.

TIP: Boneless lamb may be used, however, reduce quantity of meat to 2½ pounds and decrease cooking time in Step 4 to 15 minutes.

Lamb Chops à l'Orange

155°F

4 shoulder lamb chops (about 2 pounds)
Garlic salt
4 fresh orange slices, ½-inch thick
½ cup orange marmalade

Serves 3 to 4

1. Place chops in a 10-inch, heat-resistant, non-metallic skillet.

2. Sprinkle chops with garlic salt.

3. Place fresh orange slice on top of each chop. Spread orange marmalade over each chop and orange slice.

4. Heat, covered, on ROAST for 25 minutes or until chops are tender.

Ham Loaf

175°F

¾ pound ham
½ pound veal
¼ pound pork
2 eggs, beaten
¾ cup soft bread crumbs
¾ cup milk
Dash of pepper
¼ cup firmly packed brown
    sugar
2 teaspoons prepared mustard
⅓ cup pineapple juice

Serves 4

1. Grind ham, veal and pork together into a large mixing bowl. Add eggs, bread crumbs, milk and pepper. Combine ingredients well.

2. Pat mixture into a 1½-quart, heat-resistant, non-metallic loaf pan.

3. In a small bowl combine brown sugar and mustard. Spread top of loaf with mustard mixture.

4. Pour pineapple juice over loaf.

5. Heat, covered with plastic wrap, on ROAST for 30 minutes. Allow to stand 5 minutes before serving.

Sweet And Sour Lamb Chops

155°F

2 tablespoons butter or
    margarine
2 pounds shoulder lamb chops
Salt and pepper
1 (8-ounce) can pineapple
    chunks in unsweetened juice,
    undrained
¼ cup firmly packed dark brown
    sugar
¼ cup white vinegar
1 tablespoon cornstarch
½ teaspoon brown bouquet
    sauce
2 carrots, peeled and thinly
    sliced
1 large green pepper, cut into
    1-inch squares

Serves 3 to 4

1. Melt butter in a heat-resistant, non-metallic 10-inch skillet on a conventional surface unit. When butter is hot, sear lamb chops on both sides until lightly browned. Sprinkle with salt and pepper to taste.

2. While the chops are browning, drain pineapple juice into a small heat-resistant, non-metallic bowl. Reserve pineapple chunks; add brown sugar, vinegar, cornstarch and brown bouquet sauce to pineapple juice. Stir to combine.

3. Heat pineapple juice mixture, uncovered, on FULL POWER 2 minutes or until thickened and clear.

4. Pour thickened sauce over browned lamb chops.

5. Add carrot slices and heat, covered, on ROAST for 7 minutes. Add pineapple chunks and heat, covered, on ROAST for 3 minutes. Add green pepper squares and heat, uncovered, on ROAST for 4 to 5 minutes, or until lamb and vegetables are tender.

Variations: Pork chops, veal chops, boneless chicken pieces or shrimp may be substituted for the lamb chops; however, cooking times will have to be adjusted for pork, chicken, and shrimp. Pork chops will require an extra 3 minutes in Step 5, as pork should always be cooked to well-done. Chicken should be cooked for only 5 minutes in Step 5 and shrimp for 2 minutes.

Moussaka (Lamb And Eggplant Casserole)

4 (7 to 8-inch) eggplants, washed
1 tablespoon salt
2 tablespoons olive oil
2 pounds lean ground lamb
Vegetable oil
⅔ cup finely chopped onion
1 (8-ounce) can sliced mushrooms, drained
1 teaspoon salt
1 teaspoon dried rosemary leaves
½ teaspoon dried thyme leaves
1 clove garlic, peeled and crushed
⅔ cup beef stock or broth
1½ teaspoons cornstarch
3 tablespoons tomato paste, (save remainder for sauce)
3 eggs, slightly beaten
Tomato Sauce (see recipe on next page)

Serves 6

1. Remove green caps from eggplants and slice eggplants in half lengthwise. Make deep slashes in eggplant pulp, but do not cut through skins. Sprinkle eggplant halves with the 1 table-spoon salt and allow to stand at room temperature ½ hour.

2. Squeeze moisture out of eggplant halves and brush cut surfaces with the 2 tablespoons of olive oil. Heat 4 eggplant halves at a time on FULL POWER 7 minutes or until pulp is tender. Repeat with remaining eggplant halves.

3. Scoop pulp out of eggplant, being careful not to rip skins. Set skins aside. Chop eggplant pulp coarsely. Place pulp in a medium-sized, heat-resistant, non-metallic bowl and heat, un-covered, on FULL POWER 4 minutes or until tender. Stir occasionally.

4. In a large heat-resistant, non-metallic bowl, crumble the lamb. Heat, uncovered, on ROAST for 7 minutes stirring frequently to break up pieces.

5. Liberally oil a deep, 2-quart, heat-resistant, non-metallic cas-serole. Line casserole with the reserved eggplant skins. Ar-range skins with the purple sides toward the outside and wide ends of eggplant skins at the top of the casserole.

6. Drain the lamb juice and discard. Add chopped eggplant, onion, mushrooms, the 1 teaspoon salt, thyme, rosemary and garlic to the cooked lamb. Stir to combine well. Heat, un-covered, on ROAST for 7 minutes or until onion is tender.

7. In a small heat-resistant, non-metallic bowl combine beef stock and cornstarch until smooth. Heat, uncovered, on FULL POWER 1 minute or until thickened and clear; stir occasionally.

8. Add thickened beef stock with remaining ingredients, except tomato sauce, to lamb mixture. Pour lamb-eggplant mixture into eggplant-skin-lined casserole.

9. Fold eggplant skins over filling. Heat, covered, on ROAST for 11 minutes or until a knife inserted in the center of the mixture comes out clean.

10. Invert onto platter for serving. Serve with tomato sauce.

Tomato Sauce For Moussaka

180°F

3 tablespoons vegetable oil
½ cup finely chopped onion
1 clove garlic, peeled and
   crushed
1 (15-ounce) can tomato sauce
1 (6-ounce) can tomato paste
   minus 3 tablespoons
2 teaspoons sugar
½ teaspoon dried thyme leaves
½ teaspoon dried rosemary
   leaves
½ teaspoon salt
¼ teaspoon pepper

1. Place oil and onions in a deep, 1½-quart, heat-resistant, non-metallic casserole. Heat, uncovered, on FULL POWER 3 minutes or until onions are tender.

2. Add remaining ingredients; stir to combine well. Heat, covered, on FULL POWER 6 minutes or until sauce bubbles.

Serves 6

Note: If time permits, tomato sauce may be heated on SIMMER 12 to 15 minutes to develop flavor.

Veal Chops Italienne

160°F

9

2 tablespoons vegetable oil
Large clove garlic, peeled and
   crushed
4 (1-inch thick) veal chops
   (approximately 2 pounds)
Salt and pepper, to taste
1 (8-ounce) can tomato sauce
2 tablespoons red wire
1 teaspoon dried oregano leaves
1 teaspoon chopped, freeze-
   dried chives
½ teaspoon sugar
¼ cup grated Parmesan cheese

1. In a heat-resistant, non-metallic 10-inch skillet, place 2 table-spoons vegetable oil. Add crushed garlic.

2. Heat oil on top of a conventional surface unit. Sear veal chops in hot oil until brown on both sides. Season veal chops to taste with salt and pepper. Set aside.

3. In a medium-sized bowl, combine tomato sauce, red wine, oregano, chives and sugar. Blend thoroughly.

4. Pour sauce over veal chops. Heat, uncovered, on ROAST for 15 to 18 minutes.

5. Sprinkle top of chops with ¼ cup Parmesan cheese and heat on ROAST for 2 minutes.

Serves 4

Veal Continental

1½ pounds veal, cut up for
   stewing
2 tablespoons butter or
   margarine
2 tablespoons flour
1½ cups beef bouillon
1 large tomato, sliced
1 cup thinly sliced fresh
   mushrooms
1 onion, minced
1 bay leaf
1 tablespoon tomato paste
Salt and pepper, to taste

1. Brown veal in butter in a heat-resistant, non-metallic skillet on top of a conventional surface unit.

2. Remove veal. Blend in flour. Gradually stir in beef bouillon.

3. Add tomato, mushrooms, onion, bay leaf and tomato paste to beef bouillon mixture.

4. Heat, uncovered, on FULL POWER for 10 minutes or until mixture begins to bubble.

5. Season with salt and pepper, to taste. Add browned veal.

6. Heat, uncovered, on SIMMER for 25 minutes or until veal is fork-tender. Serve with rice or noodles.

Serves 4

Veal Scallopini

1 pound veal steak, cut ¼-inch
  thick
⅔ teaspoon salt
⅔ teaspoon paprika
⅓ cup vegetable oil
3 tablespoons lemon juice
1 clove garlic, peeled and
  crushed
⅔ teaspoon prepared mustard
½ teaspoon sugar
⅛ teaspoon nutmeg
3 tablespoons flour
Vegetable oil
1 small onion, sliced
1 green pepper, cut in thin
  strips
1 cup chicken bouillon
¼ cup thinly sliced fresh
  mushrooms

Serves 4

1. Cut veal into serving pieces.

2. Combine salt, paprika, oil, lemon juice, garlic, mustard, sugar and nutmeg in a shallow bowl. Stir to combine.

3. Dip each piece of veal into sauce and then coat well with flour. Reserve any remaining sauce. Brown veal in a small amount of oil in a 10-inch, heat-resistant, non-metallic skillet, on top of a conventional surface unit.

4. Drain excess fat.

5. Add onion and green pepper to veal.

6. Combine chicken bouillon with remaining sauce and pour over veal, pepper and onions.

7. Heat, covered, on ROAST for 12 minutes.

8. Add mushrooms to veal mixture. Spoon sauce over veal.

9. Heat, covered, on ROAST for an additional 6 minutes.

Veal à la Madelon

3 tablespoons vegetable oil
¼ cup flour
1 teaspoon salt
¼ teaspoon pepper
1 clove garlic, peeled and
  crushed
2 pounds boneless veal, cut into
  bite-sized pieces
1 cup boiling water
2 (1-inch strips) lemon rind
½ teaspoon sage
Dash cayenne pepper
1 cup heavy cream
2 tablespoons finely chopped
  parsley

Serves 4

1. In a heat-resistant, non-metallic 10-inch skillet, heat 3 tablespoons oil on top of a conventional surface unit.

2. While oil is heating, combine flour, salt and pepper in a paper or plastic bag.

3. Coat veal pieces with seasoned flour.

4. Add crushed garlic to hot oil.

5. Brown coated veal pieces in hot oil.

6. When veal pieces are browned, add boiling water, lemon rind, sage and cayenne pepper. Stir to combine.

7. Heat, covered, on ROAST for 15 minutes or until veal is tender.

8. Remove lemon rind and stir cream into veal mixture gradually.

9. Heat, covered, on ROAST, an additional 8 minutes. Stir once.

10. Garnish with chopped parsley before serving.

Tip: Boil the water in your Microwave Oven! Heat water in a glass measuring cup on FULL POWER for 3 minutes or until water boils.

Pictured: Steamed Lobster

Cooking Hints

Your family's enjoyment of fish and seafood will be increased by the enhanced flavor and texture from microwave cooking.

Fish and seafood require only a short cooking time since there is no tough tissue. Baked fish may be brushed with melted butter and sprinkled with paprika for enhanced flavor and appearance.

Most fish and seafood should be covered during cooking and standing time. Avoid overcooking! After several minutes of standing time, fish should be easily flaked with a fork. This indicates that the fish is done.

Shellfish has completed cooking when the meat appears opaque and the shell is pink.

Fish is generally cooked on FULL POWER. If a white sauce is added, reducing the setting to ROAST is suggested.

Recommended temperature for fish is 130° to 135°F. Fish should not register over 145°F, even after standing time.

Baked Fish

1 (2-ounce) package seasoned
  coating mix for fish
1 pound fish fillets or serving
  size pieces of fish
Water

Serves 3 to 4

1. Lightly grease a shallow, 10-inch, heat-resistant, non-metallic baking dish.

2. Empty seasoned coating mix into the plastic shaker bag.

3. Moisten fillets with water. Shake off excess water.

4. Shake 1 or 2 fillets at a time in the bag until evenly coated.

5. Arrange in greased baking dish.

6. Heat, uncovered, on FULL POWER 7 minutes or until fish is easily flaked with a fork.

Note: If frozen fillets are used, partially defrost in Microwave Oven and do not moisten with water.

Fish In Wine Casserole

2 tablespoons butter or
  margarine
1 medium onion, thinly
  sliced
½ cup dry white wine
2 pounds halibut fillets, cut into
  2-inch pieces
Milk
3 tablespoons butter or
  margarine
3 tablespoons flour
1½ teaspoons salt
⅛ teaspoon pepper
1 (8½-ounce) can small peas,
  drained
1½ cups Chinese fried noodles

Serves 4 to 6

1. In a shallow, 1½-quart, heat-resistant, non-metallic casserole melt the 2 tablespoons of butter on FULL POWER 30 seconds.

2. Add onion and heat, uncovered, on FULL POWER 3 minutes or until onion is tender but not browned.

3. Add wine and fish and heat, covered, on FULL POWER 6 minutes or until fish flakes easily with fork.

4. Drain pan juices into a measuring cup and add enough milk to pan juices to equal 2 cups. Set fish and liquid aside.

5. In a small, heat-resistant, non-metallic bowl, melt the 3 tablespoons of butter or margarine on FULL POWER for 30 seconds.

6. Stir in flour, salt and pepper. Gradually stir in reserved fish liquid mixture.

7. Heat, uncovered, on ROAST for 8 minutes, stirring twice until thickened and smooth.

8. Add peas to sauce.

9. Add sauce to fish in the casserole and stir gently.

10. Heat, uncovered, on ROAST for 3 minutes.

11. Sprinkle noodles over fish and heat, uncovered, on ROAST for 2 minutes.

10

Poached Fish

Butter or margarine
2½ pounds fish fillets
Salt and pepper
¼ cup finely chopped onion
1 cup dry white wine

Serves 4 to 6

1. Lightly butter a shallow, heat-resistant, non-metallic baking dish.

2. Place fillets in baking dish.

3. Sprinkle with salt and pepper to taste. Sprinkle with onions and pour wine over fish.

4. Heat, covered tightly with clear plastic wrap, on FULL POWER 10 minutes or until fish flakes easily. Baste fish with wine and onions several times during cooking.

Variation: Tomato juice, water, chicken broth or clam juice may be substituted for wine.

Stuffed Fillet Of Sole With Mushroom Sauce

Butter or margarine
2½ pounds salmon-stuffed sole
  fillets
Salt and pepper, to taste
¼ cup finely chopped onion
1 cup dry white wine
⅓ cup butter or margarine
1 cup thinly sliced fresh
  mushrooms
4 tablespoons flour
1½ cups light cream
Paprika

Serves 6

1. Butter a shallow, heat-resistant, non-metallic baking dish lightly. Place stuffed-sole fillets in baking dish. Sprinkle with salt and pepper to taste.

2. Sprinkle onions over fish fillets and pour wine over fish. Heat, covered with clear plastic wrap, on FULL POWER 7 to 8 minutes or until fish flakes easily with a fork. Baste fish with wine and onions several times during cooking. Set poached fish aside.

3. In a medium-sized, heat-resistant, non-metallic bowl melt the ⅓ cup butter or margarine on FULL POWER 45 seconds. Add mushroom slices and heat, uncovered, on FULL POWER 2 minutes.

4. Blend in flour until smooth. Gradually add cream, stirring until smooth. Return sauce to Microwave Oven and heat on ROAST, uncovered, 6 to 7 minutes or until mixture is thickened and smooth. Stir occasionally.

5. Add ½ cup fish liquid from baking dish to mushroom sauce and stir until well blended.

6. Place fish fillets on a heat-resistant, non-metallic serving platter. Spoon mushroom sauce over fish. Heat, uncovered, on ROAST for 3 to 4 minutes or until heated through. Sprinkle with paprika just before serving.

Note: Many fish markets sell sole pre-stuffed with salmon. However, if this is not available, you can roll a piece of fresh salmon (about 1 inch in diameter and 4 inches long) in a small fillet. Fasten each roll with a wooden pick. Unstuffed sole or sole that has been stuffed with shrimp, clams, scallops or crab meat can also be used for this recipe. It is advisable to roll sole fillets even though they may not be stuffed.

Poached Sole With Shrimp Sauce

Butter or margarine
2 (16-ounce) packages frozen
  sole fillets
2 tablespoons finely chopped
  green onion or shallots
Salt and pepper
¾ cup dry white wine
4 tablespoons butter or
  margarine
2 tablespoons flour
1 cup light cream or milk
1 (4½-ounce) can medium-sized
  shrimp, rinsed and drained
Chopped parsley

Serves 4

1. Butter a shallow, heat-resistant, non-metallic baking dish lightly.

2. Place frozen fish fillets in baking dish and heat, covered, on DEFROST for 10 minutes.

3. Separate fish fillets and arrange in baking dish. Sprinkle fish with chopped green onion, salt and pepper to taste. Pour wine over the fish. Heat, covered with clear plastic wrap, on FULL POWER 10 minutes or until fish flakes easily with a fork. Baste fish several times during heating. Fish should be 130°–135°F.

4. Place cooked fish on a heat-resistant, non-metallic serving platter and set aside. Reserve liquid.

5. In a small, heat-resistant, non-metallic bowl, melt the 4 tablespoons butter on FULL POWER 30 seconds.

6. Blend in flour until smooth.

7. Gradually stir in cream until smooth.

8. Return sauce to Microwave Oven and heat, uncovered, on ROAST, 4 to 5 minutes or until thickened and smooth. Stir occasionally. Set sauce aside.

9. Return reserved fish liquid to Microwave Oven and heat, uncovered, on ROAST, 4 to 6 minutes or until liquid has been reduced to ½ cup.

10. Stir fish liquid and shrimp into reserved sauce until well blended.

11. Spoon shrimp sauce over fish. Heat, uncovered, on ROAST for 2 to 3 minutes or until heated through.

12. Garnish with chopped parsley.

10

Fillet Of Flounder In Lemon Parsley Butter

½ cup butter or margarine,
  melted
2 tablespoons cornstarch
3 tablespoons lemon juice
1 tablespoon chopped fresh
  parsley
2 pounds flounder or sole fillets
Celery salt, to taste
Pepper, to taste

Serves 6

1. Melt butter in a 12 x 7-inch, heat-resistant, non-metallic baking dish on FULL POWER for 1 minute. Add cornstarch, lemon juice and parsley. Stir to blend well.

2. Dip each fillet in butter sauce. Arrange in baking dish.

3. Sprinkle fillets with celery salt and pepper, to taste. Cover loosely with clear plastic wrap and heat on FULL POWER for 7 minutes or until fish flakes easily with a fork.

4. Let stand covered for 2 minutes to finish cooking. Spoon sauce over each serving.

Fillet Of Flounder With Broccoli

¼ cup butter or margarine
¼ cup flour
1 teaspoon salt
1 teaspoon dried tarragon leaves
⅛ teaspoon pepper
1 cup milk
¼ cup dry white wine
¼ cup water
2 (10-ounce) packages frozen chopped broccoli
Lemon juice
2 (16-ounce) packages frozen flounder fillets, thawed
Salt and pepper
2 tablespoons grated Parmesan cheese

Serves 6 to 8

1. In a medium-sized, heat-resistant, non-metallic bowl, heat butter on FULL POWER 1 minute or until melted.

2. Add flour, salt, tarragon leaves and pepper. Stir until smooth. Add milk, a little at a time, stirring after each addition. Heat, uncovered, on ROAST for 6 minutes or until thickened and smooth. Stir occasionally.

3. Stir in wine. Heat, uncovered, an additional 3 minutes on ROAST. Set sauce aside.

4. In a deep, 1½-quart, heat-resistant, non-metallic casserole place ¼ cup water and chopped broccoli. Heat, covered, on FULL POWER 5 minutes. Stir. Heat, covered, an additional 5 minutes on FULL POWER or until broccoli is heated through. Drain excess water.

5. Add 1 cup of sauce and 2 tablespoons lemon juice to cooked broccoli, mixing gently to combine.

6. Brush fillets with lemon juice and sprinkle with salt and pepper, to taste.

7. Arrange fillets in a 3-quart, heat-resistant, non-metallic baking dish, with fillets overlapping. Spoon brocooli mixture around the edge of fillets. Spoon remaining sauce over fish.

8. Heat, uncovered, on ROAST for 10 to 11 minutes. Sprinkle Parmesan cheese over top of fish and heat, uncovered, an additional 6 minutes on ROAST or until cheese is melted.

Tuna Shrimp Delight
160°F

1 (10¾-ounce) can cream of mushroom soup
1 (9¼-ounce) can chunk tuna, drained
8 ounces frozen shrimp
1 (8-ounce) can pitted black olives, drained and sliced in half
¼ cup cooking sherry
1 (10½-ounce) package frozen asparagus spears, defrosted
2 slices white bread, conventionally toasted

Serves 6

1. Place first 4 ingredients in a shallow, 1½-quart, heat-resistant, non-metallic casserole. Pour sherry over ingredients and mix gently.

2. Arrange asparagus spears over mixture and heat on FULL POWER 8 minutes or until mixture bubbles.

3. Cut conventionally toasted bread into 9 squares per slice. Arrange toast squares on top of casserole filling during last 30 seconds of cooking time.

Note: Thaw frozen asparagus spears on the DEFROST setting of your Microwave Oven. Canned asparagus may be substituted but cooking time will be reduced slightly.

Trout Almondine

⅓ cup butter or margarine
½ cup slivered blanched
  almonds
4 (8-ounce) trout
4 tablespoons butter or
  margarine
1½ teaspoons lemon juice
  Salt and pepper

Serves 4

1. In a small, heat-resistant, non-metallic bowl, melt the ⅓ cup butter on FULL POWER 30 seconds.

2. Add almonds and heat, uncovered, on FULL POWER 3 minutes or until lightly browned; stir occasionally. Set almonds aside.

3. Arrange fish in a shallow, 10-inch, heat-resistant, non-metallic baking dish.

4. Place 1 tablespoon of butter on each fish and sprinkle with lemon juice and salt and pepper, to taste.

5. Heat, covered with wax paper, on FULL POWER 8 to 10 minutes or until fish flakes easily with a fork.

6. Spoon browned almonds over fish and heat, uncovered, on FULL POWER 2 minutes or until heated through.

Teriyaki Fish

¾ cup soy sauce
½ cup sugar
1 teaspoon grated fresh ginger
  root
1 clove garlic, peeled and
  crushed
¼ teaspoon monosodium
  glutamate (optional)
1 tablespoon sake (Japanese
  rice wine) or cooking sherry
1½ pounds fish fillets

Serves 3 to 4

1. In a shallow, 2-quart, heat-resistant, non-metallic baking dish combine soy sauce, sugar, ginger root, garlic, monosodium glutamate and sake. Stir to combine well.

2. Place fish fillets in sauce mixture and marinate for one half hour.

3. Heat, uncovered, on FULL POWER for 9 minutes basting occasionally with sauce.

10

Baked Tuna Chow Mein Casserole

160°F

2 tablespoons butter or
  margarine
1 cup chopped celery
¼ cup chopped onion
2 tablespoons chopped green
  pepper
1 tablespoon butter
1 (7-ounce) can tuna
1 (10½-ounce) can cream of
  mushroom soup
1 cup chow mein noodles
⅛ teaspoon pepper
⅓ cup chow mein noodles

Serves 4

1. In a deep, 1½-quart, heat-resistant, non-metallic casserole, melt 2 tablespoons butter or margarine on FULL POWER 30 seconds.

2. Add celery, onion and green pepper to melted butter. Heat, uncovered, on FULL POWER 4 minutes or until vegetables are tender.

3. Combine remaining ingredients except ⅓ cup chow mein noodles with vegetables. Blend well. Top with ⅓ cup of chow mein noodles. Heat on ROAST for 12 minutes or until sauce bubbles.

Shrimp Creole

3 tablespoons butter or
   margarine
1 cup finely chopped onion
¾ cup finely chopped green
   pepper
¼ cup finely chopped celery
2 tablespoons flour
2 tablespoons dried parsley
   flakes
1 (15-ounce) can tomatoes
1 teaspoon sugar
1 teaspoon salt
⅛ to ¼ teaspoon Tabasco sauce
Few leaves dried thyme
⅛ teaspoon pepper
1 (12-ounce) package frozen
   raw shrimp, shelled and
   deveined

Serves 4

1. Melt butter in a deep, 3-quart, heat-resistant, non-metallic casserole 30 seconds on FULL POWER.

2. Add onion, green pepper, and celery and heat, uncovered, on FULL POWER 4 minutes or until vegetables are crisp-tender. Stir occasionally.

3. Add flour and parsley flakes and stir until well blended.

4. Stir in tomatoes and heat, uncovered, on FULL POWER 3 minutes.

5. Add remaining ingredients and stir to blend. Heat, covered, on FULL POWER 7 minutes or until shrimp are pink and tender. Do not overcook as shrimp will become tough.

6. Let stand 3 to 5 minutes before serving. Serve over hot rice.

Shrimp Scampi

1 pound fresh jumbo shrimp
½ cup butter or margarine
2 tablespoons lemon juice
2 tablespoons dried parsley
   flakes
1 to 2 cloves garlic, peeled and
   crushed
½ teaspoon salt
Paprika (optional)

Serves 3 to 4

1. Under cold running water, remove the shells from the shrimp, leaving last tail section attached. Using a sharp, thin-bladed knife make a shallow cut lengthwise down the back of each shrimp and wash out the sand vein. If desired, the shrimp may be butterflied (cut lengthwise down the back of each shrimp, cutting almost completely through the shrimp, removing sand vein).

2. In a shallow, 2-quart, heat-resistant, non-metallic baking dish place butter, lemon juice, parsley flakes, garlic, to taste and salt.

3. Heat, uncovered, on FULL POWER 2 minutes.

4. Add shrimp and stir to coat well. If desired, sprinkle with paprika.

5. Heat, uncovered, on FULL POWER 6 minutes. Stir shrimp occasionally. Cook just until shrimp are pink and tender. Do not overcook shrimp as they will become tough.

Variation: If desired, lobster, scallops, crab meat or any combination of these may be substituted for shrimp.

Salmon Loaf

4 cups cooked or canned salmon
2 tablespoons lemon juice
1 cup milk
3 cups soft bread crumbs
2 eggs, beaten
¼ cup minced onion
½ teaspoon salt
¼ teaspoon pepper
1 tablespoon dried parsley flakes

Serves 4 to 6

1. In a large bowl sprinkle lemon juice over salmon.
2. In medium-sized bowl combine remaining ingredients. Pour over salmon and blend well.
3. Pour into a greased, heat-resistant, non-metallic loaf dish.
4. Heat, uncovered, on FULL POWER 10 minutes.
5. Cool 5 minutes. Place on serving platter.

Seafood Tetrazzini

150°F

2 tablespoons butter or margarine
3 tablespoons finely chopped onion
1 (10½-ounce) can cream of mushroom soup
½ cup water
1 cup elbow macaroni, cooked and drained
1 cup flaked, drained tuna, Shrimp or crab meat
½ cup grated Parmesan cheese, divided
⅓ cup sliced ripe olives
2 teaspoons lemon juice
⅛ teaspoon dried thyme leaves
⅛ teaspoon dried marjoram leaves

Serves 4

1. In a shallow, 1½-quart, heat-resistant, non-metallic baking dish, place 2 tablespoons butter.
2. Heat, uncovered, on FULL POWER 30 seconds.
3. Add onion to melted butter and heat, uncovered, on FULL POWER 2 minutes or until onion is tender.
4. Add soup, water and cooked macaroni to onions. Blend well.
5. Add remaining ingredients, except ¼ cup. Parmesan cheese to macaroni mixture. Combine well. Sprinkle remaining Parmesan cheese on top.
6. Heat, uncovered, on ROAST for 12 minutes.
7. If desired, top can be browned by placing under conventional broiler 3 minutes.

10

Steamed Clams

2 pounds steamers
¼ cup water

Serves 4

1. Place steamers and ¼ cup water in a cooking bag.
2. Tie the top of the bag with string. Do not use metal fasteners.
3. Pierce 3 holes near the top of the bag to allow the steam to escape.
4. Heat on FULL POWER 6 minutes or until shells open.

Tip: The live clams can be placed in a shallow pan with enough water to cover. Sprinkle a handful of corn meal over them and let stand a few hours or overnight. They will absorb the corn meal into their systems and it will clean out any sand as well as help in whitening the clam meat.

Scalloped Oysters

2 cups oysters, drained;
reserve liquid
1½ cups fine dry bread crumbs
⅔ cup liquid (half oyster liquid,
half milk or cream)
2 tablespoons chopped parsley
¼ cup finely chopped celery
½ teaspoon salt
¼ teaspoon pepper
1½ cups croutons

Serves 4

1. Combine all of the ingredients, except croutons, in a shallow, 2-quart, heat-resistant, non-metallic casserole.

2. Heat, uncovered, on FULL POWER 12 minutes.

3. Sprinkle croutons on top of casserole and heat, uncovered, on FULL POWER an additional 1 to 2 minutes or until heated through.

Oyster Stew

165°F

2 tablespoons butter or
margarine
1 (8-ounce) can oysters or
½ pint shucked oysters
Milk
⅛ teaspoon celery salt
Dash cayenne pepper
Paprika

Serves 2

1. Melt butter or margarine in a deep, 1-quart, heat-resistant, non-metallic casserole on FULL POWER 30 seconds.

2. While butter or margarine is melting, drain oysters and reserve liquid.

3. Add drained oysters to butter or margarine and heat, covered, on FULL POWER 2 minutes or until edges of oysters are curled.

4. Pour oyster liquid into a 2-cup heat-resistant, non-metallic measuring cup, and add enough milk to measure 1½ cups.

5. Add milk mixture to oysters with celery salt and cayenne pepper.

6. Heat, covered, on ROAST for 5 minutes or until serving temperature is reached.

7. Sprinkle with paprika and serve in soup bowls with crackers.

Steamed Lobster

½ cup water
½ teaspoon salt
1 lemon, sliced
2 (1½-pound) live lobsters,
pegged

Serves 2

1. In a deep, 3-quart, heat-resistant, non-metallic casserole place water, salt and lemon.

2. Heat, uncovered, on FULL POWER 3 minutes or until water boils.

3. Place live lobsters, head first, into boiling water to render them immobile.

4. Heat, covered, on FULL POWER 12 minutes.

5. Let stand, covered, 4 minutes to finish cooking.

6. Drain. With a sharp, heavy knife, split tail. If meat is still translucent in center, heat, covered, about 1 minute longer or until meat is opaque. Continue to cut up the center towards the head. Remove the stomach and the intestinal tract. The green liver and the red roe are considered to be delicacies.

144

Lobster Newburg

2 (9-ounce) lobster tails, removed from shells
Melted butter or margarine
¼ cup butter or margarine
2 tablespoons flour
½ teaspoon salt
Dash cayenne pepper
1½ cups light cream or milk
2 egg yolks
¼ cup sherry or dry white wine
1 teaspoon lemon juice

Serves 4

1. Place lobster tails in a shallow, heat-resistant, non-metallic baking dish and brush liberally with melted butter.

2. Heat, covered, on FULL POWER 4 minutes or until tender. Cut lobster into bite-sized pieces. Set aside.

3. In a deep, 1½-quart, heat-resistant, non-metallic casserole melt the ¼ cup butter on FULL POWER 30 seconds.

4. Blend in flour, salt and cayenne.

5. In a small bowl, beat cream and egg yolks until well blended.

6. Gradually stir cream mixture into flour mixture until smooth.

7. Heat, covered, on ROAST for 6 to 7 minutes or until sauce thickens. Stir occasionally.

8. Stir in lemon juice, lobster pieces and wine. If necessary, heat on ROAST for 2 to 3 minutes or until heated to 150°F.

9. Serve over rice or toast points.

Variation: If desired, shrimp, scallops, crab meat or any combination of these may be substituted for lobster.

Lobster En Casserole

2 tablespoons butter or margarine
1 cup soft bread crumbs
1 tablespoon butter or margarine
2 tablespoons finely chopped onion
½ clove garlic, peeled and crushed
⅔ cup canned Cheddar cheese soup
1 (4-ounce) can sliced mushrooms, drained
¼ cup milk
2 tablespoons dry sherry
1 tablespoon chopped parsley
½ cup cooked peas, drained
1½ cups canned, fresh or frozen cooked lobster, cubed

Serves 4

1. In a small, heat-resistant, non-metallic bowl melt the 2 tablespoons butter on FULL POWER for 30 seconds.

2. Place soft bread crumbs in melted butter and coat with butter. Set aside.

3. In deep, 2½-quart, heat-resistant, non-metallic casserole place the 1 tablespoon butter. Heat 30 seconds on FULL POWER.

4. Add onion and garlic to melted butter and heat, uncovered, on FULL POWER 2 minutes or until onion is tender.

5. Stir soup and mushrooms into onions and garlic.

6. Gradually blend in milk, sherry and parsley.

7. Add peas to soup mixture.

8. Add lobster and bread crumb mixture to soup mixture. Stir to combine all ingredients.

9. Heat, uncovered, on ROAST for 7 minutes or until sauce bubbles.

10

Lobster Tails

4 (8-ounce) lobster tails, frozen
2 tablespoons melted butter or
margarine

Serves 4

1. Place frozen lobster tails in a shallow, 1½-quart, heat-resistant, nonmetallic baking dish. Face meatiest part of lobster tails toward the outside of the dish.

2. To thaw lobster tails heat, uncovered, on FULL POWER 3½ minutes. Let stand at room temperature 10 minutes.

3. With a sharp, heavy knife, open shell on underside of tail and brush with melted butter.

4. Heat, uncovered, on FULL POWER 7 minutes or until lobster flesh is opaque and the shells are red.

Pictured: Roast Stuffed Turkey

Cooking Hints

The natural tenderness and moisture of poultry are preserved with microwave cooking. Most poultry requires less attention and retains more moisture when cooked on the ROAST setting of your Microwave Oven.

The time required for cooking chicken or turkey is dependent upon the age and size of the bird. Aged or more tender poultry will cook more quickly.

Poultry should be completely thawed before cooking.

Poultry should be roasted in a heat-resistant, non-metallic baking dish, placed on an inverted saucer or plastic roasting rack so that the food is raised above the drippings.

For best results, whole poultry should be started breast–side–down, turning over halfway during cooking.

Poultry may be brushed with melted butter and covered with waxed paper or paper toweling to prevent spattering and help in basting. Butter will aid in browning the surface of poultry. Additional color may be attained by basting with diluted Kitchen Bouquet® or other browning agents. Dried bread crumbs or coating mixes will also enhance the color of chicken pieces. Larger volumes, such as a turkey, will brown nicely because of the longer cooking times.

Standing times are essential for poultry. The internal temperature of poultry will increase 5° to 10°F, during standing time. Cover whole birds with aluminum foil during standing time.

To use a thermometer, insert into the thick part of the inner thigh. DO NOT USE A CONVENTIONAL MEAT THERMOMETER IN THE MICROWAVE OVEN DURING OPERATION; use only following end of cooking time. The metal clip which secures the legs on many turkeys may be left in place during cooking. Thinner sections, such as the tips of wings and legs, may need to be "shielded" with aluminum foil to prevent overcooking before thicker portions are done.

Poultry Roasting Chart

11

CUT	Variable Cooking Control Setting	Approx. Cooking Time	Internal Temp. At End Of Cooking Time	Internal Temp. At End Of Standing Time
Baked Whole Chicken	ROAST	8 min./lb.	180°–185°F	190°–195°F
Chicken Parts	ROAST	8 min./lb.	180°–185°F	190°–195°F
Turkey **Whole** **Breast, bone in**	ROAST ROAST	8 min./lb. 8 min./lb.	170°–175°F 170°–175°F	180°–185°F 180°–185°F
Cornish Game Hen **Whole**	ROAST	8 min./lb.	175°–180°F	185°–190°F

Roast Stuffed Turkey

170°F

1 (12-pound) turkey
Salt and pepper
4 cups bread stuffing

Serves 8 to 10

1. If turkey is frozen, it may be defrosted in the Microwave Oven as directed in the Defrosting Chapter, or it may be defrosted according to package directions. Turkey should be completely thawed before cooking.

2. Wash turkey and sprinkle inside cavity with salt and pepper.

3. Stuff turkey loosely. Tie legs together. Tie wings and legs to body.

4. Use a microwave trivet or invert a heat-resistant, non-metallic saucer or small casserole cover in a shallow, heat-resistant, non-metallic baking dish.

5. Place turkey breast-side-down on saucer or trivet.

6. Turkey should be cooked 8 minutes per pound on ROAST. Heat, covered, for ¾ of cooking time (about 72 minutes).

7. Turn turkey breast-side-up. Insert temperature probe or microwave thermometer into fleshy portion of the turkey, not touching any bones. Continue cooking for the remaining ¼ of the cooking time (about 24 minutes). Small pieces of aluminum foil may be used for shielding if needed.

8. Internal temperature should reach 170°F.

9. If temperature is not 170°F, return turkey to Microwave Oven for an additional few minutes until correct temperature is reached.

10. Let turkey stand covered with aluminum foil at room temperature 20 to 30 minutes to finish cooking. The internal temperature of the turkey should be 180°F after standing.

Tip: Turkey can be basted with margarine or butter to increase browning, or Kitchen Bouquet® and water can be used to give a darker color. The Orange Glaze (page 112) gives a beautiful glaze for turkey.

Oven-Fried Chicken

180°F

2 (2½ pound) broiler-fryer chickens, cut up
2 cups seasoned bread crumbs, cornflake crumbs or packaged coating mix
2 teaspoons paprika
⅔ cup milk

Serves 6

1. Wash chickens and pat dry.

2. Combine desired crumb coating with paprika. Coat each piece of chicken with milk, then crumb mixture.

3. Place coated chicken pieces in a shallow, heat-resistant, non-metallic baking dish or on turntable with the larger pieces along the outside edges of the dish and the smaller pieces in the center.

4. Heat, uncovered, on ROAST for 20 minutes. Rearrange chicken pieces and heat on ROAST for 15 minutes or until chicken is fork-tender.

5. Cover chicken with aluminum foil and let stand at room temperature 5 minutes.

6. Serve either hot or cold.

Roast Capon With Rye Bread Stuffing

170°F

1 (6-pound) capon or roasting chicken
4 tablespoons butter or margarine
½ cup finely chopped onion
½ cup finely chopped celery
½ teaspoon salt
¼ teaspoon pepper
½ teaspoon caraway seeds (optional)
1 envelope instant chicken broth or 1 cube chicken bouillon, crumbled
6 cups cubed day-old rye bread
¼ cup finely chopped parsley
¼ cup boiling water
Salt and pepper, to taste
Seasoned coating for chicken

Serves 6

1. Wash capon and pat dry with paper toweling and set aside.

2. Melt butter or margarine in a deep, 2-quart, heat-resistant, non-metallic casserole on FULL POWER 30 seconds.

3. Add onion and celery and heat, uncovered, 4 minutes on FULL POWER or until vegetables are tender.

4. Stir salt, pepper, caraway seeds and chicken broth mix into vegetable mixture. Add rye bread cubes and parsley; toss until well combined.

5. Moisten bread mixture with the water.

6. Rub inside cavity of capon with salt and pepper to taste. Stuff capon lightly with stuffing mixture. Close body cavity with wooden skewers or sew with string. Sprinkle capon with seasoned coating for chicken as bottle instructions direct.

7. Place capon, breast-side-up in a shallow, heat-resistant, non-metallic baking dish. Use an inverted saucer or microwave trivet to keep capon out of pan drippings.

8. Heat, uncovered, for 8 minutes per pound on ROAST (about 48 minutes) or until temperature probe or microwave thermometer inserted in the thickest part of the bird (not touching any bones) registers 170°F. DO NOT PLACE CONVENTIONAL THERMOMETER IN MICROWAVE OVEN. Wrap in aluminum foil and allow to stand 15 minutes before carving. If it is necessary to reheat capon, DO NOT PLACE ALUMINUM FOIL IN MICROWAVE OVEN.

11

Barbecue Chicken

180°F

1 (3-pound) broiler-fryer, cut into serving pieces
1 (8-ounce) can tomato sauce
¼ cup vinegar
2 tablespoons finely chopped onion
2 tablespoons butter or margarine
2 tablespoons firmly packed dark brown sugar
1 tablespoon Worcestershire sauce
1 tablespoon paprika
1 teaspoon sugar
1 teaspoon salt
½ teaspoon pepper

Serves 4

1. Wash chicken pieces and pat dry. Set aside.

2. In a deep, 2½-quart, heat-resistant, non-metallic casserole, combine all ingredients except chicken.

3. Heat, uncovered, on FULL POWER 4 minutes, stirring occasionally.

4. Add chicken pieces to sauce and heat, covered, on ROAST for 12 minutes. Stir.

5. Heat, covered, on ROAST an additional 9 minutes or until chicken is tender.

Herbed Drumsticks

½ cup butter or margarine
2 tablespoons chopped parsley
2 teaspoons chopped chives
1 teaspoon dried tarragon leaves
Salt and pepper
8 chicken drumsticks

Serves 4

1. In a shallow, heat-resistant, non-metallic baking dish, melt butter on FULL POWER 1 minute.

2. Add herbs, salt and pepper to taste. Stir to combine.

3. Place drumsticks in baking dish and toss lightly to coat drumsticks well with butter mixture.

4. Heat, uncovered, on ROAST for 16 minutes or until chicken is done. Turn drumsticks occasionally.

Variation: If desired, drumsticks can be partially cooked over charcoal, then transferred to Microwave Oven to finish cooking. The Microwave cooking time would have to be adjusted because of the conventional cooking time.

Chicken Breasts Supreme

180°F

3 pounds chicken breasts
2 tablespoons butter
 or margarine
½ cup finely chopped onion
1 (10½-ounce) can cream of
 mushroom soup
1 cup milk
1 teaspoon salt
⅛ teaspoon pepper

Serves 6

1. Place chicken breasts, skin-side-down in a shallow, heat-resistant, non-metallic, 10-inch baking dish.

2. Heat, uncovered, on FULL POWER 12 minutes. Set chicken aside.

3. In a deep, heat-resistant, non-metallic casserole, melt 2 tablespoons butter on FULL POWER 15 seconds.

4. Add onion to melted butter and heat, uncovered, on FULL POWER 2½ minutes or until onion is tender.

5. Add soup, milk and seasonings to onions. Stir well to combine all ingredients.

6. Heat, uncovered, on ROAST for 5 minutes.

7. Pour sauce over chicken and heat, covered, on ROAST for 10 minutes or until chicken is tender.

Chicken Marengo

180°F

1 (1½-ounce) package spaghetti
 sauce mix
½ cup dry bread crumbs
¼ teaspoon seasoned salt
1 (3-pound) broiler-fryer
 chicken, cut into 8 pieces,
 skinned
1 (17-ounce) can whole peeled
 tomatoes with basil leaf, undrained, cut into pieces
½ cup sauterne wine
1 cup thinly sliced fresh
 mushrooms

Serves 4

1. Combine sauce mix, bread crumbs and seasoned salt in plastic bag. Shake chicken pieces in mixture to coat. Reserve crumb mixture.

2. Arrange coated chicken pieces in a shallow, 2-quart, heat-resistant, non-metallic casserole with the thickest portions toward outside of casserole. Heat, covered loosely with a paper towel, on ROAST for 10 minutes.

3. Add tomatoes with liquid, wine, mushrooms and reserved crumb mixture.

4. Cover loosely with plastic wrap and heat on ROAST for 16 minutes or until chicken is tender.

Chicken Curry

1 tablespoon vegetable oil
2 large onions, thinly sliced
1 medium green pepper, diced
2 cloves garlic, peeled and
   crushed
1 tablespoon allspice
1 tablespoon curry powder
1 tablespoon turmeric powder
1 teaspoon ginger
1 teaspoon salt
¼ teaspoon pepper
1 (3-pound) broiler-fryer
   chicken, cut into 8 pieces
2 large tomatoes peeled and
   thinly sliced
2 cups chicken stock or
   4 chicken bouillon cubes and
   2 cups hot water
½ cup chopped tart apple
1 cup green peas

Serves 4 to 6

1. In a deep, 3-quart, heat-resistant, non-metallic casserole add 1 tablespoon vegetable oil. Add onion, green pepper and garlic to vegetable oil. Heat on FULL POWER, uncovered, 5 minutes or until onion and pepper are tender.

2. In a small mixing bowl combine allspice, curry, turmeric powder ginger, salt and pepper.

3. Rub spice mixture onto chicken with hands until chicken is evenly covered. Add chicken, tomatoes and 1 cup of chicken stock to onion-pepper mixture.

4. Heat, covered, on ROAST for 14 minutes. Add an additional cup of chicken stock, tart apples and heat, covered, on ROAST for 14 minutes or until chicken is tender.

5. Add green peas and heat, covered, on ROAST for 5 minutes or until mixture is heated through. Serve over rice.

Chicken Cacciatore

180°F   **11**

1 (2½ to 3 pound) broiler-fryer
   chicken
1 (15-ounce) can tomato sauce
1 (6-ounce) can tomato paste
1½ cups water
½ cup red wine
½ cup finely chopped onion
2 cloves garlic, peeled and
   crushed
1½ teaspoons dried oregano leaves
1½ teaspoons dried parsley flakes
1 teaspoon sugar
1 teaspoon salt
¼ teaspoon pepper
¼ teaspoon dried thyme leaves
1 (4-ounce) can mushroom
   slices, drained

Cooked rice or spaghetti

Serves 4

1. Wash chicken and pat dry. Cut chicken into eight pieces. Set aside.

2. Combine tomato sauce, paste, water, wine, onion, garlic, oregano, parsley, sugar, salt, pepper and thyme in a deep 3-quart heat resistant, non-metallic casserole.

3. Add chicken pieces. Make sure all pieces are coated with sauce.

4. Heat, covered, on FULL POWER 10 minutes. Stir.

5. Heat, covered, on FULL POWER for an additional 10 minutes. Stir occasionally.

6. Add mushroom slices and heat, uncovered, on FULL POWER 15 to 20 minutes or until chicken is tender.

7. Serve with rice or spaghetti.

Chicken Breasts Parmesan

180° F

½ cup seasoned dry bread crumbs

¼ cup grated Parmesan cheese

1½ pounds boneless chicken breasts

2 eggs, beaten

3 tablespoons olive oil

1 (8-ounce) can tomato sauce

1 teaspoon dried Italian seasoning

¼ teaspoon garlic salt

1 cup shredded mozzarella cheese

Grated Parmesan cheese

Serves 4

1. On wax paper combine bread crumbs and ¼ cup grated Parmesan cheese. Dip chicken breasts first in egg and then in bread crumb mixture until well coated.

2. Heat oil in a large, heat-resistant, non-metallic skillet over high heat on top of a conventional surface unit. Quickly brown coated chicken pieces on both sides.

3. In a small bowl combine tomato sauce, Italian seasoning and garlic salt. Spoon tomato sauce over chicken.

4. Sprinkle the shredded mozzarella cheese over the tomato sauce.

5. Heat, loosely covered with wax paper, on ROAST for 7 to 9 minutes or until sauce is bubbly and chicken is tender. Sprinkle with grated Parmesan cheese and heat, uncovered, on ROAST for 1 minute or until cheese is melted.

Pictured: Chicken Breasts Parmesan

Teriyaki Chicken

¼ cup soy sauce
¼ cup sugar
¼ cup sake (Japanese rice wine) or cooking sherry
¼ teaspoon salt
¼ teaspoon monosodium glutamate (optional)
1 tablespoon vegetable oil
1 teaspoon grated fresh ginger root
1 (2½-pound) broiler-fryer chicken, cut into 8 pieces

Serves 4

1. In a large bowl combine all ingredients. Marinate chicken pieces 3 to 4 hours.
2. Place chicken skin-side-down in a deep, 3-quart, heat-resistant, non-metallic baking dish and heat on ROAST for 12 minutes.
3. Turn chicken skin-side-up and heat on ROAST for 6 to 8 minutes or until chicken is fork-tender. Baste occasionally with sauce.

Chicken And Dumplings

1 (2 to 3 pound) broiler-fryer chicken, cut into serving pieces
2 cups water
6 whole black peppercorns
2 bay leaves
1 teaspoon salt
3 medium carrots, peeled and thinly sliced
6 tablespoons flour
¾ cup cold water
1 teaspoon sage
1 cup buttermilk biscuit mix
⅓ cup milk
2 tablespoons dried parsley flakes
1 (4-ounce) can button mushrooms, drained
1 (10-ounce) package frozen peas, thawed

Serves 4 to 6

1. Wash chicken and pat dry.
2. Place chicken, the 2 cups water, peppercorns, bay leaves and salt in a deep, 2½ to 3-quart, heat-resistant, non-metallic casserole. Heat, covered, on FULL POWER 10 minutes. Stir. Heat, covered, on FULL POWER an additional 5 minutes.
3. Add carrot slices and heat, covered, on FULL POWER 5 minutes longer.
4. Remove chicken pieces from broth and set chicken aside until cool enough to handle. Reserve broth.
5. Remove chicken from bones and cut into bite-sized pieces.
6. Discard bones, bay leaves and peppercorns. Skim any excess fat from chicken broth.
7. Return chicken to casserole.
8. In a small bowl combine flour, the ¾ cup cold water and the sage until smooth. Gradually stir flour mixture into chicken mixture.
9. Heat, covered, on FULL POWER for 16 to 18 minutes or until gravy is thickened and smooth. Stir occasionally.
10. Prepare dumpling dough in a small bowl by combining biscuit mix, milk and parsley flakes; stir with a fork until just blended.
11. Add mushrooms and peas to chicken and gravy mixture.
12. Drop dumpling dough by spoonfuls onto hot chicken mixture to form 6 dumplings and heat, covered, on ROAST for 6 minutes.
13. Uncover casserole and heat on ROAST for 3 to 5 minutes or until dumplings are no longer doughy on the underside.

11

Coq Au Vin

2 (2½-pound) broiler-fryer
  chickens, cut into serving
  pieces
4 tablespoons flour
2 teaspoons salt
½ teaspoon pepper
6 tablespoons butter or
  margarine
12 small white onions, peeled
4 tablespoons brandy
1 clove garlic, peeled
1 bay leaf
1 stalk celery, cut into 4 pieces
3 cups red wine
½ pound fresh mushrooms,
  thinly sliced

Serves 4 to 6

1. Wash chickens and pat dry. Combine flour, salt and pepper in a plastic bag. Put chicken pieces in bag to coat with flour mixture.

2. Melt butter or margarine in skillet on a conventional surface unit. Lightly brown chicken pieces on all sides.

3. Place browned chicken pieces in a deep, 3-quart, heat-resistant, non-metallic casserole.

4. Brown onions lightly in skillet and set aside.

5. Remove skillet from surface unit. Gradually pour brandy into skillet, scraping pan to loosen any browned particles. Add brandy mixture to chicken casserole. Add garlic, bay leaf, celery, onions and red wine. Heat, covered, on ROAST for 15 minutes stirring occasionally. (Place meatiest portion of chicken to outside of casserole.)

6. Add mushrooms and heat, uncovered, on ROAST for 10 minutes or until chicken and onions are tender. Remove garlic, bay leaf and celery pieces.

7. If sauce is not thick enough, it may be thickened with a little flour mixed with cold water. Heat, uncovered, on FULL POWER for an extra 1 to 2 minutes if flour mixture is added.

Chicken Fricassee

2 tablespoons vegetable oil
1 medium onion, thinly
  sliced
1 (3-pound) broiler-fryer
  chicken, cut into 8 pieces
1½ teaspoons salt
¼ teaspoon pepper
1 bay leaf
3 cups water
3 tablespoons butter or
  margarine
¼ cup flour
1 teaspoon paprika
½ cup milk
Finely chopped parsley

Serves 4 to 6

1. In a deep, 3-quart, heat-resistant, non-metallic casserole heat oil on FULL POWER 2 minutes. Add onion and heat, uncovered, on FULL POWER 3 minutes or until onion is tender.

2. Add chicken pieces, salt, pepper, bay leaf and water and heat, tightly covered, on FULL POWER 10 minutes. Stir occasionally. Continue cooking on FULL POWER 9 minutes or until chicken is tender. Chicken parts should be cooked to 180°F.

3. Remove chicken pieces and set aside.

4. Strain stock and reserve 1½ cups for sauce.

5. In a medium-sized, heat-resistant, non-metallic bowl melt butter on FULL POWER 30 seconds. Blend in flour and paprika until smooth.

6. Gradually stir in milk and reserved chicken stock. Heat, uncovered, on FULL POWER 4 to 5 minutes stirring frequently, until thickened and smooth.

7. Place reserved chicken pieces on a heat-resistant, non-metallic serving dish and spoon sauce over chicken pieces. Heat, uncovered, on ROAST for 5 minutes or until heated through.

8. Sprinkle with parsley before serving.

Brunswick Stew

1 (2 to 3 pound) broiler-fryer
  chicken, cut into serving
  pieces
2 cups water
6 whole peppercorns
2 bay leaves
1 teaspoon salt
3 ripe tomatoes, peeled and cut
  into 8 wedges each
1 medium onion, thinly sliced
1 (10-ounce) package frozen
  lima beans, thawed
1 (10-ounce) package whole
  kernel corn, thawed
1 (10-ounce) package frozen
  okra, thawed and sliced into
  ½-inch pieces

Serves 4 to 6

1. Wash chicken and pat dry.

2. Place chicken, water, peppercorns, bay leaves and salt in a deep, 3-quart, heat-resistant, non-metallic casserole. Stir to combine.

3. Heat, covered, on FULL POWER 10 minutes. Stir. Heat, covered, on FULL POWER an additional 8 minutes.

4. If desired, remove chicken from bone and cut into 1-inch pieces.

5. Discard bay leaves and peppercorns.

6. Return chicken to broth and add remaining ingredients.

7. Heat, covered, on FULL POWER 10 minutes.

8. Uncover and heat on FULL POWER 5 minutes or until chicken and vegetables are tender.

9. Serve in soup bowls. Serving temperature should be 160°F.

Tip: Vegetables may be thawed in your Microwave Oven. Place package directly on turntable and thaw on DEFROST for 10 minutes.

11

Chicken And Shrimp In Red Wine Sauce

1 (2½ to 3-pound) broiler-fryer
  chicken, cut into serving
  pieces
¼ cup flour
1 teaspoon salt
¼ teaspoon pepper
½ cup butter or margarine
1 large finely chopped onion
2 cloves garlic, peeled and
  crushed
3 tablespoons chopped parsley
¾ cup red wine
½ teaspoon Italian seasoning
1 (8-ounce) can tomato sauce
1 teaspoon dried basil leaves
1 pound raw, shelled, deveined
  shrimp

Serves 4 to 5

1. Wash chicken and pat dry. Set aside.

2. In a plastic bag combine flour, salt and pepper. Coat each piece of chicken with seasoned flour.

3. In a large, heat-resistant, non-metallic skillet melt butter on top of a conventional surface unit.

4. Add chicken pieces and brown on all sides until golden brown.

5. Remove chicken pieces and set aside. Add onion and garlic to skillet. Heat, uncovered, on FULL POWER 1½ minutes or until onion is tender.

6. Add chopped parsley, wine, Italian seasoning, tomato sauce, and basil to sautéed onion mixture. Stir to combine.

7. Add reserved chicken pieces and heat, covered, on ROAST for 12 to 15 minutes or until chicken is tender.

8. Remove chicken pieces and place on serving platter.

9. Add shrimp to wine sauce and heat, uncovered, on FULL POWER 3 minutes or until sauce bubbles and shrimp turn pink. (Do not overcook shrimp as they will become tough.)

10. Skim any fat from surface of sauce. Pour shrimp sauce over chicken pieces.

Chicken Livers And Mushrooms

5 slices raw bacon
1½ pounds chicken livers
2½ tablespoons flour
1 teaspoon salt
⅛ teaspoon pepper
¼ cup finely chopped onion
2 (10½-ounce) cans chicken giblet gravy or cream of chicken soup
1 (4-ounce) can sliced mushrooms, drained

Serves 4

1. Place 5 slices of bacon in a 10-inch, heat-resistant, non-metallic skillet. Cover with a paper towel and heat on FULL POWER 5 minutes or until bacon is crisp.

2. Remove bacon and set aside.

3. In a plastic bag combine flour, salt and pepper. Coat chicken livers with seasoned flour and place in hot bacon fat. Add minced onion.

4. Heat, uncovered, on ROAST for 6 minutes. Turn chicken livers over and heat on ROAST for 6 minutes or until chicken livers are browned.

5. Add the canned chicken giblet gravy and heat, covered, on ROAST for 8 minutes.

6. Add mushrooms, stir and heat, uncovered, on ROAST for 2 minutes.

> **Tip:** If chicken livers begin to pop, pierce them with the tines of a fork before continuing to cook. The popping is just the steam escaping through the thin membrane surrounding the livers.

Wine And Chicken Livers

2 tablespoons butter or margarine
1½ pounds chicken livers
2½ tablespoons flour
½ teaspoon salt
⅛ teaspoon pepper
¼ cup minced onion
2 tablespoons catsup
¾ cup dry white wine

Serves 3 to 4

1. Place 2 tablespoons butter in a 10-inch, heat-resistant, non-metallic skillet. Heat, uncovered, on FULL POWER 30 seconds.

2. In a plastic bag combine flour, salt and pepper. Coat each chicken liver with seasoned flour and place in skillet with melted butter.

3. Heat, uncovered, on ROAST for 6 minutes.

4. Turn livers and heat, uncovered, on ROAST for 5 minutes or until chicken livers are browned.

5. Add onion, catsup and wine. Heat, covered, on ROAST for 3 minutes. Stir.

6. Heat, uncovered, on ROAST for an additional 3 to 5 minutes. Serve with cooked rice.

> **Tip:** If chicken livers begin to pop, pierce them with the tines of a fork before continuing to cook. The popping is just the steam escaping through the thin membrane surrounding the liver.

Pictured: Eggs Benedict

Cheese And Eggs

Cooking Hints

Due to their delicate nature, both cheese and eggs are very sensitive to microwave power. The Variable Cooking Control gives the flexibility you need to cook these foods without requiring careful attention, and the Carousel assures even cooking results. Both eggs and cheese are high protein foods and are sensitive to heat. Some cooking will continue even after removal from the oven, so standing times are important to prevent overcooking. Overcooking can cause the egg to pop or burst.

Because of the high fat content of the egg yolk, the yolk will tend to cook faster than the white. It is difficult to cook an egg so that the yolk is less cooked than the white.

Do not attempt to cook eggs ir. the shell. Due to the build up of pressure within the shell, they are very likely to explode.

Cheese Fondue

1 clove garlic, peeled and cut in half
1 pound shredded Swiss cheese
¼ cup flour
¼ teaspoon salt
Dash pepper
¼ teaspoon nutmeg (optional)
1½ cups dry white wine
2 tablespoons kirsch (optional)
French bread, cut in 1-inch cubes

Serves 4 to 6

1. Rub the insides and bottom of a deep, 1½-quart, heat-resistant, non-metallic casserole or heat-resistant, non-metallic fondue pot with garlic. Discard garlic.

2. Combine cheese, flour, salt, pepper and nutmeg in the prepared dish. Add wine and mix well.

3. Heat, covered, on SIMMER for 12 minutes stirring during last half of cooking time.

4. If cheese is not completely melted, heat on SIMMER for 1 to 2 minutes. If desired, stir in kirsch.

5. Spear squares of French bread with fondue forks or regular forks and dip in fondue.

6. If necessary, fondue pot may be placed on a warmer stand over low heat or returned to Microwave Oven to reheat fondue.

Browning Dish Fried Eggs

1 tablespoon butter or margarine
2 eggs

1. Preheat browning dish on FULL POWER for 2 minutes.

2. Add butter to hot browning dish, stirring to melt. Place eggs in browning dish. Puncture yolks.

3. Heat, covered, on ROAST for 2 minutes, 15 seconds.
Do not overcook as eggs will continue cooking while standing.

Cheesy Noodle Omelet

12

8 eggs
1 teaspoon salt
¼ teaspoon pepper
2 cups cooked noodles
1 cup shredded Cheddar cheese
2 tablespoons finely chopped green pepper
1 tablespoon finely chopped pimiento

1. In a deep, 2-quart, heat-resistant, non-metallic casserole, beat the eggs with salt and pepper.

2. Stir in cooked noodles, Cheddar cheese, green pepper and pimiento.

3. Heat, covered, on ROAST for 8 to 9 minutes stirring occasionally.

4. Let stand 2 to 3 minutes at room temperature. Cut into wedges and serve.

Poached Eggs

2 cups hot water
½ teaspoon white vinegar
½ teaspoon salt
2 eggs

Serves 1 to 2

1. Combine water, vinegar and salt in a deep, 1-quart, heat-resistant, non-metallic casserole.

2. Heat, uncovered, on FULL POWER 2 to 3 minutes or until water mixture comes to a boil.

3. Carefully break eggs, 1 at a time, into the liquid.

4. Heat, covered with plastic wrap, on FULL POWER 1 minute.

5. Let stand, covered, 1 minute or until eggs reach desired degree of doneness.

Fried Eggs

½ tablespoon butter or
    margarine
2 eggs
Salt and pepper

Serves 1 to 2

1. Grease a heat-resistant, non-metallic saucer with the butter.
2. Carefully break eggs onto saucer. Sprinkle with salt and pepper. Puncture egg yolk with a wooden pick.
3. Heat, uncovered, on ROAST for 1 minute. Shake to loosen eggs from sides of saucer.
4. Heat, uncovered, 1 to 1½ minutes longer. Do not overcook as eggs will continue cooking while standing. Let eggs stand, covered, 1 minute to finish cooking.

> **Note:** The yolk of eggs tends to cook faster than the white.

Baked Eggs

Butter or margarine
2 eggs

1. Lightly grease two glass custard cups with butter or margarine. Break one egg into each prepared cup and puncture yolk and white with the tines of a fork.
2. Heat, covered with plastic wrap, on SIMMER for 2 minutes, 15 seconds or until eggs appear almost done. Allow to stand for 1 minute to complete cooking.

Scrambled Eggs

1 tablespoon butter or
    margarine
2 eggs
2 tablespoons light cream or
    milk
⅛ teaspoon salt
Dash pepper

Serves 1

1. Melt butter in a heat-resistant, non-metallic bowl on FULL POWER 30 seconds.
2. Beat remaining ingredients until well-blended. Pour egg mixture into bowl.
3. Heat, covered with plastic wrap or a saucer on ROAST for 1½ minutes. Stir.
4. Heat, covered, on ROAST an additional 1½ minutes. Stir.
5. Stop cooking eggs when they are slightly softer than desired, as they will continue to cook after they are removed from the Microwave Oven. Allow to stand 1 to 2 minutes before serving.

For four scrambled eggs:

2 tablespoons butter or
    margarine
4 eggs
4 tablespoons light cream or
    milk
¼ teaspoon salt
Dash pepper

Serves 2

1. Melt butter in a heat-resistant, non-metallic bowl on FULL POWER for 30 seconds.
2. Beat remaining ingredients until well-blended. Pour egg mixture into bowl.
3. Heat, covered with plastic wrap or a saucer, on ROAST for 1½ to 2 minutes. Stir.
4. Heat, covered, on ROAST an additional 2 minutes. Stir.
5. Allow to stand 1 to 2 minutes before serving.

Welsh Rarebit

3 eggs, at room temperature
1 (12-ounce) can or bottle beer or ale
3 cups Cheddar cheese, cubed (approximately 1 pound)
3 tablespoons butter or margarine
1½ teaspoons dry mustard
1½ teaspoons Worcestershire sauce
⅛ teaspoon Tabasco sauce
12 toast triangles (made from 6 slices of bread)
6 slices of ham cut in triangles the size of bread triangles

Serves 6

1. In a deep, 1½-quart, heat-resistant, non-metallic casserole beat eggs until well blended. Stir in remaining ingredients except toast and ham.

2. Heat, uncovered, on SIMMER for 12 to 14 minutes or until cheese has melted and mixture has thickened. Stir mixture occasionally.

3. Beat mixture with rotary beater or electric mixer until very smooth.

4. Spoon rarebit over toast triangles that have been topped with ham triangles.

Omelets

4 eggs
4 tablespoons milk or light cream
¼ teaspoon salt
Dash pepper
1 tablespoon butter or margarine

Serves 2

1. In a medium-sized bowl combine eggs, milk, salt and pepper; beat until well blended.

2. Melt butter in a 10-inch, heat-resistant, non-metallic pie plate on ROAST for 30 seconds. Rotate plate so it is completely coated with butter.

3. Pour egg mixture into pie plate and cover tightly with plastic wrap.

4. Heat on ROAST for 2½ minutes.

5. With a rubber spatula or fork, move cooked eggs toward center.

6. Heat, covered with plastic wrap, on ROAST for 2 minutes.

7. Let stand, covered, at least 1½ minutes.

8. Loosen egg from pie plate with a rubber spatula. Fold omelet in half and place on a heat-resistant, non-metallic serving platter. If omelet is not cooked enough, heat omelet on ROAST for an additional 30 seconds to 1 minute.

Variations:

Cheese Omelet: Sprinkle omelet with ½ cup shredded cheese after Step 6. Cover and heat on ROAST for an additional 30 seconds to melt cheese. Continue with Step 7.

Bacon Omelet: Cook bacon before preparing omelet. Crumble bacon into egg mixture during Step 1. If desired, some of the bacon drippings may be used in place of the butter.

Western Omelet: Heat ¼ cup chopped onion, ¼ cup chopped green pepper and ¼ cup diced ham in 1 tablespoon butter or margarine on ROAST for 2 minutes. Stir into egg mixture in Step 1.

Onion Omelet: Heat ½ cup chopped onion in 1 tablespoon butter or margarine on ROAST for 1 minute. Add to egg mixture in Step 1.

Eggs Benedict

¼ cup butter or margarine
¼ cup light cream
2 egg yolks, beaten
1 tablespoon cider vinegar
½ teaspoon dry mustard
¼ teaspoon salt
Dash cayenne pepper
1 (17-ounce) can asparagus
   spears, drained
4 English muffins, split and
   toasted conventionally
4 slices ham
4 poached eggs (see recipe page
   161)

Serves 4

1. In a 2 cup, non-metallic measuring cup melt butter on FULL POWER 1 minute. Add light cream, egg yolks, vinegar, mustard, salt and cayenne; stir to blend thoroughly.

2. Heat, uncovered, on ROAST for 2 minutes or until thickened. Stir frequently. Be careful not to overcook as sauce will curdle.

3. Beat sauce until light and fluffy. Set aside.

4. Place asparagus in a shallow, heat-resistant, non-metallic baking dish and heat, uncovered, on FULL POWER 1 to 2 minutes or until heated through.

5. Arrange toasted English muffin halves on a heat-resistant, non-metallic serving platter. Place 1 slice of ham over 2 halves of the English muffin. Divide asparagus among the 4 muffins.

6. Heat, uncovered, on FULL POWER 2½ to 3 minutes or until muffins and ham are heated through.

7. Carefully place poached eggs on asparagus. Top with reserved sauce and heat, uncovered, on ROAST for 1 minute or until hot.

Ham Quiche

3 eggs
1 cup half and half
½ teaspoon salt
¼ teaspoon nutmeg
⅛ teaspoon pepper
⅛ teaspoon cayenne pepper
½ pound cooked ham, cut into
   thin strips
2 cups shredded Swiss cheese
1 baked 10-inch pastry shell
   (in a heat-resistant, non-
   metallic pie plate)

Serves 6 to 8

1. In a medium-sized bowl beat eggs, cream, salt, nutmeg, pepper and cayenne pepper until well blended.

2. Stir in ham and cheese.

3. Pour mixture into baked pastry shell.

4. Heat, uncovered, on SIMMER for 10 minutes.

5. Move cooked edges toward center and continue to heat on SIMMER for 20 minutes or until a knife inserted in center comes out clean.

6. Let stand at room temperature 3 to 4 minutes to finish cooking.

Quiche Lorraine

½ pound bacon
1 baked 10-inch pastry shell
   (in a heat-resistant, non-
   metallic pie plate)
3 eggs
1 cup half and half
¼ cup finely chopped onion
½ teaspoon salt
¼ teaspoon nutmeg
⅛ teaspoon pepper
⅛ teaspoon cayenne pepper
2 cups shredded Swiss cheese

1. Place bacon between two layers of paper toweling and cook on FULL POWER for 8 to 9 minutes or until crisp.

2. Crumble bacon into pastry shell.

3. In medium-sized bowl beat eggs, cream, onion, salt, nutmeg, pepper and cayenne pepper until well blended.

4. Stir in Swiss cheese.

5. Proceed with steps 3 through 6 in Ham Quiche recipe above.

Pictured: Macaroni and Cheese Casserole

164

CASSEROLES

Cooking Hints

Casseroles are ideal for microwave cooking. Since they can be prepared, cooked and served all in the same dish, you will find that both the preparation and cooking times are shortened.

Casseroles may be prepared in advance and refrigerated or frozen. Why not prepare two recipes and freeze the second or freeze the leftover portion for future use? Thawing and reheating of casseroles is quick and easy using microwave energy.

TO THAW CASSEROLES			TO REHEAT CASSEROLES		
VARIABLE COOKING			VARIABLE COOKING		
	CONTROL	TIME		CONTROL	TIME
1 cup	ROAST	4 minutes	1 cup	ROAST	4 minutes
2 cups	SIMMER	6 minutes	2 cups	ROAST	6 minutes
3 cups	SIMMER	8 minutes	3 cups	ROAST	8 minutes
4 cups	DEFROST	10 minutes	4 cups	ROAST	12 minutes
8 cups	DEFROST	16 minutes	8 cups	ROAST	18 minutes

Using the ROAST setting for reheating casseroles allows the food to heat more thoroughly without the edges becoming overcooked before the center is heated. Suggested serving temperature for casseroles is 140° to 160°F.

Some casseroles may be defrosted and reheated in one step. Much depends on the amount of time you have to spare and the consistency of the casserole. Heating times are approximate, depending on the ingredients.

If a brown crust is desired, the casserole may be placed under a preheated broiler or in a hot oven for a few minutes.

Your own favorite casseroles can easily be converted to microwave cooking, or you can use your Microwave Oven for preparing parts of casseroles. For example:

Sauté onions, celery or green pepper

1 cup	3 minutes on FULL POWER
2 cups	5–6 minutes on FULL POWER

Brown ground beef

1 pound	6 minutes on ROAST

Cheese Casserole

1 (4-ounce) can green chili peppers
2 tablespoons butter or
  margarine
1 medium onion, finely chopped
1 (8-ounce) can tomato sauce
½ teaspoon salt
2 eggs, beaten
1 cup half and half
1 (6-ounce) package corn chips
½ pound shredded Cheddar cheese
1 cup dairy sour cream
½ cup shredded Cheddar cheese
3 ripe tomatoes, sliced

Serves 6

1. Drain chili peppers. Remove seeds and chop peppers coarsely.

2. In a medium-sized, heat-resistant, non-metallic bowl melt butter on FULL POWER 30 seconds.

3. Add onion and heat, uncovered, on FULL POWER 3 minutes or until tender. Add chili peppers, tomato sauce and salt to onion.

4. Heat, uncovered, on FULL POWER 6 minutes.

5. In a small bowl beat eggs and half and half together until well blended.

6. Gradually add egg mixture to heated sauce mixture, very little at a time, stirring constantly.

7. Layer ½ of corn chips, ½ of tomato mixture and half of the ½-pound shredded Cheddar cheese in a shallow, 1½-quart, heat-resistant, non-metallic casserole.

8. Repeat with remaining corn chips, tomato mixture and the remainder of the ½ pound cheese.

9. Carefully spread the sour cream over the top of the entire casserole.

10. Heat, uncovered, on ROAST for 7 minutes or until mixture begins to set.

11. Sprinkle the ½ cup of Cheddar cheese over the sour cream.

12. Arrange tomatoes in a ring around the outside edge of the casserole.

13. Heat, uncovered, on ROAST for 7 to 8 minutes or until cheese melts and tomatoes are cooked.

13

Macaroni Sauté

½ cup vegetable oil
1 (8-ounce) box or 2 cups
  uncooked elbow macaroni
½ cup finely chopped onion
½ cup finely chopped green
  pepper
1 clove garlic, peeled and
  crushed
1 (20-ounce) can tomato juice
1 teaspoon salt
¼ teaspoon pepper
2 tablespoons Worcestershire
  sauce

Serves 6

1. In a 1½-quart, heat-resistant, non-metallic casserole, place vegetable oil, macaroni, onion, green pepper and garlic. Heat, uncovered, on FULL POWER 5 minutes or until macaroni turns slightly yellow. Stir occasionally. Set aside.

2. In a 1-quart, heat-resistant, non-metallic measuring cup, heat tomato juice, uncovered, on FULL POWER for 6 minutes or until tomato juice comes to a boil.

3. Add salt, pepper and Worcestershire sauce to tomato juice. Stir to combine.

4. Pour tomato juice mixture into macaroni mixture. Heat, covered, on ROAST for 18 minutes or until macaroni is tender.

Marzetti

5 cups hot water
1 tablespoon salt
3 cups uncooked egg noodles
¼ cup butter or margarine
1 cup dry bread crumbs
1 pound lean ground beef
½ cup finely chopped onion
¼ cup finely chopped green
   pepper
1 teaspoon salt
½ teaspoon garlic salt
⅛ teaspoon pepper
1 cup shredded Swiss cheese
1 (8-ounce) can tomato sauce
1 (4-ounce) can mushroom
   stems and pieces, drained

Serves 4 to 6

1. In a deep, 3-quart, heat-resistant, non-metallic casserole place 5 cups water, 1 tablespoon salt and 3 cups uncooked noodles. Heat, covered, on FULL POWER 12 minutes or until noodles are tender. Stir occasionally.

2. Drain noodles and set aside.

3. In a large, heat-resistant, non-metallic mixing bowl, melt ¼ cup butter or margarine on FULL POWER 30 seconds.

4. Add bread crumbs and heat, uncovered, on FULL POWER 1½ minutes or until bread crumbs are golden brown.

5. Add meat to bread crumb mixture and mix well. Heat on ROAST, uncovered, 6 minutes or until meat is browned, stirring occasionally so meat crumbles.

6. Add onions, green pepper, salt, garlic salt and pepper. Blend into meat mixture thoroughly. Heat, uncovered, on ROAST for 4 minutes.

7. In a 2-quart, heat-resistant, non-metallic casserole layer cooked noodles with meat mixture. Top with cheese, tomato sauce and mushrooms (in that order). Heat, uncovered, on ROAST for 10 minutes or until cheese melts.

Macaroni And Cheese Casserole

3 tablespoons butter or
   margarine
3½ tablespoons flour
2 teaspoons dry mustard
¾ teaspoon salt
¼ teaspoon pepper
3 cups milk
½ pound shredded sharp Cheddar
   cheese
1 (8-ounce) package elbow
   macaroni, cooked and drained
1 (12-ounce) can luncheon
   meat, cut into ¼-inch strips
3 tablespoons melted butter
   or margarine
½ cup seasoned dry bread crumbs

Serves 6

1. In a deep, 2½-quart, heat-resistant, non-metallic casserole melt butter or margarine on FULL POWER 30 seconds.

2. Blend in flour, dry mustard, salt and pepper stirring until smooth.

3. Gradually stir in milk until smooth.

4. Heat, uncovered, on ROAST for 12 minutes or until thickened and smooth. Stir occasionally during last half of cooking time.

5. Add shredded cheese and stir until melted.

6. Add cooked macaroni and luncheon meat. Stir until well blended.

7. In a small, heat-resistant, non-metallic bowl combine melted butter or margarine and bread crumbs and heat, uncovered, on FULL POWER 3 minutes or until bread crumbs are lightly browned.

8. Sprinkle bread crumb mixture over macaroni mixture.

9. Heat, uncovered, on ROAST for 7 minutes or until heated through.

Variation: 2½ cups of ham, tongue, turkey, other leftover meat or other luncheon meat may be substituted for the canned luncheon meat.

Noodles Romanoff

140°F

3 cups cooked egg noodles
1 cup cottage cheese
1 cup dairy sour cream
¼ cup finely chopped onion
1 clove garlic, peeled and
   crushed
1½ teaspoons Worcestershire
   sauce
 Few drops Tabasco sauce
½ teaspoon salt
½ cup shredded sharp Cheddar
   cheese

Serves 4

1. Combine all of the ingredients except the Cheddar cheese in a greased, 8-inch, heat-resistant, non-metallic square baking dish.

2. Sprinkle the cheese over the top and heat, uncovered, on ROAST for 14 to 16 minutes or until cheese melts.

Specialty Casserole

160°F

1 pound lean ground beef
½ cup chopped onion
1 (8-ounce) package cream
   cheese, cubed
1 (10½-ounce) can cream of
   mushroom soup
1 (12-ounce) can whole kernel
   corn, drained
1 (2-ounce) jar pimiento,
   drained and chopped
1 teaspoon salt
Dash of pepper

Serves 4

1. In a 2-quart, heat-resistant, non-metallic casserole, brown meat and onions, uncovered, on ROAST for 4 minutes. Stir occasionally to break up meat chunks.

2. Drain excess fat.

3. Blend cream cheese and soup in a small bowl.

4. Heat, uncovered, on ROAST for 5 minutes.   Stir once.

5. Add cream cheese mixture, corn and pimiento to hamburger. Stir to combine.

6. Heat, uncovered, on ROAST for 10 minutes.

13

Full O' Boloney

1½ cups raw potatoes, cubed
   (about 1½ potatoes)
1½ cups cubed bologna
   (½ pound)
2 tablespoons minced green
   pepper
1 (10½-ounce) can cream of
   mushroom soup
2 large slices of American
   cheese, quartered

Serves 4

1. Combine all the ingredients except the American cheese, in a deep, 1½-quart, heat-resistant, non-metallic casserole.

2. Heat, covered, on ROAST for 17 minutes or until tender. Stir occasionally.

3. Top casserole with cheese slices and heat, uncovered, on ROAST an additional 1 minute or just until cheese melts.

Franks And Macaroni

140°F

1 pound beef frankfurters
1 (8-ounce) package macaroni,
cooked and drained
1 (8-ounce) jar processed
cheese spread
¼ cup finely chopped onions
1 tablespoon prepared brown
mustard

Serves 4 to 5

1. Place frankfurters on a paper plate. Heat, uncovered, on FULL POWER for 3 minutes.

2. Slice each cooked frankfurter into five diagonal slices.

3. Combine cooked macaroni, sliced frankfurters, cheese spread, onion, and mustard in a deep, 2½-quart, heat-resistant, non-metallic casserole.

4. Heat, uncovered, on ROAST for 7 minutes, or until sauce is bubbly.

Salmon Casserole

150°F

4 cups cooked noodles
1 (16-ounce) can salmon,
drained and flaked
1 (4-ounce) can mushroom
slices, drained
1 (10¼-ounce) can cream of
celery soup
½ cup thinly sliced celery
1 (5¼-ounce) can sliced water
chestnuts, drained
1 (17-ounce) can green peas,
drained
1 cup coarsely crushed potato
chips

Serves 4 to 6

1. In a deep, 2½-quart, heat-resistant, non-metallic casserole, combine noodles, salmon, mushroom slices, celery soup, celery, water chestnuts and green peas until well blended.

2. Heat, covered, on ROAST for 8 to 10 minutes or until heated through. Stir occasionally.

3. Just before serving, sprinkle with potato chips.

Variation: A number of substitutions may be made in this casserole.
1. Tuna may be substituted for salmon.
2. Cream of mushroom or cream of asparagus soup may be substituted for cream of celery soup.
3. Green beans or corn may be used in place of peas.
4. Pimientos or green pepper may be added for color and flavor.
5. Chinese noodles, fried onion rings, crushed crackers or nuts may be used in place of potato chips.

Tip: When making substitutions, try to keep the volume about the same so that the cooking times will be unchanged.

Franks And Beans

150°F

1 pound frankfurters
1 (32-ounce) can pork and
beans
1 (8-ounce) can crushed
pineapple in unsweetened
juice, undrained
¼ cup chili sauce
¼ cup finely chopped onion

Serves 4 to 6

1. Slice frankfurters into ¼-inch rounds.

2. Place frankfurters, beans, pineapple, chili sauce and onions in a 2-quart, heat-resistant, non-metallic casserole.

3. Heat, covered, on ROAST for 10 minutes stirring after 5 minutes.

4. Allow to stand covered for 2 minutes before serving.

Baked Bean Casserole

150°F

2 strips bacon
1 (16-ounce) can old fashioned baked beans in molasses and brown sugar sauce
2 tablespoons minced onion
2 tablespoons catsup
2 tablespoons firmly packed brown sugar
1 teaspoon prepared mustard

Serves 3 to 4

1. Place bacon on a paper-towel-lined paper plate. Heat on FULL POWER, covered with paper toweling, 3 minutes or until crisp.

2. In a deep, 1½-quart, heat-resistant, non-metallic casserole combine beans, onion, catsup, brown sugar and mustard. Mix thoroughly.

3. Crumble bacon and sprinkle over baked bean mixture.

4. Heat, uncovered, on ROAST for 12 minutes or until sauce is bubbly.

Variation: Add 6 franks or 4 slices (½-inch thick) ham and heat an additional 2 minutes in Step 4.

South Of The Border Eggplant

4 slices raw bacon
1 pound lean ground beef
1 medium onion, finely chopped
1 clove garlic, peeled and crushed
1 medium green pepper, finely chopped
1 medium eggplant, peeled and cut into ½-inch slices
1 teaspoon salt
⅛ teaspoon pepper
1 (15-ounce) can tomato sauce
½ cup crumbled feta cheese
1 cup seasoned croutons

Serves 4 to 6

1. In a deep, 2-quart, heat-resistant, non-metallic casserole heat bacon, covered with paper toweling, on FULL POWER 4 minutes or until crisp. Reserve bacon fat.

2. Remove bacon. Set aside.

3. Add beef, onion, garlic and green pepper to reserved bacon fat. Heat on ROAST, uncovered, 7 to 8 minutes or until vegetables are tender and meat is browned.

4. Add eggplant, salt, pepper, tomato sauce, feta cheese and reserved bacon. Stir to blend.

5. Heat, covered, on ROAST for 10 minutes or until eggplant is tender.

6. Sprinkle with croutons and heat on ROAST, uncovered, an additional 2 minutes or until heated through. Serving temperature should be 150° to 160°F.

13

Enchilada Casserole

160°F

1 pound lean ground beef
1 tablespoon instant minced onion
1 clove garlic, peeled and crushed
2½ teaspoons chili powder
1 teaspoon pepper
⅔ cup water
1 (8-ounce) can tomato sauce
2 cups shredded sharp Cheddar cheese
¼ teaspoon salt
6 tortillas or taco shells

Serves 4 to 6

1. Crumble beef into a shallow, 2½-quart, heat-resistant, non-metallic casserole. Sprinkle meat with minced onion and crushed garlic.

2. Heat, uncovered, on ROAST for 6 minutes. Stir occasionally to break up meat.

3. Drain excess fat. Add chili powder, pepper, water and tomato sauce. Stir to combine. Heat, uncovered, 5 minutes on ROAST.

4. Alternately layer tortillas, meat sauce and cheese in a round, 1½-quart, heat-resistant, non-metallic casserole. Last layer should be cheese.

5. Heat, covered, on ROAST for 9 to 11 minutes or until cheese is melted.

Sausage And Cabbage Casserole

160°F

2 pounds bulk breakfast sausage
1 medium onion, coarsely chopped
2 pounds cabbage, cored and coarsely chopped
1 (16-ounce) can whole peeled tomatoes, undrained
1 tablespoon sugar
½ teaspoon dried oregano leaves
1½ teaspoons salt
¼ teaspoon pepper
2 tablespoons flour
¼ cup cold water

Serves 6 to 8

1. Crumble sausage into a deep, 4-quart, heat-resistant, non-metallic casserole and add onion.

2. Heat, uncovered, on ROAST for 14 minutes or until sausage is cooked and onion is tender. Stir frequently. Drain off excess fat and crumble.

3. Add cabbage, tomatoes, sugar, oregano, salt and pepper. Stir to combine.

4. Heat, covered, on ROAST for 25 to 30 minutes or until cabbage is tender.

5. In a small cup mix flour and water until smooth.

6. Gradually stir flour mixture into sausage mixture.

7. Heat, uncovered, on ROAST for 4 minutes, stirring frequently until thickened.

Chili Pie

160°F

1½ pounds lean ground beef
1 medium onion, thinly sliced
1 (12-ounce) can, whole kernel corn, drained
1 (16-ounce) can whole peeled tomatoes, undrained
1 (8-ounce) can tomato sauce with cheese
1 to 2 teaspoons chili powder
1 teaspoon salt
¼ teaspoon pepper
⅓ cup sliced stuffed olives
½ cups shredded Cheddar cheese
1½ cups coarsely crumbled tortilla chips or corn chips

Serves 4 to 6

1. Crumble meat into a deep, 2-quart, heat-resistant, non-metallic casserole.

2. Add onions and heat, uncovered, on ROAST for 8 to 9 minutes or until meat is browned and onions are tender. Stir occasionally. Drain off excess fat.

3. Add corn, tomatoes, tomato sauce, chili powder to taste and salt and pepper. Stir to combine.

4. Heat, uncovered, on ROAST for 5 minutes, stirring occasionally.

5. Arrange olive slices on top of meat mixture and sprinkle with cheese.

6. Heat, uncovered, on ROAST for 5 minutes.

7. Sprinkle with tortilla chips and heat, uncovered, on ROAST for 1 minute.

Baked Ziti

140°F

1 (8-ounce) package ziti, cooked conventionally or according to spaghetti recipe on page 199.
Italian Tomato Sauce (see recipe on page 111)
¾ cup shredded mozzarella cheese

Serves 4

1. In a deep, 2-quart, heat-resistant, non-metallic casserole combine ziti, tomato sauce and ⅓ cup shredded cheese.

2. Sprinkle remainder of cheese on top of casserole and heat, uncovered, on ROAST for 7 to 10 minutes or until cheese is melted and sauce is bubbly.

Pictured: Hot Turkey Salad, Turkey Tetrazzini, Turkey Divan.

Leftovers

LEFTOVERS

Cooking Hints

Leftovers can become exciting new dishes with your Sharp Microwave Oven. Reheating with microwaves retains the fresh appearance and fresh-cooked flavor of leftovers without drying them out. Therefore, they return to your table looking and tasting just as good as when first cooked. This results in a saving in food costs and grocery bills, as well as saving your own time and energy.

Cover foods with clear plastic wrap if you wish to retain moisture.

Dense foods reheat most successfully using the ROAST setting. However, if the food contains a large amount of liquid, FULL POWER may be used. Your own experience and time limitations will help you decide which setting is best for each particular food. If using FULL POWER rather than ROAST, decrease the cooking time by 2 to 3 minutes.

Bread products should be wrapped in paper toweling to absorb excess moisture and prevent sogginess. Reheat bread products on ROAST for best results.

Place thin portions of food toward the center of the plate. Thicker portions should be placed toward the outside edge of the plate.

Serving temperature for leftovers is 150° to 160°F.

Approximate times for reheating casserole-type foods:

AMOUNT	VARIABLE COOKING CONTROL SETTING	TIME
1 cup	ROAST	4 minutes
2 cups	ROAST	6 minutes
3 cups	ROAST	8 minutes
4 cups	ROAST	10 minutes
8 cups	ROAST	18 minutes

To reheat a plate of food, use the following time guide. Cover plate with clear plastic wrap to retain moisture.

1 plate of food (room temperature) 2 minutes on ROAST
1 plate of food (refrigerated)   3 minutes on ROAST

Quick Beef Stew

2 tablespoons vegetable oil
1 medium onion, finely chopped
1 bay leaf
1 (8-ounce) can sliced carrots, drained
1 (16-ounce) can tiny white potatoes, drained
½ teaspoon salt
⅛ teaspoon pepper
¼ teaspoon celery salt
2 cups beef gravy (see recipe page 109)
2 to 3 cups cubed cooked beef
1 (8-ounce) can green peas, drained
Serves 4 to 6

1. In a deep, 2-quart, heat-resistant, non-metallic casserole, heat oil on FULL POWER 2 minutes.
2. Add onion and heat, uncovered, on FULL POWER 3 minutes or until tender. Stir occasionally.
3. Add bay leaf, carrots, potatoes, salt, pepper, celery salt, beef gravy and beef; stir to combine.
4. Heat, covered, on ROAST for 8 to 9 minutes or until almost heated. Salt and pepper to taste.
5. Remove bay leaf and discard.
6. Add peas and heat, covered, on ROAST for 4 to 5 minutes or until heated through.

Note: For a thicker stew, add additional flour to beef gravy recipe.

Saucy Pork N' Noodle Bake

1 tablespoon butter or margarine
1 cup cubed cooked pork
½ cup uncooked noodles
1 (10½-ounce) can cream of chicken soup
1 (8¾-ounce) can whole kernel corn, undrained
1 tablespoon sliced pimiento
½ cup shredded sharp Cheddar cheese
¼ cup finely chopped green pepper
Serves 2 to 3

1. Place 1 tablespoon butter in a deep, 1½-quart, heat-resistant, non-metallic casserole. Heat, uncovered, on FULL POWER 30 seconds.
2. Add pork and heat, uncovered, on FULL POWER 2 minutes. Drain off excess fat.
3. Add remaining ingredients and mix well.
4. Heat, covered, on ROAST for 14 to 17 minutes or until noodles are tender. Stir occasionally.

Layered Dinner

1 (16-ounce) can cut green beans, drained
8 slices cooked ham
1 (10½-ounce) can cream of celery soup
¼ cup mayonnaise
1 teaspoon prepared mustard
5 slices American cheese
⅓ cup seasoned croutons
1 tablespoon butter or margarine, melted
Serves 6 to 8

1. Place green beans in a 1½-quart, heat-resistant, non-metallic casserole. Top with slices of ham.
2. In a small bowl, combine soup, mayonnaise and mustard. Blend together well.
3. Pour soup mixture over ham slices.
4. Top with cheese.
5. In a small, heat-resistant, non-metallic bowl, melt butter on FULL POWER 30 seconds.
6. Toss croutons in melted butter.
7. Sprinkle buttered croutons over cheese.
8. Heat, uncovered, on ROAST 12 minutes. Let stand for 5 minutes before serving.

14

Shepherd's Pie

2 tablespoons vegetable oil
1 medium onion, thinly sliced
3 medium tomatoes, peeled and
  thinly sliced
3 tablespoons butter or margarine
2 tablespoons flour
¼ teaspoon salt
¼ teaspoon pepper
1 cup chicken stock or 2 envelopes instant chicken broth
  and 1 cup water
1½ pounds cooked lamb, cut into
  1-inch cubes
2 cups mashed potatoes; leftover, fresh or from packaged
  instant potatoes

Serves 4 to 6

1. In a deep, 2-quart, heat-resistant, non-metallic casserole, place vegetable oil, onion and tomatoes and heat, uncovered, on FULL POWER for 4 minutes or until tender. Set aside.

2. In a small, heat-resistant, non-metallic bowl melt butter on FULL POWER for 30 seconds.

3. Blend in flour, salt, pepper and chicken stock.

4. Heat, uncovered, on FULL POWER for 3 minutes or until thickened and smooth. Stir occasionally.

5. Add sauce and cooked lamb to onion-tomato mixture. Stir to combine.

6. Heat, covered, on ROAST for 6 to 8 minutes or until almost heated through (time will depend on temperature of cooked lamb). Top with mashed potatoes and heat, uncovered, on ROAST for an additional 5 to 7 minutes or until serving temperature is reached.

Variation: Cooked beef chunks, ground beef or ground lamb may be substituted for cooked lamb.

Ham-Broccoli Rolls

4 rectangular slices boiled ham
  (¼-inch thick)
4 slices Swiss cheese (⅛-inch
  thick)
1 (10-ounce) package frozen
  broccoli spears, cooked and
  drained
1 tablespoon butter or margarine
1 tablespoon flour
¼ teaspoon salt
1 tablespoon prepared horseradish
2 teaspoons prepared mustard
½ teaspoon Worcestershire sauce
½ teaspoon instant minced onion
2 egg yolks, slightly beaten
1 cup pineapple juice
½ cup milk
4 slices canned pineapple, drained

Serves 4

1. In a shallow, heat-resistant, non-metallic baking dish, place ham slices. Top each ham slice with cheese.

2. Place cooked broccoli spears on top of each cheese topped ham slice. Set aside.

3. In a medium-sized, heat-resistant, non-metallic bowl, melt butter, uncovered, on FULL POWER 30 seconds.

4. Blend in the flour, salt, horseradish, mustard, Worcestershire sauce and onion. Set aside.

5. Combine beaten egg yolk and pineapple juice.

6. Add pineapple juice mixture to butter mixture. Blend well.

7. Stir in milk.

8. Heat, uncovered, on ROAST for 7 minutes, stirring occasionally until sauce is thick and bubbly.

9. Spoon about 1 tablespoon of sauce over broccoli.

10. Roll ham and cheese around broccoli and secure with wooden picks.

11. Heat, covered, on ROAST for 10 minutes.

12. Spoon remaining sauce over ham rolls. Top with pineapple slices.

13. Heat, uncovered, on ROAST for 3 to 4 minutes or until sauce is bubbly.

Chicken à la King

3 tablespoons butter or margarine
5 tablespoons flour
1 teaspoon salt
⅛ teaspoon pepper
1¾ cups chicken stock
3 cups cooked chicken
1 (4-ounce) can mushroom stems
and pieces, drained
¼ cup finely chopped
pimiento
8 puff pastry shells, baked

Serves 8

1. In a deep, 2-quart, heat-resistant, non-metallic casserole melt butter on FULL POWER 30 seconds.

2. Blend in flour, salt and pepper.

3. Gradually stir in chicken stock.

4. Heat, uncovered, on FULL POWER 4 minutes or until thickened and smooth. Stir occasionally.

5. Add remaining ingredients except pastry shells and heat, uncovered, on FULL POWER 3 minutes or until heated to 160°F.

6. Heat pastry shells on a heat-resistant, non-metallic serving platter on FULL POWER 2 minutes or until heated through.

7. Fill each with some of the chicken mixture.

Oven Chicken Salad

140°F

2 cups cubed cooked chicken
2 cups thinly sliced celery
1 cup croutons
1 cup mayonnaise
½ cup toasted chopped or slivered almonds
2 tablespoons lemon juice
2 teaspoons finely chopped onion
½ teaspoon salt
½ cup shredded sharp Cheddar
cheese
1 cup croutons or crushed
potato chips

Serves 4

1. Combine all ingredients except cheese and the second 1 cup of croutons in a 1½-quart, heat-resistant, non-metallic casserole.

2. Sprinkle with cheese and the 1 cup of croutons or crushed potato chips.

3. Heat, uncovered, on ROAST for 8 to 10 minutes or until bubbly.

14

Hot Turkey Salad

140°F

1 cup mayonnaise
2 tablespoons lemon juice
½ teaspoon salt
2 tablespoons finely chopped
onion
2 cups cooked turkey
2 cups chopped celery
½ cup sliced almonds
½ cup shredded sharp Cheddar
cheese
Crushed potato chips

Serves 4

1. In a large mixing bowl, blend all ingredients together, except cheese and crushed potato chips.

2. Place turkey mixture in a shallow, heat-resistant, non-metallic 8-inch square baking dish. Sprinkle top with cheese and potato chips.

3. Heat, uncovered, on ROAST for 8 minutes or until cheese melts.

Variation: Shrimp, tuna or chicken may be substituted for turkey.

Turkey Divan

2 tablespoons butter or margarine

2 tablespoons flour

2 envelopes instant chicken broth or 2 cubes chicken bouillon, crumbled

¾ cup hot water

2 tablespoons dry sherry

⅛ teaspoon nutmeg

¼ cup heavy cream, chilled and whipped

¼ cup grated Parmesan cheese

1 (10-ounce) package frozen broccoli, cooked

1 pound cooked turkey or chicken slices

¼ cup grated Parmesan cheese

Paprika (optional)

Serves 3 to 4

1. In a medium-sized, heat-resistant, non-metallic bowl melt butter on FULL POWER 30 seconds.

2. Blend in flour and instant chicken broth. Gradually add water, stirring until smooth.

3. Heat, uncovered, on FULL POWER 2 minutes or until thickened and smooth.

4. Add sherry and nutmeg.

5. Gently fold in whipped cream and ¼ cup Parmesan cheese.

6. Line a heat-resistant, non-metallic serving dish with cooked broccoli. Arrange turkey or chicken slices over broccoli.

7. Spoon sauce over turkey slices. Sprinkle with the ¼ cup Parmesan cheese and paprika, if desired.

8. Heat, uncovered, on ROAST for 6 to 7 minutes or until heated through.

Turkey Tetrazzini

¼ cup butter or margarine

¼ cup flour

¼ teaspoon salt

¼ teaspoon pepper

1 chicken bouillon cube, crumbled or 1 envelope instant chicken broth

1 cup boiling water

1 cup heavy cream

2 tablespoons sherry

1 (8-ounce) package spaghetti, cooked and drained

2 cups cubed, cooked turkey

1 (4-ounce) can sliced mushrooms

½ cup grated Parmesan cheese

Serves 4 to 6

1. Melt butter in a large, heat-resistant, non-metallic bowl on FULL POWER for 1 minute.

2. Blend in flour, salt, pepper and crumbled bouillon cube.

3. Gradually stir in boiling water and cream.

4. Heat, uncovered, on ROAST for 6 minutes or until thickened and smooth, stirring occasionally.

5. Stir in sherry, spaghetti, turkey and mushrooms.

6. Pour mixture into a deep, 2-quart, heat-resistant, non-metallic casserole.

7. Sprinkle with grated cheese and heat, uncovered, on ROAST for 6 minutes or until heated through.

Pictured: Ratatouille

Vegetables

VEGETABLES

Cooking Hints

Vegetables are superb when cooked by microwaves!
Microwave cooking retains more of the color, flavor and nutritional value of vegetables. Since very small amounts of water are used to cook vegetables in your Microwave Oven, it is not necessary to drain before serving. Water soluble vitamins and minerals are retained and quick cooking means less loss of other valuable nutrients.

Most frozen vegetables need little or no water added. The ice crystals often provide enough moisture for cooking, and rarely is more than ¼ cup water needed. Frozen vegetables may be cooked directly in the paper carton in which they are packaged. The container should be vented before cooking.

If you wish to add seasonings to frozen vegetables before cooking, place vegetables and seasonings in serving bowl and cook, covered with a glass cover or plastic wrap, for recommended cooking time. Salt should either be added following cooking, or placed in water in the bottom of the bowl and the vegetable placed over this liquid. Salt tends to dehydrate and toughen microwave cooked vegetables.

Vegetables should be covered when cooking to help steam them in the smallest amount of water possible.

Vegetables in cooking pouches work well in the Microwave Oven, and directions for microwave cooking are on many packages. The cooking pouch should be slit or punctured before cooking to allow excess steam to escape. Otherwise, the bag will give way at the seam.

Most vegetables cook best on FULL POWER. See recipes and charts for specific recommendations.

Commercially canned vegetables heat rapidly. You may wish to stir halfway through cooking time. Draining part of the liquid before cooking will shorten heating times. Serving temperature for canned vegetables is 150°F.

8½-ounce can	2–3 minutes on FULL POWER
15–16-ounce can	4 minutes on FULL POWER

Vegetables should still be a little firm when removed from the oven. They will continue to cook somewhat during the standing time. Allow vegetables to stand, covered, for a few minutes before serving.

Vegetables should be cooked until they are fork tender.
Overcooking will not yield a softer (or mushy) vegetable, but rather one that is tough and dehydrated.

Fresh vegetables can be blanched in your Microwave Oven for freezing. Place vegetables in ¼ to ½ cup water and cover. Heat in the Microwave Oven on FULL POWER approximately ⅓ the recommended microwave cooking time for that fresh vegetable. Vegetables should become hot and begin to change color. After heating, vegetable should be immersed in ice water to cool and then packaged for freezing. No more than 4 cups should be blanched at once.

We do not recommend canning in your Sharp Microwave Oven. Canning in a Microwave Oven is similar to canning in a conventional oven, another procedure which is not recommended.

Vegetables should be cooked until desired degree of tenderness is reached, not according to temperature.

15

Frozen Vegetable Cooking Chart
Vegetables should be cooked on FULL POWER for best results

Vegetable	Amount	Cooking Procedure	Minutes On FULL POWER
Asparagus, green spears	10 oz. pkg.	Separate after 3 min.	5–6
Beans, green cut or wax French cut	10 oz. pkg.	Add 2 tbsp. hot water Stir after 4 min.	7–8
Beans, green diagonal cut	10 oz. pouch	Slit pouch with knife	5–6
Beans, green French	10 oz. pouch	Slit pouch with knife	6–7
Beans, lima Fordhook	10 oz. pkg.	Add ¼ cup hot water Stir after 4 min.	8–9
Beans, lima	10 oz. pouch	Slit pouch with knife	6–7
Broccoli	10 oz. pkg.	Separate after 4 min.	8–9
Broccoli, spears	10 oz. pouch	Slit pouch with knife	6½–7½
Broccoli, in cheese sauce	10 oz. pouch	Slit pouch with knife	7½–8½
Brussel Sprouts	10 oz. pkg.	Add 2 tbsp. hot water	5–6
	10 oz. pouch	Slit pouch with knife	6–7
Carrots	10 oz. pkg.	Add 2 tbsp. hot water Stir after 3 min.	6–7
Carrots, nuggets	10 oz. pouch	Slit pouch with knife	6–7
Cauliflower	10 oz. pkg.	Add 2 tbsp. hot water	5–6
Cauliflower, in cheese sauce	10 oz. pouch	Slit pouch with knife	7½–8½
Corn, cut off cob	10 oz. pkg.	Add ¼ cup hot water	4–5
Corn, niblets and white shoe peg	10 oz. pouch	Slit pouch with knife	6–7
Corn, cream style	10 oz. pouch	Slit pouch with knife	5½–6½
Corn, on cob	1 ear	Place in small flat covered casserole	4–4½
	2 ears	Place in small flat covered casserole	6–7
	4 ears	Place in small flat covered casserole	10–11
Okra	10 oz. pkg.	Add 2 tbsp. hot water	6–7
Onions, in cream	10 oz. pouch	Slit pouch with knife	6–7
Peas, Black eyed	10 oz. pkg.	Add ¼ cup water	8–10
Peas, green	10 oz. pkg.	Add 2 tbsp. hot water	4½–5½
	10 oz. pouch	Slit pouch with knife	6–7
Peas & Carrots	10 oz. pkg.	Add 2 tbsp. hot water	5–6
Spinach, leaf or chopped	10 oz. pkg.	Add 2 tbsp. hot water	4½–5½
	10 oz. pouch	Slit pouch with knife	6½–7½
Squash, Hubbard	10 oz. pkg.	Add 2 tbsp. hot water	4–6
Vegetables, mixed	10 oz. pkg.	Add ¼ cup hot water	5–6
	10 oz. pouch	Slit pouch with knife	6–7

Fresh Vegetable Cooking Chart

Vegetable	Amount	Cooking Procedure	Minutes On FULL POWER
Artichokes	2 medium	Add ¼ cup water and 1 tsp. salt	5–7
Asparagus	15 stalks (¾ lb.)	Add ¼ cup water. Stir after 3 min.	4–5
Beans	1 lb.	Add ½ cup water. Stir after 4 min.	12–14
Beans, yellow wax	1 lb.	Add ½ cup water. Stir during cooking.	10–12
Beans, lima	1 lb. (2 cups shelled)	Add ½ cup water. Stir after 4 min.	7–8
Beets (whole)	4 medium	Cover with water.	16–17
* Broccoli	1 small bunch (1½ lbs.)	Remove tough part of stalk. Split tender ends. Add ¼ cup water.	8–9
Brussel Sprouts	½ lb. (2 cups)	Add 2 tbsp. water. Stir after 3 min.	4–5
Cabbage	1 medium head	Wash, remove outer leaves, quarter and chop. Add 2 tbsp. of water.	12–13
Carrots	4 medium sliced	Add 2 tbsp. water.	6–7
* Cauliflower	1 medium head	Add ½ cup water.	10–12
Celery	4 cups sliced (6 stalks)	Add ¼ cup water	7–8
Corn, on cob	2 ears 4 ears 6 ears	See recipe for fresh corn on the cob in this chapter.	4 8 12
Eggplant	1 medium	Peel and dice. Add ¼ cup water and ¼ tsp. salt.	5–6
Onions	2 large	Cut in quarters. Add ¼ cup water.	6–7
Parsnips	4 medium	Add ¼ cup water.	8–9
Peas, green	2 cups	Shell and add 2 tbsp. water. Stir after 3 min.	5–6
Potatoes, baked	4 medium	Place on paper towel.	13–15
Potatoes, boiled	4 medium	Peel and quarter. Cover with hot water.	16–17
Potatoes, sweet	2 medium	Prepare as you would regular baking potatoes.	8–11
Rutabaga	1 lb.	Wash, peel and cube. Add ½ cup water. Stir during cooking.	8–9
Spinach	10 oz. package	Wash and remove thick stems. Shake off excess water.	5
Squash, Acorn	1 lb.	Pierce skin. Cook on paper plate.	7–8
Tomatoes	4 large	Clean, peel and halve. Add 2 tbsp. water.	4–6
Turnips	2 or 3 medium	Wash, peel and cube. Add ¼ cup water. Stir after 5 min.	7–9
Zucchini or Summer Squash	2 medium	Cut into thin slices. Add 1 tbsp. water. Stir after 4 min.	6½–7½

* Broccoli and whole cauliflower give excellent results on ROAST due to their density.
        Broccoli (1½ lbs.)   15 to 16 minutes on ROAST
        Whole cauliflower   12 to 15 minutes on ROAST

15

Artichoke Hearts Vinaigrette

2 (14-ounce) cans artichoke
 hearts
¼ cup butter or margarine
 Flour
⅓ cup butter or margarine,
 melted
Vinaigrette Dressing (recipe
 below)

Serves 6

1. Drain liquid from artichoke hearts and discard.

2. In a small, heat-resistant, non-metallic bowl melt the ¼ cup butter or margarine on FULL POWER 30 seconds.

3. Dip artichoke hearts in melted butter and then lightly coat with flour.

4. Place the ⅓ cup melted butter or margarine in a 10-inch, heat-resistant, non-metallic pie plate or non-metallic skillet.

5. Place flour-coated artichokes in melted butter and heat, uncovered, on FULL POWER 8 minutes. Turn artichoke hearts as needed to brown lightly.

6. While artichoke hearts are cooking, prepare Vinaigrette Dressing.

7. Just before serving, pour dressing over artichoke hearts.

Vinaigrette Dressing

¼ cup wine vinegar
¼ cup olive oil
¼ cup finely chopped parsley
2 tablespoons finely chopped
 chives
1 tablespoon finely chopped
 pimiento
1 teaspoon salt
⅛ teaspoon pepper

Makes 1 cup

1. Combine all ingredients in a small bowl. Stir until well blended.

Scalloped Asparagus

¼ cup butter or margarine
¼ cup flour
1 teaspoon salt
2 cups milk
1½ cups shredded sharp Cheddar
 cheese
2 (10-ounce) packages frozen
 cut-up asparagus, thawed
½ cup toasted slivered almonds
 Paprika

Serves 6 to 8

1. In a 1-quart, heat-resistant, non-metallic measuring cup place butter. Heat, uncovered, on FULL POWER 1 minute or until melted.

2. Stir in flour and salt until smooth. Gradually add milk, stirring constantly.

3. Heat, uncovered, on ROAST for 7 minutes or until thickened and smooth. Stir occasionally.

4. Stir in cheese until melted.

5. Place 1 package of asparagus in a deep, 2-quart, heat-resistant, non-metallic baking dish.

6. Sprinkle ½ of toasted almonds over asparagus. Pour half of sauce over almonds.

7. Repeat layers with remaining asparagus, almonds and sauce.

8. Heat, uncovered, on ROAST for 10 to 12 minutes or until heated through.

9. Before serving, sprinkle with paprika, if desired.

Tip: Thaw frozen asparagus using the DEFROST setting of your Microwave Oven. Fresh asparagus may be substituted for frozen.

Fresh Green And Wax Beans

1 pound fresh beans (green, wax or a combination of both)
¼ cup water

Serves 4

1. Wash and cut beans into 1½-inch pieces.
2. Place in a deep 2-quart, heat-resistant, non-metallic casserole with the water.
3. Heat, covered, on FULL POWER 12 minutes or until tender. Stir occasionally during cooking.
4. Drain water and season to taste.

Green Beans Almondine

2 pounds fresh green beans
½ cup water
3 tablespoons butter or margarine
⅓ cup slivered, blanched almonds
1 teaspoon salt
¼ teaspoon pepper
¼ teaspoon nutmeg (optional)

Serves 6

1. Wash beans and cut off ends. Place in a deep, 2-quart, heat-resistant, non-metallic casserole with water.
2. Heat, covered, on FULL POWER 10 to 12 minutes or until beans are crisp-tender. Drain beans.
3. Add remaining ingredients to drained green beans.
4. Stir to combine.
5. Heat, uncovered, on FULL POWER 5 minutes or until butter has melted and beans are tender.

Broccoli-Mushroom Scallop

1½ pounds fresh broccoli, washed, split and cut into 2-inch pieces or 1 (10-ounce) package frozen broccoli spears
2 tablespoons butter or margarine
1 cup sliced fresh mushrooms or 1 (4-ounce) can sliced mushrooms, drained
1 teaspoon finely chopped onion
2 tablespoons flour
¼ teaspoon salt
⅛ teaspoon pepper
1 cup milk
1 cup shredded sharp Cheddar cheese
Paprika

Serves 3 to 4

1. Heat fresh broccoli in a deep, 2½-quart, heat-resistant, non-metallic casserole, covered, on FULL POWER 8 to 9 minutes. (Note: If frozen broccoli spears are used, cook, covered, on FULL POWER 7 to 8 minutes.)
2. In a small, heat-resistant, non-metallic bowl, combine butter, mushrooms and onion. Heat, uncovered, on FULL POWER 3 minutes. Stir occasionally.
3. Blend flour and seasonings into butter-mushroom mixture. Heat, uncovered, on FULL POWER 3 minutes, stirring after 1½ minutes.
4. Gradually add milk, stirring until mixture is smooth. Heat, uncovered, on ROAST for 5 minutes. Stir once.
5. Pour hot mushroom sauce over cooked broccoli. Sprinkle with 1 cup cheese and paprika. Heat, uncovered, on ROAST for 5 to 6 minutes or until cheese is melted.

15

Note: Fresh broccoli gives excellent results when cooked on the ROAST setting, particularly if it has large stems. Cook 1½ pounds fresh broccoli on ROAST for 15 to 16 minutes.

Broccoli In Lemon Sauce

2 (10-ounce) packages frozen broccoli spears
2 tablespoons butter or margarine
1 tablespoon flour
½ cup milk
1 teaspoon grated lemon rind
1 tablespoon lemon juice
¼ teaspoon salt
¼ teaspoon ginger

Serves 4 to 6

1. Cook broccoli in a shallow, heat-resistant, non-metallic 1½-quart baking dish. Two packages will cook on FULL POWER in 14 to 16 minutes. Drain and set aside.

2. In a small, heat-resistant, non-metallic bowl melt butter or margarine on FULL POWER 30 seconds.

3. Blend in flour with a fork until smooth. Gradually stir in milk. Heat, uncovered, on ROAST for 2 to 3 minutes or until thickened and smooth.

4. Gradually stir in lemon rind and juice so that the mixture does not curdle. Stir in salt and ginger until well blended.

5. Spoon sauce over drained broccoli spears. Heat, uncovered, on ROAST 2 to 3 minutes or until heated through.

Candied Carrots

4 large carrots
⅓ cup butter or margarine
½ cup sugar
1 teaspoon salt
⅓ teaspoon cinnamon
1 tablespoon water

Serves 4

1. Scrape and cut carrots into thin strips. Place carrots in a deep, 1½-quart, heat-resistant, non-metallic casserole. Set aside.

2. In a small, heat-resistant, non-metallic bowl combine remaining ingredients. Heat, uncovered, on FULL POWER 1 minute or until butter is melted.

3. Spoon butter-sugar mixture over carrots. Heat, covered, on FULL POWER 7 minutes.

4. Spoon sauce over carrots and heat, uncovered, on FULL POWER an additional 3 minutes.

Cauliflower Scramble

2 (10-ounce) pouches of cauliflower, frozen in cheese sauce
1 medium zucchini, sliced
¼ cup finely chopped onion
2 tablespoons butter
2 tomatoes, cut into 8 wedges each
½ teaspoon salt
⅛ teaspoon thyme leaves, crushed

Serves 6

1. Heat cauliflower in pouches on FULL POWER for 9 to 10 minutes or until thawed. (Pierce holes in pouches with the tines of a fork to allow steam to escape.)

2. In a deep, 2-quart, heat-resistant, non-metallic casserole place zucchini, onion and butter and heat, uncovered, on FULL POWER 3 minutes or until zucchini and onion are tender.

3. Add cauliflower in cheese sauce and tomatoes to onion-zucchini mixture. Add salt and thyme leaves to mixture.

4. Heat, covered, on FULL POWER 5 minutes or until tomatoes are tender.

Pictured: Broccoli in Lemon Sauce

Orange Spirited Carrots

4 medium carrots, slivered
⅓ cup vodka
1 tablespoon grated orange ring
1 teaspoon sugar
¼ cup butter or margarine

1. In a deep, 1½-quart, heat-resistant, non-metallic casserole place slivered carrots and vodka. Grated orange rind and sprinkle sugar over carrots. Dot with ¼ cup butter or margarine.

2. Heat, covered, on FULL POWER 10 to 12 minutes or until carrots reach desired degree of tenderness. Stir occasionally.

Serves 4

Fresh Cauliflower Au Gratin

1 medium head cauliflower
2 tablespoons water
1 tablespoon butter or margarine
1 tablespoon flour
¼ teaspoon salt
½ cup milk
½ cup shredded sharp Cheddar cheese
Paprika

Serves 4

1. Wash cauliflower and separate into flowerets.

2. Place flowerets and water in a deep, 1½-quart, heat-resistant, non-metallic casserole.

3. Heat, covered, on FULL POWER 9 to 10 minutes. Set aside.

4. In a medium-sized, heat-resistant, non-metallic bowl melt butter, uncovered, on FULL POWER 30 seconds.

5. Blend in flour and salt. Stir until smooth. Gradually add milk.

6. Heat, uncovered, on ROAST for 2 to 3 minutes or until sauce is thickened and smooth. Stir once.

7. Stir cheese into sauce.

8. Pour sauce over cauliflower and heat, uncovered, on ROAST 2 to 3 minutes or until cauliflower is heated through.

9. Sprinkle paprika over sauce before serving.

> **Note:** Whole cauliflower gives excellent results when cooked on ROAST. If time allows, cook fresh cauliflower on ROAST for 12 to 15 minutes. Flowerets can be cooked on FULL POWER.

Corn Custard

2 cups evaporated milk
1½ tablespoons butter or margarine
2 eggs, slightly beaten
2 teaspoons sugar
1½ teaspoons salt
¼ teaspoon pepper
1 (17-ounce) can whole kernel corn, drained

Serves 6

1. In a deep, 1½-quart, heat-resistant, non-metallic casserole, heat evaporated milk, uncovered, on FULL POWER 2½ minutes or until scalded. Add butter and stir until butter has melted.

2. Stir in eggs, sugar, salt and pepper. Stir to blend well.

3. Stir in corn.

4. Heat, uncovered, on ROAST for 16 to 17 minutes.

5. Set aside 5 minutes to finish cooking.

Pimientos Stuffed With Corn

1 (8-ounce) can whole kernel
  corn
1 cup soft bread crumbs
1 tablespoon chili sauce
3 tablespoons melted butter or
  margarine
Salt and pepper, to taste
6 whole pimientos, well
  drained

Serves 6

1. Combine the corn, bread crumbs, chili sauce, butter or margarine and salt and pepper, to taste, in a small bowl.

2. Stuff the pimientos with the corn mixture and place in a shallow, heat-resistant, non-metallic baking dish.

3. Heat, uncovered, on FULL POWER 4 minutes or until heated through.

Succotash

2 (10-ounce) packages frozen
  Fordhook lima beans, thawed
2 (10-ounce) packages frozen
  whole kernel corn, thawed
⅓ cup chopped pimiento
2 teaspoons salt
½ teaspoon sugar
¼ teaspoon pepper
6 tablespoons butter or margarine
½ cup light cream

Serves 6

1. Place lima beans and corn in a large, heat-resistant, non-metallic bowl.

2. Heat, covered, on FULL POWER 12 minutes or until vegetables are hot.

3. Add remaining ingredients and stir to combine. Heat, uncovered, on ROAST for 5 minutes or until heated through.

Fresh Corn On The Cob

4 ears fresh corn, unhusked
Butter or margarine, melted

Serves 4

1. Peel back the husks and remove the silk, leaving the husks intact.

2. Brush the ears with melted butter. Replace the husks and fasten with string or rubber bands.

3. Place in Microwave Oven, leaving at least 1-inch between ears. Cook 4 minutes on FULL POWER.

4. Turn ears over and cook an additional 4 minutes on FULL POWER. Allow to stand 2 to 3 minutes with the husks in place.

5. Turn back the husks and use as a handle. Season corn to taste.

15

Variation: If desired, husks can be removed and corn wrapped in wax paper or placed in a covered casserole and cooked as in recipe above.

Corn Casserole

1 (10-ounce) package frozen
  cut corn, defrosted
1 (17-ounce) can cream-style
  corn
3 eggs, well beaten
½ cup whole milk
1 teaspoon salt
¼ teaspoon pepper
½ cup cracker crumbs or
  dry bread crumbs
Butter or margarine

Serves 6

1. In a medium-sized bowl place cut corn. Add can of cream-style corn and mix well. To corn mixture add beaten eggs, milk, salt and pepper. Stir until thoroughly blended.

2. Lightly butter a 2-quart, heat-resistant, non-metallic casserole.

3. Pour ⅓ of corn mixture into casserole. Cover with ⅓ of the crumbs. Dot with butter. Repeat until all ingredients are used. Be sure to end with crumbs dotted with butter.

4. Heat, covered, on ROAST for 8 to 9 minutes. Remove cover and heat on ROAST for an additional 2 minutes.

Tip: If a browner crust is desired, place in a hot oven (425°F) for 5 minutes.

Scalloped Corn

2 tablespoons butter or margarine
¼ cup finely chopped onion
2 tablespoons flour
½ teaspoon salt
½ teaspoon paprika
¼ teaspoon dry mustard
Dash pepper
¾ cup milk
1 (17-ounce) can whole kernel
  corn, drained
1 egg, slightly beaten

Serves 6

1. Place 2 tablespoons butter in a deep, 1-quart, heat-resistant, non-metallic casserole. Heat, uncovered, on FULL POWER 45 seconds.

2. Add chopped onion and heat, uncovered, on FULL POWER 2 minutes or until onion is tender.

3. Blend in flour, salt, paprika, dry mustard and pepper. Heat, uncovered, on FULL POWER 1 minute or until bubbly.

4. Gradually add milk, stirring constantly.

5. Add remaining ingredients. Blend thoroughly.

6. Heat, uncovered, on ROAST for 12 to 14 minutes or until set.

Ratatouille

1 (1½-pound) eggplant, cut into
  ½-inch cubes
2 small zucchini, thinly sliced
  (about 1 pound)
¼ cup olive oil
2 medium onions, thinly sliced
1 clove garlic, peeled and crushed
1 large green pepper, thinly
  sliced
3 large ripe tomatoes, washed
  and cut into 8 wedges each
2 teaspoons dried basil leaves
2 teaspoons dried marjoram
  leaves
1 teaspoon salt
½ teaspoon pepper
1 (8-ounce) can sliced mushrooms, drained

Serves 6 to 8

1. In a large bowl cover eggplant and zucchini with salted water (about 1 teaspoon salt to 1 quart water). Soak for 30 minutes; drain.

2. In a deep, 3-quart, heat-resistant, non-metallic casserole, heat olive oil, onions and garlic, uncovered, on FULL POWER 5 minutes or until onions and garlic are tender.

3. Add green pepper, drained eggplant and zucchini.

4. Heat, covered, on FULL POWER 5 minutes.

5. Add remaining ingredients and stir to combine well.

6. Heat, uncovered, on FULL POWER 5 minutes longer or until vegetables are tender.

7. Ratatouille may be served either hot or cold.

Cucumber-Onion Bake

2 (8-inch) cucumbers, sliced
¼-inch thick
2 medium onions, thinly sliced
and separated into rings
4 tablespoons flour
Salt and pepper, to taste
2 cups catsup
2 tablespoons butter or margarine

Serves 6

1. Alternate layers of cucumbers and onions in a deep, 2½-quart, heat-resistant, non-metallic casserole. Sprinkle each layer with flour, salt and pepper.

2. Pour catsup over cucumber-onion mixture.

3. Place chunks of butter on top.

4. Heat, covered, on FULL POWER 20 minutes or until onions are tender.

Chived Mashed Potatoes

1½ cups hot water
½ teaspoon salt
⅛ teaspoon pepper
3 tablespoons butter or margarine
½ cup milk or light cream
1½ cups instant mashed potato
flakes
⅓ cup dairy sour cream
¼ cup finely chopped parsley
3 tablespoons freeze-dried
chives
1 egg, slightly beaten

Serves 4

1. Combine water, salt, pepper and butter in a deep, 1½-quart, heat-resistant, non-metallic casserole.

2. Heat, uncovered, on FULL POWER 4 minutes or until mixture boils.

3. Add milk.

4. Stir in potato flakes with a fork.

5. Stir in remaining ingredients until well blended.

6. Heat, uncovered, on FULL POWER for 5 minutes or until heated to 160°F.

Scalloped Potatoes Au Gratin

4 medium potatoes, peeled and
thinly sliced
1 cup cheese sauce (recipe on
page 109)
Pepper
Paprika

Serves 4

1. Arrange ½ of the potatoes in the bottom of lightly buttered, shallow, 1½-quart, heat-resistant, non-metallic baking dish. Pepper potatoes.

2. Pour half of the cheese sauce over potatoes.

3. Repeat with remaining potatoes and cheese sauce. Sprinkle pepper and paprika over top of casserole.

4. Heat, uncovered, on ROAST for 14 to 16 minutes or until potatoes are tender when tested with a fork.

Variation: If desired, 1½ pounds of fresh broccoli may be substituted for potatoes. Heat, un-covered, on ROAST for 16 to 18 minutes in Step 4. If you prefer to use frozen broccoli, thaw on DEFROST before using. The cooking time will be reduced to 6 to 7 minutes in Step 4.

15

Hot German Potato Salad

6 to 8 medium potatoes,
cooked and peeled
8 slices raw bacon, cooked
and crumbled
⅓ cup olive oil or bacon fat
½ cup finely chopped onion
¼ cup wine vinegar
2 tablespoons finely chopped
green onion
¼ cup chopped parsley

Serves 6

1. Slice potatoes into a large, heat-resistant, non-metallic bowl.
2. Add crumbled bacon.
3. Place oil or bacon fat in a medium-sized, heat-resistant, non-metallic bowl.
4. Add the ½ cup chopped onion and heat, uncovered, on FULL POWER 5 minutes or until lightly browned.
5. Add vinegar and cook an additional 3 minutes on FULL POWER.
6. Combine remaining ingredients with the potatoes; toss lightly.
7. Serve hot. Serving temperature should be 150°F.

Squash Parmesan

1 small onion, peeled and
chopped
3 small yellow squash, sliced
¼-inch thick (about 1 pound)
¼ cup water
3 slices white bread with crusts
removed, crumbled
1 cup milk
1 teaspoon salt
½ teaspoon monosodium
glutamate (optional)
2 tablespoons melted butter
or margarine
½ cup grated Parmesan cheese
Italian flavored dry bread crumbs

Serves 6

1. Place chopped onions and sliced squash in a 2-quart, heat-resistant, non-metallic casserole with water. Cover tightly and heat on FULL POWER 7 minutes or until squash is tender. Drain excess water.
2. Soak crumbled slices of white bread in 1 cup milk for 5 minutes.
3. Add salt, monosodium glutamate, melted butter and grated cheese to bread mixture. Stir to combine.
4. Pour bread and cheese mixture over squash and stir to mix together thoroughly.
5. Sprinkle top of mixture with Italian flavored dry bread crumbs. Cook, uncovered, on ROAST for 12 minutes or until cheese is melted. Thermometer should register 160°F.

Variation: Zucchini may be substituted for yellow squash.

Fresh Spinach

1 (10-ounce) package fresh
spinach

Serves 2 to 3

1. Wash spinach and remove any bruised leaves or thick stems. Shake excess water off leaves.
2. Place spinach in a 2-quart, heat-resistant, non-metallic casserole.
3. Heat, tightly covered, on FULL POWER 5 minutes. Stir after 2 minutes.
4. Drain excess water and season to taste.

Wilted Spinach Salad

1 pound fresh spinach
6 slices raw bacon
3 tablespoons finely chopped onion
⅓ cup wine vinegar
⅓ cup water
3 tablespoons finely chopped pimiento
2 tablespoons sugar
¼ teaspoon pepper

Serves 4

1. Wash spinach very carefully and remove any thick stems and bruised leaves. Drain well and place in a salad bowl.
2. Place bacon slices in a 9-inch, heat-resistant, non-metallic pie plate.
3. Heat, covered with a paper towel, on FULL POWER 6 minutes or until crisp. Remove bacon slices, crumble and set aside.
4. Add finely chopped onion to bacon fat and heat, uncovered, on FULL POWER 2 minutes or until lightly browned.
5. To make dressing, add remaining ingredients and heat, uncovered, on FULL POWER 4 minutes or until mixture comes to a boil.
6. Just before serving, pour boiling dressing over spinach. Add crumbled bacon and toss well. Serve immediately.

Cheese Spinach Timbales

2 (10-ounce) packages frozen chopped spinach, cooked and drained well
½ cup feta cheese, crumbled
3 slices bacon, cooked and crumbled
5 egg yolks, slightly beaten
1 teaspoon salt
1 teaspoon sugar
½ teaspoon pepper
1 hard-cooked egg, cut in 8 slices

Serves 8

1. In a medium-sized bowl combine all ingredients except hard-cooked egg slices. Blend well.
2. Lightly grease 8 (6-ounce) heat-resistant, non-metallic custard cups (coffee cups may be substituted).
3. Place slice of hard boiled egg in bottom of each custard cup. Spoon spinach mixture on top of egg slice. Fill custard cups ¾ full.
4. Place custard cups on outside edge of glass turntable.
5. Heat, uncovered, on ROAST for 14 minutes or until knife inserted in the center of custard cup comes out clean.
6. To serve, invert timbales on serving plate. Run a sharp knife around edge of cooked spinach to loosen timbales from custard cups.

Tip: To cook 2 (10-ounce) packages of frozen chopped spinach, heat, covered, on FULL POWER 8 to 10 minutes.

Zucchini

2 pounds small fresh zucchini
⅓ cup water
½ teaspoon salt
4 tablespoons butter or margarine
3 tablespoons finely chopped parsley

Serves 4

1. Wash zucchini, but do not peel. Cut into ¼-inch slices.
2. Place zucchini and water in a deep, 2-quart, heat-resistant, non-metallic casserole.
3. Cover and heat on FULL POWER 7 minutes or until tender. Add remaining ingredients and stir to combine.
4. Heat, uncovered, on FULL POWER for an additional 2 minutes.

15

Zesty Squash And Zucchini Casserole

¼ cup butter or margarine
1 large clove garlic, peeled and crushed
½ teaspoon salt
⅛ teaspoon pepper
1 teaspoon dried oregano leaves
½ teaspoon dried basil leaves
1 large yellow summer squash, cut into ¼-inch slices
2 small zucchini, cut into ½-inch slices
1 large onion, cut into 16 pieces
1 cup thinly sliced fresh mushrooms
1 large fresh tomato, cut into eighths

Serves 8

1. Place butter or margarine, garlic and seasonings in a deep, 2½-quart, heat-resistant, non-metallic casserole. Heat, uncovered, on FULL POWER 1 minute. Mix well.

2. Add sliced squash, zucchini, onions and mushrooms to seasoned butter mixture. Toss lightly until all vegetables are coated with seasoned butter mixture.

3. Cover tightly and heat on FULL POWER 8 minutes. Add tomatoes and heat on FULL POWER an additional 6 minutes or until vegetables have reached desired degree of doneness.

Stuffed Zucchini

4 small zucchini (about 1 pound)
½ pound lean ground beef
2 tablespoons finely chopped onion
1 teaspoon parsley flakes
½ teaspoon salt
Pepper, to taste
1 egg, beaten
1 slice white bread, crusts removed and crumbled
¼ cup grated Parmesan cheese
1 (15-ounce) can tomato sauce
3 tablespoons chopped onion
1 clove garlic, peeled and crushed
1 teaspoon dried parsley flakes
1 teaspoon dried oregano leaves
½ teaspoon dried basil leaves
½ teaspoon sugar
½ teaspoon salt
Pepper, to taste

Serves 4

1. Place zucchini in the Microwave Oven and heat on FULL POWER 7 minutes, or until soft. Cut each zucchini in half and scoop out pulp and seeds and save.

2. In a medium-sized bowl combine pulp and seeds, ground beef, the 2 tablespoons of onion, parsley flakes and salt and pepper, to taste.

3. In a small bowl combine beaten egg, crumbled white bread and grated Parmesan cheese.

4. Add egg-bread mixture to ground beef mixture and mix thoroughly.

5. Stuff each zucchini half with some of the ground beef mixture.

6. Place zucchini, stuffing side up, in a shallow, 3-quart, heat-resistant, non-metallic baking dish, leaving about ½-inch between each zucchini half. Sprinkle top of zucchini with Parmesan cheese.

7. In a medium-sized, heat-resistant, non-metallic bowl combine remaining ingredients. Heat, uncovered, 5 minutes on FULL POWER or until sauce bubbles. Spoon sauce over zucchini.

8. Heat, uncovered, on ROAST for 16 to 18 minutes.

Pictured: Rice Pilaf

194

Cereals And Grains

Cooking Hints

Cereal is fast and easy to cook in the Microwave Oven since it can be cooked in individual serving dishes.

For large servings always use a bowl larger than necessary and stir several times during cooking to prevent lumping.

Some cereals will be thin when removed from the oven, but will thicken when allowed to stand for several minutes.

When reheating cereals, cover with plastic wrap and heat only for a few minutes.

Cooking rice and pasta in your Microwave Oven may not save a tremendous amount of time, but these products are very convenient to cook by microwaves and give good results. Rice can be cooked to perfection without sticking or scorching.

Most grain products such as rice give best results on the SIMMER setting. See individual recipes for timing suggestions.

Pasta should be cooked on FULL POWER. To reduce cooking time to a minimum, bring recommended amount of water to a boil on FULL POWER and then add pasta.

Rice

2 cups hot water
1 cup long grain rice
1 tablespoon butter or margarine
1 teaspoon salt

Serves 4

1. Combine all ingredients in a deep, 3-quart, heat-resistant, non-metallic casserole. Heat, covered, on SIMMER for 20 minutes. Allow rice to stand at room temperature, covered, 5 to 6 minutes.

2. Fluff with a fork before serving.

3. If necessary, rice may be returned to Microwave Oven for a few minutes additional cooking on SIMMER.

Brown Rice

1 cup brown rice
3 cups hot water
1 teaspoon salt

Serves 4

1. Combine all ingredients in a deep, 3-quart, heat-resistant, non-metallic casserole.

2. Heat, covered, on SIMMER for 25 minutes or until rice is almost tender.

3. Allow rice to stand, covered, 10 minutes.

4. Pour rice into a colander and rinse with hot water.

Commercial Pre-Cooked Rice

1 teaspoon salt
1¼ cups water
1¼ cups pre-cooked rice

Serves 3 to 4

1. Combine water, rice and salt in a 2-quart, heat-resistant, non-metallic casserole.

2. Heat, covered, on FULL POWER 4 minutes, or until water boils.

3. Allow to stand 6 to 8 minutes before serving.

Tip: If a larger serving is desired, use equal amounts of water and rice. Cook until water boils. Allow to stand after cooking before serving.

Rice Pilaf

2 tablespoons butter or margarine
½ cup long grain rice
2 tablespoons finely chopped onion
2 tablespoons finely chopped parsley
2 tablespoons finely chopped celery
1 (4-ounce) can mushroom slices, drained
⅓ cup water
⅓ cup condensed chicken broth
⅛ teaspoon salt

Serves 2

1. In a deep, 1-quart, heat-resistant, non-metallic casserole combine butter, rice, onion, parsley and celery. Heat, uncovered, on FULL POWER 3 minutes or until vegetables are almost tender.

2. Add remaining ingredients and heat, tightly covered, on SIMMER for 18 minutes or until rice is almost tender.

3. Stir at end of 10 minutes. Allow to stand covered 5 minutes to finish cooking.

16

Fried Rice

2 tablespoons finely chopped onion
2 tablespoons butter or margarine
2 cups pre-cooked rice
1⅔ cups water
2 beef bouillon cubes
½ teaspoon salt
Dash pepper
2 eggs, slightly beaten
¼ cup chopped green onion
2 teaspoons soy sauce

Serves 4 to 5

1. Sauté the 2 tablespoons chopped onion in butter or margarine on FULL POWER for 2 minutes, using a 2-quart, heat-resistant, non-metallic casserole.
2. Add rice, water, bouillon cubes, salt and pepper.
3. Bring to a rolling boil on FULL POWER (about 5 minutes). Stir well, cover, and heat on FULL POWER 2 minutes.
4. Stir and let stand, covered, 5 minutes until water is absorbed.
5. Add eggs and chopped green onion.
6. Heat on ROAST for 2½ minutes, stirring several times until edges are set.
7. Stir in soy sauce.

Risi Bisi

2 tablespoons butter or margarine
½ cup long grain rice
2 tablespoons finely chopped onion
2 tablespoons finely chopped celery
⅓ cup water
⅓ cup condensed chicken broth
⅛ teaspoon salt
1 (8-ounce) can baby peas, drained

Serves 2

1. In a deep, 1-quart, heat-resistant, non-metallic casserole combine butter, rice, onion and celery.
2. Heat, uncovered, on FULL POWER 3 minutes.
3. Add remaining ingredients except peas. Heat, covered, on SIMMER for 18 minutes.
4. Add peas and stir to combine.
5. Heat on SIMMER 2 minutes or until rice is almost tender.
6. Allow to stand, covered, 5 minutes to finish cooking.
7. Fluff with fork before serving.

Polenta

1 recipe Corn Meal Mush (see recipe page 200)
1 cup shredded sharp Cheddar cheese
⅛ teaspoon paprika
Cayenne pepper

Serves 6

1. Add cheese, paprika, sprinkle of cayenne pepper to cooked corn meal mush.
2. Heat on ROAST for 2 minutes; let stand, covered, 5 minutes.
3. Pour mixture into a square cake dish.
4. Cover with wax paper. Chill.
5. Cut Polenta into slices.
6. Coat each slice lightly with flour.
7. Sauté slowly in hot bacon drippings or oil.
8. Serve with syrup, if desired.

Macaroni, Spaghetti And Noodles

4 cups hot water
1 teaspoon salt
2 cups macaroni, noodles, etc.

1. Mix water and salt in deep, 3-quart, heat-resistant, non-metallic casserole.
2. Bring water to a boil (approximately 6 to 8 minutes).
3. Add pasta and stir.
4. Heat on FULL POWER 15 minutes or until cooked completely.
5. Drain in a colander.

Orange Dressing

1½ cups dried bread cubes
½ cup boiling water
⅔ cup diced orange pulp
½ cup finely chopped celery
¼ cup melted butter or margarine
2 teaspoons grated orange rind
¼ teaspoon salt
⅛ teaspoon poultry seasoning
Dash pepper

Makes 1½ cups stuffing

1. In a medium-sized bowl place bread cubes. Add ½ cup boiling water to soften bread cubes. Let stand 10 minutes.
2. Add remaining ingredients.
3. Stuff chicken, cornish hen or duck just before cooking.

Saucepan Stuffing

1 (7-ounce) package saucepan stuffing mix
Water

Serves 6

1. Combine contents of vegetable/seasoning packet and 1¾ cups water in a deep, 1½-quart, heat-resistant, non-metallic casserole.
2. Heat, covered, on FULL POWER 6 minutes or until water boils.
3. Heat an additional 1 minute, covered, on FULL POWER.
4. Add stuffing crumbs; stir just to moisten. Cover and let stand 5 minutes before serving.
5. Fluff with a fork before serving.

Almond Stuffing

⅓ cup butter or margarine
½ cup (1 stalk) chopped celery
½ cup chopped almonds
¼ cup chopped onion or 1 tablespoon instant minced onion
4 cups (4 slices) soft bread cubes
⅓ cup water
1 tablespoon parsley flakes
¼ teaspoon salt
1 cube or teaspoon chicken bouillon (crumble cube)

1. In a heat-resistant, non-metallic bowl, combine butter, celery, onion and almonds.
2. Heat, uncovered, on FULL POWER 2 minutes, stirring once.
3. Stir in remaining ingredients.

16

Corn Meal Mush

1 cup white or yellow corn meal
4 cups water (room temperature)
1½ teaspoons salt

Serves 6 to 8

1. Measure corn meal into a deep, 2½-quart, heat-resistant, non-metallic glass casserole.
2. Add water and salt. Stir well.
3. Heat, uncovered, on FULL POWER 5 minutes. Stir. Heat on FULL POWER 5 minutes longer.
4. Stir well, cover and let stand 5 to 6 minutes before serving.

Regular Oatmeal

1½ cups hot water
½ teaspoon salt
⅔ cup quick or old fashioned oats, uncooked

Serves 2

1. Place water and salt into a deep, 2-quart, heat-resistant, non-metallic casserole. Be sure to use a large container as oatmeal increases in volume substantially.
2. Heat, uncovered, on FULL POWER for 3½ minutes or until boiling.
3. Add oats and cook on FULL POWER for 3½ minutes. Cover and let stand for a few minutes before serving.

Instant Oatmeal

1 individual package instant oatmeal
Water as called for on package directions

Serves 1

1. Pour oatmeal into a 10-ounce heat-resistant, non-metallic bowl. Add water and stir to combine.
2. Heat, covered, on FULL POWER for 1½ minutes or until water boils.
3. Stir and heat, covered, an additional 1 minute.
4. Let stand 3 to 5 minutes to finish cooking.

Instant Cream Of Wheat

1 individual package instant cream of wheat
Water as called for on package directions

Serves 1

1. Pour water into a 10-ounce bowl.
2. Add 1 package of instant cream of wheat
3. Heat, covered, on FULL POWER for 1½ minutes.
4. Let stand 2 minutes.

Pictured: Dutch Carrot Bread, Sticky Buns.

BREADS

Cooking Hints

A variety of breads can be cooked in your Microwave Oven. All breads rise well in the oven.

When reheating breads, the center will be hotter than the outside, since the center contains more moisture than the crust. Overcooking can make bread items tough and rubbery. Breads should be reheated on a paper napkin or towel to absorb moisture.

Muffins may be prepared in plastic microwave muffin or cupcake pans, coffee cups lined with paper muffin liners, or lined plastic coffee cup holders. Custard cups may also serve as holders. Fill with batter no more than halfway, as the volume of baked goods is greater when cooked by microwaves.

Breads and baked goods are not usually covered. Leaving uncovered prevents the surface from being too moist.

The surface of breads does not brown; doneness cannot be based on surface appearance. Color will depend on ingredients and toppings. If more browning or crisping is desired, breads may be placed in a hot conventional oven or under a conventional broiler for a few minutes.

Opening the oven door while baking will not cause the bread to fall permanently as it would when baked conventionally.

Cooking continues during cooling, so breads should be slightly damp when removed. As bread cools, it may pull away from the sides of the dish.
Loaf breads should cool 10 to 15 minutes in the baking dish. Muffins should be removed immediately from the cooking containers.

Day old or slightly dry rolls or breads may be freshened very quickly in your Microwave Oven. Fully baked breads, rolls, and pastries should be reheated on paper toweling to absorb excess moisture. Reheat bread products on ROAST. Approximate serving temperature is 120°F. Eight ounces of rolls reheat in approximately 1 minute, 15 seconds on ROAST.

Frozen baked goods may be defrosted and heated on SIMMER.

The texture and volume of most bread products is best when either the ROAST or SIMMER setting is used for baking.

White Bread

1 envelope active dry yeast
½ cup warm water
½ cup butter or margarine
¼ cup sugar
1 teaspoon salt
½ cup evaporated milk
3½ cups sifted flour

Makes 1 loaf

1. Sprinkle yeast over warm water (105° to 115°F) in a large bowl. Stir until yeast dissolves.

2. In a medium-sized, heat-resistant, non-metallic bowl melt butter on FULL POWER 1 minute. Add sugar, salt and evaporated milk and stir until sugar dissolves. Stir into yeast mixture.

3. Add flour all at once and beat until batter is smooth and very stiff. Knead until smooth and elastic.

4. Cover and let rise in a warm place until double in bulk.

5. Punch dough down and place in a heat-resistant, non-metallic loaf dish. Cover and let rise again until double in bulk.

6. Heat, uncovered, on SIMMER for 14 to 16 minutes.

Tip: If desired, bread may be placed in a very hot conventional oven (475°F) for a few minutes to brown.

Whole Wheat Bread

1 cup milk
2 tablespoons shortening
4 tablespoons sugar
1 teaspoon salt
1 envelope active dry yeast
2 tablespoons lukewarm water
2 cups all-purpose flour
1½ to 2 cups whole wheat flour

Makes 1 loaf

1. In a medium-sized, heat-resistant, non-metallic bowl, heat milk, uncovered, on FULL POWER 2½ to 3 minutes or until bubbles form around edge.

2. Add shortening, sugar and salt to milk. Let cool until lukewarm.

3. In a small bowl place the 2 tablespoons lukewarm water (105° to 115°F). Sprinkle yeast on top of water and stir until dissolved.

4. Add yeast mixture to lukewarm milk mixture. Stir to combine.

5. Add 2 cups flour to yeast-milk mixture and beat until smooth.

6. Cover and set in a warm place to rise until almost double in bulk.

7. Punch down dough.

8. Gradually add the 1½ cups whole wheat flour and knead on a wooden pastry board, until the dough is smooth and elastic and does not stick to the board.

9. Grease a medium-sized bowl. Place dough in bowl and turn so that top of dough is greased. Cover and let rise in warm place until doubled in bulk.

10. Knead again until free from air bubbles.

11. Place dough in a 1½-quart, heat-resistant, non-metallic loaf dish. Cover and place in warm place to rise until double in bulk.

12. Heat, uncovered, on SIMMER for 12 to 14 minutes or until a wooden pick inserted in the center comes out clean.

Tip: If desired, bread may be placed in a very hot conventional oven (475°F) for a few minutes to brown.

17

Irish Soda Bread

4 cups flour
¼ cup sugar
1 tablespoon baking powder
1 teaspoon salt
½ cup butter or margarine
2 cups dark raisins
1⅓ cups buttermilk
1 egg
1 teaspoon baking soda
1 egg yolk
1 tablespoon water

1. Grease a deep, 2½-quart, heat-resistant, non-metallic casserole and set aside.

2. Sift flour, sugar, baking powder and salt together into a large bowl.

3. With a pastry blender or 2 knives, cut in butter until mixture resembles corn meal.

4. Stir in raisins.

5. Combine buttermilk, egg and baking soda in a small bowl until thoroughly blended.

6. Stir buttermilk mixture into dry ingredients until well blended.

7. Turn out onto a lightly floured board and knead lightly about 3 minutes or until dough is smooth.

8. Shape dough into a ball and place in prepared casserole.

9. With a sharp knife cut an "X" about ½-inch deep into the top of the dough.

10. Beat egg yolk and water together.

11. Brush mixture over top of dough.

12. Heat, uncovered, on ROAST for 14 to 16 minutes or until a wooden pick inserted in the center comes out clean. Cool 10 minutes in casserole; turn out of pan and allow to cool completely.

> **Tip:** If desired, bread may be placed in a very hot conventional oven (475°F) for a few minutes to brown.

Corn Meal Molasses Bread

¾ cup boiling water
3 tablespoons vegetable shortening
¼ cup dark molasses
½ cup corn meal
2 teaspoons salt
1 envelope active dry yeast
¼ cup lukewarm water
1 egg, beaten
3 cups sifted flour

Makes 1 large loaf

1. Combine boiling water and shortening in a large bowl and set aside until shortening has melted. Add molasses, corn meal and salt. Let stand until mixture is lukewarm.

2. Sprinkle yeast over the ¼ cup lukewarm water (105° to 115°F) and stir to dissolve. Stir dissolved yeast, egg and half of the flour into the corn meal mixture. Beat until thoroughly mixed.

3. Stir in remaining flour and mix until dough forms a soft ball. Transfer dough to a greased, 1½-quart, heat-resistant, non-metallic loaf dish.

4. Cover with greased wax paper and place cloth on top. Set in warm place to rise until dough is double in bulk.

5. Heat, uncovered, on SIMMER for 18 to 20 minutes or until bread tests done with a wooden pick. Cool before slicing.

> **TiP:** If desired, bread may be placed in a very hot conventional oven (475°F) for a few minutes to brown.

Chili Cheese Corn Bread

1 cup corn meal
1 cup whole kernel corn
1 cup dairy sour cream
2 eggs
¼ cup melted butter or
   margarine
1 tablespoon baking powder
1½ teaspoon salt
¼ teaspoon pepper
3 drops Tabasco sauce
   (optional)
1½ cups shredded sharp Cheddar
   cheese
2 to 4 ounces canned green
   chilies, drained and chopped

Serves 8 to 10

1. In a large bowl, thoroughly blend together all but the last two ingredients.

2. Grease a shallow, 8-inch, round, heat-resistant, non-metallic baking dish.

3. Pour half the batter into the greased baking dish.

4. Spread chopped chilies and ½ cup of cheese over the batter.

5. Top with remaining batter, then cheese. Heat, uncovered, on ROAST for 14 to 16 minutes. Let stand 5 minutes before serving.

Corn Bread From A Mix

1 (8½-ounce) package corn
   bread mix

Serves 6 to 8

1. Prepare corn bread according to package instructions.

2. Grease an 8-inch, round, heat-resistant, non-metallic baking dish.

3. Heat, uncovered, on ROAST for 7 to 8 minutes or until a wooden pick inserted in center comes out clean. Let stand 3 to 4 minutes before serving.

Corn Bread

1 cup sifted flour
1 cup corn meal
¼ cup sugar
1 teaspoon baking powder
1 teaspoon baking soda
1 teaspoon salt
1 egg
1 cup sour milk*
2 tablespoons melted vegetable
   shortening

Serves 6

1. Sift flour, corn meal, sugar, baking powder, baking soda and salt together into a large mixing bowl.

2. In a medium-sized bowl beat the egg. Add the sour milk to the egg and blend together well.

3. Add milk mixture to flour mixture. Stir to combine.

4. Add melted shortening to flour-milk mixture and beat well.

5. Pour into an 8-inch, round, heat-resistant, non-metallic baking dish.

6. Heat, uncovered, on ROAST for 9 to 10 minutes or until done.

17

---

* **To make sour milk:** Place 2 tablespoons lemon juice into glass measuring cup. Add milk until it measures 1 cup. Let stand 5 minutes.

Quick Muffins

¾ cup milk
¼ cup sugar
1 egg
2 tablespoons vegetable oil
2 cups sifted buttermilk biscuit
mix

Makes 12 muffins

1. In a medium-sized bowl, combine milk, sugar, egg and oil. Blend well.

2. Add sifted biscuit mix to milk mixture and stir vigorously until all the flour is moistened.

3. Divide batter into 12 lined plastic coffee cup holders, custard cups, or use a plastic muffin pan.

4. Place 6 of the muffins on outside edge of glass turntable. Heat, uncovered, on ROAST for 3 to 4 minutes or until wooden pick inserted in the center of muffin comes out clean. Place remaining 6 muffins on outside edge of glass turntable and heat, uncovered, on ROAST for 3 to 4 minutes.

Muffin Gems

½ cup flour
¼ cup sugar
4 teaspoons baking powder
½ teaspoon salt
1 cup whole wheat flour
1 egg, beaten
1 cup milk
3 tablespoons butter or margarine, melted

Makes 12 muffins

1. Sift flour, sugar, salt and baking powder together. Stir in whole wheat flour.

2. Combined beaten egg, milk and melted butter.

3. Make a well in dry ingredients and add liquid ingredients all at once. Stir just until flour mixture is moistened.

4. Spoon batter into paper muffin lined plastic coffee cup holders, custard cups or plastic muffin pan.

5. Place 6 muffins at a time around outside edge of turntable, leaving center of turntable empty. Heat, uncovered, on ROAST for 3½ to 4 minutes or until muffins test done with a wooden pick.

6. Repeat step 5 for the remaining muffins.

Banana Bread

3½ cups flour
3 teaspoons baking powder
1 teaspoon baking soda
1 teaspoon salt
2 cups mashed ripe banana
2 tablespoons lemon juice
¾ cup butter or margarine,
softened
1½ cups sugar
3 eggs
¾ cup milk
1 cup coarsely chopped walnuts

Makes 2 loaves

1. Lightly grease two 8½ x 4½ x 2½-inch, heat-resistant, non-metallic loaf dishes and set aside.

2. Sift together flour, baking powder, baking soda and salt; set aside. In a small bowl, combine mashed banana and lemon juice and set aside.

3. In the large bowl of an electric mixer, cream butter and sugar until light and fluffy. Add eggs, one at a time, beating well after each addition.

4. Add milk and dry ingredients alternately, beginning and ending with dry ingredients.

5. Fold in walnuts and banana mixture.

6. Pour batter into prepared loaf dishes and bake each loaf, uncovered, on ROAST for 12 to 14 minutes.

7. Bread is done when a wooden pick inserted in the bread comes out clean.

8. Allow bread to cool 10 minutes before removing from loaf dishes.

Dutch Carrot Bread

2 cups flour
1½ cups sugar
2 teaspoons baking soda
1 teaspoon cinnamon
3 eggs
1½ cups vegetable oil
2 teaspoons vanilla
2 cups finely grated carrots

Makes 2 loaves

1. Lightly grease two 8½ x 4½ x 2½-inch, heat-resistant, non-metallic loaf dishes and set aside.

2. Sift flour, sugar, baking soda and cinnamon together into a large bowl.

3. Stir with a spoon. Make a well in center with the back of the spoon.

4. Place eggs in well and beat just the eggs with a rotary beater or electric hand mixer until thoroughly blended. Try to keep dry ingredients on the side of the bowl.

5. Add vegetable oil and beat thoroughly with eggs, again trying to keep dry ingredients on the side of the bowl.

6. Add vanilla to egg-oil mixture.

7. Beat in flour mixture until all ingredients are combined and smooth.

8. Fold carrots into mixture.

9. Pour mixture into prepared loaf dishes.

10. Bake each loaf, uncovered, on ROAST for 10 to 12 minutes. Bread is done when a wooden pick inserted in the bread comes out clean.

11. Allow bread to cool 10 minutes before removing from loaf dishes.

17

Sticky Buns

1 (13¼-ounce) package hot roll
   mix
Ingredients as called for on package label
Melted butter or margarine
½ cup sugar
½ teaspoon cinnamon
¼ cup butter or margarine
½ cup firmly packed dark
   brown sugar
½ cup walnut pieces

Makes 16 buns

1. Prepare hot roll mix according to package directions.
2. Allow to rise as package directs.
3. Divide dough into 2 equal parts. Roll each part on a generous-ly floured board until it forms an 8 x 16-inch rectangle.
4. Brush each rectangle generously with melted butter.
5. In a small bowl combine granulated sugar and cinnamon.
6. Sprinkle half of sugar mixture over rectangle.
7. Roll dough up in jellyroll fashion from the long side. Cut into 8 slices and set aside.
8. Repeat procedure with remaining dough.
9. Melt 2 tablespoons butter in each of two 9-inch, heat-resistant, non-metallic pie plates on FULL POWER for 30 seconds. Plates will have to be placed in the oven one at time.
10. Divide brown sugar and walnuts between pie plates.
11. Arrange 8 slices of dough in each plate and allow to rise, covered with a clean towel, until double in bulk.
12. Heat each plate uncovered, on ROAST for 8 minutes. Test for doneness with a wooden pick.
13. Allow to cool 5 minutes before inverting onto a serving plate. Allow topping to drip over buns.

Tip: Buns may be browned for a few minutes under the broiler of a conventional oven.

Pictured: Fruit Cake

Cooking Hints

Cake baking can be more creative than ever with your Sharp Microwave Oven. You can bake cakes in dessert dishes, mixing bowls or even ice cream cones. Microwave baked cakes will not fall even if the oven door is opened. White and yellow cakes will not brown as in conventional cooking; however, because they are usually frosted, there is no noticeable difference. Cake batter may be prepared in advance and refrigerated or frozen. You may want to cook one layer and keep another in the freezer for unexpected company.

Pies of all types can also be made with your Microwave Oven. Pie crust should be pre-cooked, and then fruit or custard filling added. Since the cooking time of fruit varies according to the ripeness and amount of fruit used, the cooking time of fruit pies will vary. Test the fruit with a fork to determine doneness. To recapture that just from the oven taste, reheat individual slices of pie on FULL POWER for 30 seconds per slice. Pie a la mode can even be made in your Sharp Microwave Oven by placing a hard scoop of ice cream on a piece of pie and heating it on FULL POWER for 45 seconds. The pie will be hot and the ice cream will be just the right consistency.

The Carousel turntable on your Sharp Microwave Oven will make it possible to bake cakes with an even surface without the inconvenience of rotating the dish during cooking. Cakes should be placed in the center of the turntable unless otherwise indicated.

For best results, ingredients for cakes should be at room temperature, measured accurately, and the batter mixed and baked according to recipe directions.

The simplest and easiest way to prepare cake dishes is to lightly grease the bottom and sides of the dish with vegetable shortening and lightly dust with flour. Waxed paper may be used to cover the bottom of the dish, making layer cakes easy to remove.

Cake dishes should not be filled over half full. Microwave baked cakes increase substantially in volume and the texture is somewhat lighter than conventionally baked cakes. Save extra batter and use for cupcakes.

Bake one layer at a time and allow each to cool no longer than 5 minutes before removing from dish, unless otherwise noted in recipe.

Overcooked cakes will be dry and slightly hard or tough. It is always better to undercook and check for doneness frequently toward the end of the cooking period.

If you desire a cake with a heavier texture, place plastic wrap over the top of the cake batter.

Cake may be warmed or leftover cake may be freshened by heating in the Microwave Oven on ROAST for a few seconds.

Most cakes are less porous in texture and give best results when cooked at about 70% power. Thus, many recipes in this section recommend baking on ROAST.

Commercially frozen layer cakes may be defrosted on SIMMER. A 17-ounce cake defrosts in 1 minute, 15 seconds on SIMMER.

The ideal utensil for baking cakes in your microwave oven is doughnut-shaped. Plastic tube pans or ring molds designed for microwave cooking give excellent results.

18

211

Packaged Cake Mix

1 (17 to 18½-ounce) package
   cake mix
Ingredients as called for on
   package

1. Lightly grease two 8-inch round glass cake dishes. Line bottom of each with wax paper cut to fit.
2. Prepare cake mix according to package directions.
3. Pour 2⅔ cups batter into each prepared cake dish.
4. Heat one layer at a time, uncovered, on ROAST for 8 to 9 minutes or until wooden pick inserted in center comes out clean.
5. Allow cake to cool for 5 minutes before removing from dish.

Snack Cake Mix

1 (15½-ounce) package snack
   cake mix
Ingredients as called for on
   package

1. In either an 8-inch square glass cake dish or an 8-inch round glass cake dish, prepare mix according to package directions.
2. Heat, uncovered, on FULL POWER 8 to 9 minutes or until cake begins to pull away from the edges of the dish and a wooden pick inserted in the center comes out clean.
3. Allow to cool. Serve from baking dish.

Bundt® Cake Mix

1 (27½-ounce or 23¼-ounce)
   package Bundt® cake mix
Ingredients as called for on
   package

1. Lightly grease and flour a 10-cup heat-resistant, non-metallic tube pan.
2. Prepare cake mix according to package directions.
3. Pour batter into prepared plastic or glass tube pan until ⅔ full.
4. Heat, uncovered, in center of turntable on ROAST for 11 to 12 minutes or until a wooden pick inserted comes out clean.
5. Allow cake to cool for 5 to 10 minutes before removing from pan.

> **Note:** All of the batter may be used from the 23¼-ounce package. There will be some extra batter from the 27½-ounce package. Use extra batter for cupcakes.

Brownies From A Mix

1 (15½-ounce) package brownie
   mix
Ingredients as called for on
   package

1. Lightly grease an 8-inch square glass baking dish.
2. Prepare brownie mix according to package directions.
3. Heat, uncovered, on ROAST for 9 to 10 minutes or until a wooden pick inserted in the center comes out clean.

Two-Layer Pineapple Upside-Down Cake

4 tablespoons butter or margarine
1 cup firmly packed
   brown sugar
2 (20-ounce) cans sliced pineapple in unsweetened juice,
   drained; reserve juice
22 maraschino cherry
   halves, well drained
1 (18½-ounce) package yellow
   cake mix
Ingredients as called for on cake
   package label

Serves 8

1. Line two 8 or 9-inch cake dishes with wax paper; divide butter evenly in dishes.

2. Heat each dish, uncovered, on FULL POWER 30 seconds or until butter melts.

3. Sprinkle half of brown sugar over butter in each dish. Arrange pineapple and cherries over sugar.

4. Prepare cake mix according to package directions, substituting the reserved pineapple juice for the liquid called for on the package. Add water if necessary for full measure.

5. Pour 2⅔ cups batter over pineapple slices in both dishes. Spread evenly.

6. Elevate dish on microwave rack; cook each layer on FULL POWER 10 minutes.

7. Invert one layer onto serving plate. Invert the second layer on top of the first. Serve warm.

Tip: Any extra batter may be used for cupcakes.

Supreme White Cake

¾ cup butter or margarine,
   softened
1⅓ cups sugar
1 teaspoon vanilla
½ teaspoon lemon extract
2½ cups sifted cake flour
2 teaspoons baking powder
1 teaspoon salt
1 cup milk
5 egg whites, at room temperature
⅓ cup sugar

Serves 8 to 10

1. In a large mixing bowl, cream butter until light and fluffy. Gradually add 1⅓ cups sugar, beating until fluffy. Stir in vanilla and lemon extract.

2. Sift together cake flour, baking powder and salt.

3. Add dry ingredients alternately with milk to creamed mixture. Beat after each addition until smooth.

4. Beat egg whites until foamy. Gradually add ⅓ cup sugar, beating only until meringue will stand up in soft peaks.

5. Fold meringue into batter.

6. Divide batter evenly between two 8-inch round, lightly greased heat-resistant, non-metallic baking dishes.

7. Heat each layer separately, on ROAST for 8 to 9 minutes or until wooden pick comes out clean.

8. Allow cake to cool in the dish for 5 minutes before inverting onto cooling rack.

18

New Fudge Cake

1⅓ cups sugar
1¼ cups sifted flour
1¼ teaspoons baking powder
½ teaspoon salt
¼ teaspoon baking soda
3 tablespoons vegetable shortening
1 cup milk
½ teaspoon vanilla
1 egg
3 (1-ounce) squares unsweetened chocolate, melted
⅔ cup chopped nuts

Serves 8

1. Lightly grease two 8-inch, heat-resistant, non-metallic round baking dishes. Set aside.
2. In a large bowl, blend together sugar, flour, baking powder, salt and baking soda.
3. Add shortening, milk and vanilla.
4. Beat 2 minutes at medium speed of electric mixer. Scrape sides and bottom of bowl frequently.
5. Add egg and chocolate. Beat 2 additional minutes.
6. Stir in nuts.
7. Pour batter into prepared dishes.
8. Heat each layer separately, uncovered, on ROAST for 8 minutes or until wooden pick inserted in center comes out clean.
9. Frost with favorite icing.

Fruitcake

¾ cup flour
¾ teaspoon salt
¾ teaspoon baking powder
¾ teaspoon nutmeg
¾ teaspoon allspice
6 cups coarsely chopped walnuts
1¾ cups diced green candied cherries
1¾ cups diced red candied cherries
¾ cup butter or margarine, softened
6 tablespoons firmly packed dark brown sugar
3 tablespoons honey
6 eggs
6 tablespoons brandy

1. Sift flour, salt, baking powder, nutmeg and allspice together. Set aside.
2. In a large bowl combine walnuts and candied cherries and set aside.
3. In another large bowl cream butter until light and fluffy. Gradually beat in sugar and honey. Beat in eggs one at a time.
4. Add flour mixture and beat until smooth.
5. Beat in brandy.
6. Fold in nut mixture.
7. Pour batter into a greased tube or bund-type pan. Cover with a piece of greased wax paper. Place on microwave trivet or rack. Heat on ROAST 18 minutes. Top will be moist.
8. Let cake stand at room temperature for 20 minutes before turning out of the dish. Let cool completely before cutting.
9. If desired, a glaze may be prepared from confectioners' sugar and water.

Applesauce Cake

1½ cups sifted cake flour
½ teaspoon baking soda
½ teaspoon salt
1 teaspoon cinnamon
½ teaspoon all spice
½ teaspoon cloves
½ teaspoon nutmeg
½ cup butter or margarine, softened
1 cup firmly packed brown sugar
1 egg
1¼ cups unsweetened apple-sauce
½ cup raisins

Serves 8

1. Lightly grease a shallow, square, 1½-quart, heat-resistant, non-metallic baking dish. Set aside.
2. Sift together flour, baking soda, salt and spices. Set aside.
3. Cream butter and sugar together until thoroughly blended.
4. Add egg and beat until thoroughly blended.
5. In a small bowl combine applesauce and raisins.
6. Add dry ingredients and applesauce-raisin mixture alternately to creamed mixture.
7. Pour batter into prepared baking dish and heat, uncovered, on ROAST for 12 to 13 minutes or until wooden pick comes out clean.

Pecan Loaf

2 cups sifted cake flour
1¼ cups sugar
1½ teaspoons baking powder
1 teaspoon salt
½ cup vegetable shortening
½ cup milk
1 teaspoon vanilla
4 egg whites, at room temper-ature
½ cup coarsely chopped pecans

1. Sift flour, sugar, baking powder and salt together into a large mixing bowl.
2. Add shortening, milk and vanilla. Beat 2 minutes at medium speed of electric mixer. Scrape sides and bottom of bowl often.
3. Add egg whites; beat 2 more minutes.
4. Fold in nuts.
5. Pour batter into a lightly greased, 9 x 5 x 3-inch, heat-resistant, non-metallic loaf dish.
6. Heat, uncovered, on ROAST for 12 to 14 minutes or until wooden pick comes out clean.

Crumb Cake

2 cups sifted flour
1¼ cups sugar
2 teaspoons baking powder
1½ teaspoons cinnamon
½ cup butter or margarine, softened
2 eggs, well beaten
½ cup milk

Serves 8

1. Sift together flour, sugar, baking powder and cinnamon.
2. Add butter to dry ingredients and mix thoroughly. Set aside 1 cup of flour mixture for crumb topping.
3. To the remaining crumb mixture add eggs and milk, mixing well.
4. Pour into a lightly greased 8-inch, heat-resistant, non-metallic cake dish. Sprinkle the 1 cup reserved crumb mixture on top.
5. Heat, uncovered, on ROAST for 10 minutes, or until a wooden pick inserted in the center comes out clean.
6. Cool completely before removing from dish.

18

Sour Cream Coffee Cake

½ cup butter or margarine
1 cup sugar
2 eggs
1 cup dairy sour cream
1 teaspoon vanilla
2 cups flour
1 teaspoon baking soda
½ teaspoon baking powder
½ teaspoon salt
½ cup firmly packed dark
   brown sugar
¾ cup coarsely chopped nuts
1 teaspoon cinnamon

Serves 8 to 10

1. In the large bowl of an electric mixer, cream butter until soft. Add sugar gradually and beat until light and fluffy. Add eggs, one at a time; beat until thoroughly combined. Beat in sour cream and vanilla.

2. Sift flour, baking soda, baking powder and salt together.

3. Add flour mixture to sour cream mixture, beating until smooth.

4. Pour batter into a lightly greased and floured, 8-inch square, heat-resistant, non-metallic baking dish and heat, uncovered, on ROAST for 6 minutes.

5. While cake is baking, combine remaining ingredients in a small bowl.

6. Sprinkle topping mixture over cake and heat, uncovered, on ROAST for 4 to 5 minutes. Let stand for 1 to 2 minutes.

7. Test for doneness with a wooden pick. Serve warm.

Chocolate Frosting

4 tablespoons cocoa
⅔ cup milk
6 tablespoons butter or margarine
3½ cups confectioners' sugar
1 teaspoon vanilla

Fills and frosts two (8-inch) layers.

1. In a medium-sized, heat-resistant, non-metallic mixing bowl combine 4 tablespoons cocoa and ⅔ cup milk. Add 6 tablespoons butter or margarine.

2. Heat, uncovered, on FULL POWER 3 minutes or until mixture boils. Stir occasionally.

3. Heat, uncovered, on ROAST for 3 minutes, stirring several times.

4. Add confectioners' sugar to chocolate mixture gradually, beating at high speed on electric mixer. Beat until mixture is cooled.

5. Stir in 1 teaspoon vanilla.

Fluffy Nut Frosting

⅓ cup butter or margarine
1 teaspoon vanilla
Dash salt
3 cups confectioners' sugar
6 tablespoons milk
¼ cup chopped nuts

Frosts one (8-inch) layer

1. Cream butter until light and fluffy.

2. Blend in 1 teaspoon vanilla and dash of salt.

3. Add 3 cups confectioners' sugar alternately with milk beating until light and fluffy.

4. Stir in chopped nuts.

Cupcakes

Cake batter

1. Prepare cake batter as desired from favorite cake mix or scratch recipe. Allow to stand 10 minutes before baking in Microwave Oven.

2. Place a paper-muffin-liner in a plastic coffee cup holder; 6-ounce heat-resistant, non-metallic custard cup; heat-resistant, non-metallic coffee cup; or plastic muffin pan. Spoon or pour batter into muffin liner until ½ full.

3. Place cups with batter on the outside edge of the turntable and heat on ROAST according to chart below.

6 cupcakes	3½ to 4 minutes
4 cupcakes	2½ minutes
2 cupcakes	1½ minutes
1 cupcake	1 minute

4. Test cupcakes by inserting a wooden pick in the center. If it comes out clean, cupcakes are done.

5. Ice and decorate as desired.

Tip: When baking 3 or more cupcakes at a time, never place 1 cupcake in the center of a circle of cupcakes as it will bake more slowly.

Cupcakes may be baked using flat-bottomed ice cream cones as containers. The timing is the same as above.

Snowflake Macaroon Cupcakes

3 cups shredded coconut
⅓ cup sugar
1 egg white
6 tablespoons sifted flour
½ teaspoon baking powder
½ teaspoon almond extract
2 egg whites
⅓ cup sugar
10 candied cherries (optional)

Makes 12 cupcakes

1. Combine coconut, ⅓ cup sugar and the 1 egg white in a small, heat-resistant, non-metallic bowl. Heat on FULL POWER for 2 minutes.

2. Sift together flour and baking powder. Add to coconut mixture. Stir in almond extract. Mix thoroughly.

3. Beat remaining two egg whites until stiff but not dry. Add ⅓ cup sugar, 1 tablespoon at a time, beating until stiff peaks form. Fold meringue into coconut mixture.

4. Spoon batter into paper-muffin-lined plastic coffee cup holders or plastic muffin pan. Top each cupcake with cherry, if desired.

5. Place 6 cupcakes at a time around outside edge of turntable, leaving center of turntable empty. Heat, uncovered, on ROAST for 3 to 4 minutes, or until cupcakes test done with a wooden pick.

18

Molasses Cupcakes

**1 cup firmly packed dark
 brown sugar**
**½ cup butter or margarine,
 melted**
1 cup dark molasses
1¼ cups water
1 egg, beaten
3 cups sifted flour
2 teaspoons baking soda
1 cup sifted flour
1 cup sugar
**½ cup butter or margarine,
 softened**

Makes 36 cupcakes

1. In a large bowl combine brown sugar, melted butter, molasses, water and beaten egg.
2. Sift together the 3 cups flour and baking soda. Stir into molasses mixture and mix thoroughly.
3. Spoon batter into paper-muffin-lined plastic coffee cup holders or plastic muffin pan. Fill only half full.
4. For crumb topping combine 1 cup flour, 1 cup sugar and ½ cup butter or margarine in a small bowl.
5. Spoon 2 heaping teaspoonfuls of topping mixture on each cupcake.
6. Place 6 cupcakes at a time around outside edge of turntable, leaving center of turntable empty. Heat, uncovered, on ROAST for 4 minutes or until cupcakes test done with wooden pick.

Tip: Cupcake batter may be stored in the refrigerator up to three weeks.

Double Butterscotch Brownies

¼ cup butter or margarine
**1 cup firmly packed dark
 brown sugar**
¾ cup flour
1 egg, slightly beaten
1 teaspoon baking powder
1 teaspoon vanilla
¼ teaspoon salt
¾ cup coarsely chopped pecans
**1 (6-ounce) package butter-
 scotch pieces**

Makes 32 small bars

1. Lightly grease an 8-inch square, heat-resistant, nonmetallic baking dish.
2. Place butter in a medium-sized, heat-resistant, non-metallic bowl and heat on FULL POWER 30 seconds or until melted.
3. Mix in brown sugar, flour, egg, baking powder, vanilla and salt until smooth.
4. Stir in pecans.
5. Pour batter into prepared baking dish.
6. Heat, uncovered, on ROAST for 5 to 6 minutes.
7. Place butterscotch pieces in a small, heat-resistant, non-metallic bowl and heat on ROAST for 2 minutes.
8. Spread melted butterscotch pieces over brownies. When cool, cut into bars.

Graham Cracker Crust

⅓ cup butter or margarine
1½ cups graham cracker crumbs
**¼ cup sugar or firmly packed
 brown sugar**

1. Place butter in a 9 or 10-inch glass pie plate and heat on FULL POWER for 45 seconds.
2. Combine graham cracker crumbs and sugar with melted butter and mix thoroughly.
3. Press mixture onto sides and bottom of pie plate.
4. Heat, uncovered, on ROAST for 3 to 4 minutes.
5. Allow to cool before filling.

Raspberry Rhubarb Tart

1¼ cups sifted flour
½ cup firmly packed dark brown sugar
½ cup butter or margarine, softened
¼ teaspoon vanilla
½ cup finely chopped nuts
2 cups frozen rhubarb, cut into ¼-inch pieces
1 (10-ounce) pouch raspberries
1 cup sugar
1 egg, slightly beaten
2 teaspoons cornstarch
2 tablespoons water
Whipped cream (optional)

Serves 8 to 10

1. In medium-sized mixing bowl, place butter, flour, sugar and vanilla. Blend ingredients together using medium speed of electric mixer. When blended, stir in nuts.

2. Pat crust mixture onto bottom and up sides of a 10-inch, heat-resistant, non-metallic pie plate.

3. Heat, uncovered, on ROAST for 5 minutes. Set aside to cool.

4. Place frozen rhubarb and raspberries, sugar and egg in a large, heat-resistant, non-metallic mixing bowl. Stir to combine ingredients.

5. Heat, uncovered, on FULL POWER 8 minutes. Stir occasionally.

6. Combine 2 teaspoons cornstarch and 2 tablespoons water in a small bowl. Blend until smooth.

7. Add cornstarch mixture to raspberry-rhubarb mixture. Mix well.

8. Heat, uncovered, on FULL POWER 2 minutes or until mixture becomes clear and thickened.

9. Pour fruit mixture into cooled pie shell. Refrigerate 2 to 3 hours or until firm.

10. Garnish with whipped cream before serving.

Chocolate Pudding Pie

⅓ cup butter or margarine
1½ cups chocolate cookie crumbs
½ cup sugar
1 (3⅝-ounce) chocolate pudding and pie filling mix (not instant)
2 cups milk
1 cup miniature marshmallows

Serves 8

1. In a 9-inch, heat-resistant, non-metallic pie plate melt butter on FULL POWER 30 seconds.

2. Stir in cookie crumbs and sugar.

3. Press crumb mixture onto bottom and sides of prepared pie plate.

4. Heat, uncovered, on ROAST for 3 minutes or until crust has crunchy texture.

5. In a deep, 1-quart, heat-resistant, non-metallic casserole combine chocolate pudding mix and milk.

6. Heat, uncovered, on ROAST for 8 minutes or until mixture boils. Stir occasionally.

7. Stir in marshmallows. If marshmallows are not well-blended, heat mixture on ROAST for 1 minute.

8. Pour chocolate-marshmallow mixture into pie crust.

9. Refrigerate for 4 hours.

18

Cranberry Pie

**1 tablespoon butter or marga-
rine**
**1½ cups fresh or frozen whole
cranberries**
⅓ cup sugar
1 egg
½ cup flour
**½ cup butter or margarine,
melted**
¼ cup sugar
**¼ cup firmly packed dark brown
sugar**
**¼ cup chopped pecans or wal-
nuts**

1. Grease a 9-inch, non-metallic pie plate with the 1 tablespoon butter or margarine.

2. Mix cranberries and the ⅓ cup sugar in the greased pie plate. Cover with a paper towel and heat on FULL POWER 2 minutes or until berries are tender.

3. In small bowl beat together egg with the flour, butter, sugar and brown sugar until well blended.

4. Sprinkle chopped nuts over cranberries.

5. Pour batter over cranberry-nut mixture. Smooth batter with a spatula.

6. Heat, uncovered, on ROAST for 9 to 10 minutes or until top looks dry.

7. Cut into wedges and serve topped with ice cream.

Tip: Any variety of berries may be used in this recipe as long as the amount used remains 1½ cups.

Strawberry Shortcake

2 pints fresh strawberries
¾ cup sugar
2 cups flour
3 tablespoons sugar
1 tablespoon baking powder
1 teaspoon salt
½ cup vegetable shortening
⅓ cup light cream
1 egg, slightly beaten
Butter or margarine
Sweetened whipped cream

Serves 8

1. Wash and hull strawberries.

2. Slice strawberries into a medium-sized bowl and sprinkle with the ¾ cup sugar and toss lightly to coat berries. Refrigerate for 30 to 60 minutes.

3. Sift flour, the 3 tablespoons sugar, baking powder and salt together into a large bowl.

4. Cut in the shortening with a pastry blender or 2 knives until mixture resembles corn meal.

5. In a small bowl combine light cream and egg.

6. Stir cream mixture into flour mixture with a fork until mixture is moistened.

7. Turn dough out onto a lightly floured board and knead gently 5 times.

8. Press mixture into bottom of a lightly greased and floured 8-inch, round, heat-resistant, non-metallic baking dish.

9. Heat, uncovered, on ROAST for 6 minutes or until shortcake tests done with a wooden pick.

10. Split shortcake with a knife while it is still warm and spread with butter.

11. Fill and top with reserved strawberries.

12. Serve warm with dollops of whipped cream.

Note: Biscuit mix can be used for shortcake. Follow package directions and cook on ROAST for 6 minutes or until a wooden pick inserted in the center comes out clean.

Cherry Pie

Ingredients for a 9-inch, 2 crust pastry

2 (16-ounce) cans water-packed, pitted, tart red cherries
1 cup sugar
⅓ cup flour
⅛ teaspoon salt
½ teaspoon lemon extract
2 tablespoons butter or margarine
Water
Sugar

Serves 8

1. Prepare pie crust pastry according to package directions or favorite recipe.
2. Roll out ½ of the pastry and line a 9-inch, heat-resistant, non-metallic pie plate.
3. Roll out remaining dough and cut into 6 strips, ½-inch wide, and set aside; cover with a clean cloth towel.
4. Drain cherries and set aside. Reserve ½ cup of the liquid.
5. Mix together the 1 cup of sugar, the ⅓ cup of flour and the salt in a medium-sized, heat-resistant, non-metallic bowl.
6. Gradually add the cherry liquid; mix until smooth.
7. Heat, uncovered, on ROAST for 5 minutes or until thickened and smooth; stir occasionally.
8. Stir in lemon extract.
9. Add cherries to sauce and mix gently.
10. Pour cherries into pastry-lined pie plate. Dot with butter.
11. To make a lattice top, place 3 strips of pastry at equal intervals across the top of cherries, using one of the largest strips for the center, and the shorter ones for the sides. The ends should extend over the edges of the lower crust.
12. Lay remaining 3 strips crosswise to form lattice, weaving if desired.
13. Trim strips to fit the edge of the lower crust.
14. Turn the pastry edge from the lower crust over the ends of the strips. Pinch or flute, as desired, to seal the edge.
15. Brush strips with water and sprinkle with granulated sugar.
16. Preheat a conventional oven to 450°F.
17. Heat pie, uncovered, on FULL POWER 7 to 8 minutes, or until juice starts bubbling and fruit is just about tender.
18. Cook in the preheated conventional oven 10 to 15 minutes, or until the top crust is golden brown.

Deep Dish Apple Pie

5 cups peeled and sliced tart apples
½ cup sugar
3 tablespoons water
½ teaspoon cinnamon, or cloves or a combination of these spices
1 cup buttermilk biscuit mix
2 tablespoons sugar
½ cup milk
Whipped cream (optional)

Serves 6 to 8

1. In a deep, 2-quart, heat-resistant, non-metallic casserole combine apples, sugar, water and the ½ teaspoon of spice.
2. Heat, covered, on FULL POWER 4 minutes or until apples are almost tender.
3. While apples are cooking, prepare topping. Combine biscuit mix, sugar and milk stirring with fork until just moistened.
4. Drop mixture by spoonfuls on hot apple mixture.
5. Heat, covered, on FULL POWER 6 minutes or until topping is no longer doughy underneath. If desired, serve with dollops of whipped cream.

18

Pie Shell From A Mix

1 package pie shell mix for
  double crust
Ingredients as called for on
  package

1. Prepare pie shell according to package directions, but use entire package for one crust. This will give better results and make a more attractive shell.

2. Heat, uncovered, on ROAST for 7 to 8 minutes.

Cherry Cobbler

1 (17-ounce) can cherry pie
  filling
1 teaspoon lemon juice
½ cup butter or margarine
1 cup flour
⅔ cup coarsely chopped nuts
⅓ cup firmly packed dark
  brown sugar
¾ teaspoon cinnamon
¼ teaspoon allspice
Vanilla ice cream

Serves 4 to 6

1. Combine cherry pie filling and lemon juice in a shallow, 1-quart, heat-resistant, non-metallic casserole.

2. In a small, heat-resistant, non-metallic bowl melt butter on FULL POWER 45 seconds.

3. Combine butter, flour, brown sugar, nuts, cinnamon and allspice with a fork until crumbly.

4. Sprinkle topping mixture over cherry filling. Heat, uncovered, on FULL POWER 5 to 6 minutes or until cobbler is bubbly. Serve with scoops of ice cream.

Note: If ice cream is too hard to scoop, it may be softened on SIMMER for 45 seconds to 1 minute, depending on size of container.

Pictured: Floating Island Custard.

Desserts

DESSERTS

Cooking Hints

Desserts such as puddings and custards can be made easily in your Sharp Microwave Oven. The oven eliminates the possibility of scorching because the cooking occurs from all sides and not just the bottom. You can even measure, mix and cook right in the same heat-resistant, non-metallic measuring cup. The possibilities for desserts are limitless.

Milk can be scalded quickly and easily in your Microwave Oven, using a glass measuring cup as a container. If a recipe calls for scalded milk, heat only until tiny bubbles begin to appear around the edges of the container. Scalded milk should be heated to about 180°F; do not boil. For one cup milk, heat 2 to 2½ minutes on FULL POWER.

Floating Island Custard

2 egg yolks, at room temper-
    ature
¼ cup sugar
1½ teaspoons cornstarch
1½ cups milk
1 teaspoon vanilla, divided
2 egg whites, at room temper-
    ature
4 tablespoons sugar
1 (16-ounce) package straw-
    berries, frozen whole without
    syrup or 1 pint fresh straw-
    berries

Serves 4

1. Place egg yolks, the ¼ cup sugar and the cornstarch in a medi-um-sized, heat-resistant, non-metallic bowl; mix well.

2. Gradually stir in milk. Heat, uncovered, on ROAST for 5 minutes or until mixture just about boils. DO NOT ALLOW MIXTURE TO BOIL.

3. Stir mixture occasionally during last half of cooking. Add ½ teaspoon vanilla and chill until ready to serve.

4. Just before serving time, beat egg whites until stiff but not dry. Beat in the 4 tablespoons of sugar, 1 tablespoon at a time, until mixture forms stiff peaks. Beat in the remaining ½ teaspoon vanilla.

5. Divide the strawberries among 4 heat-resistant, non-metallic dessert dishes.

6. Pour chilled custard over berries. Place a dollop of egg white mixture in each dessert dish.

7. Place desserts in Microwave Oven and heat, uncovered, on ROAST for 1 minute or until puffs are set.

Blanc Mange

⅓ cup sugar
3 tablespoons cornstarch
¼ teaspoon salt
2¼ cups milk
1½ teaspoons vanilla

Makes 5 to 6 servings

1. Combine sugar, cornstarch and salt in a deep, 1-quart, heat-resistant, non-metallic casserole.

2. Gradually add milk, stirring constantly.

3. Heat, uncovered, on ROAST for 10 minutes, stirring oc-casionally.

4. Allow to cook just until mixture begins to boil. Stir in vanil-la.

5. Chill. Serve topped with fresh fruit or whipped cream.

Fruit-Flavored Gelatin Dessert From Prepared Mixes

1 (3½-ounce) package fruit
    flavored gelatin mix
1 cup warm water
1 cup cold water

Serves 4

1. Empty package of gelatin mix into a deep, 1-quart, heat-resistant, non-metallic casserole.

2. Gradually add warm water, stirring until thoroughly dissolv-ed.

3. Heat, uncovered, on FULL POWER for 3 minutes or until mixture comes to a boil. Stir occasionally.

4. Stir in cold water and allow to stand at room temperature ½ hour before refrigerating.

5. Refrigerate until set.

19

Easy Rice Pudding

1 (3-ounce) package vanilla pudding and pie filling mix (not instant)
2½ cups milk
½ cup dark seedless raisins
½ cup instant quick cooking rice

Serves 6

1. In a deep, 1-quart, heat-resistant, non-metallic casserole combine all ingredients. Heat, uncovered, on ROAST for 14 minutes or until mixture boils.

2. Stir mixture occasionally during last 5 minutes of cooking time.

3. Serve either hot or chilled.

Chocolate Marshmallow Pudding

½ cup cocoa
½ cup sugar
2 tablespoons cornstarch
¼ teaspoon salt
2½ cups milk
1 cup miniature marshmallows
1 egg, well beaten
1 teaspoon vanilla

Serves 6 to 8

1. Combine cocoa, sugar, cornstarch and salt in a deep, 1½-quart, heat-resistant, non-metallic casserole.

2. Add milk gradually to dry ingredients, stirring constantly.

3. Heat, uncovered, on ROAST for 6 minutes. Stir and heat, uncovered, on ROAST for an additional 2 minutes.

4. Add marshmallows to chocolate mixture and heat, uncovered, on ROAST for 2 minutes. Stir. If marshmallows are not melted, heat an additional 1 minute.

5. Add beaten egg to chocolate-marshmallow mixture.

6. Heat, uncovered, on ROAST for 2 minutes. Stir. If mixture has not thickened, heat on ROAST for 1 minute.

7. Stir in vanilla and place in refrigerator to chill.

Baked Custard

1⅔ cups milk, scalded
3 eggs
4 tablespoons sugar
¼ teaspoon salt
½ teaspoon vanilla
Dash nutmeg

Serves 5

1. To scald milk, heat in a heat-resistant, non-metallic measuring cup for 3 to 4 minutes on FULL POWER, or until tiny bubbles appear around the edges of the cup.

2. Beat eggs slightly. Add sugar, salt and vanilla. Slowly add milk. Divide custard among 5 glass custard cups or use heat-resistant, non-metallic coffee cups. Place custard dishes in a circle on the outer edge of the turntable.

3. Heat, uncovered, on ROAST for 5 to 5½ minutes or until custard just begins to boil. Center will become firm during standing time. Chill several hours before serving.

Bread Pudding

1 (3-ounce) package French
   vanilla pudding and pie filling
   (not instant)
2 cups milk
1 teaspoon cinnamon
½ cup raisins
1½ cups day-old bread cubes

Serves 4

1. In a deep, 1-quart, heat-resistant, non-metallic casserole combine all ingredients.
2. Heat, uncovered, on ROAST for 8 minutes or until mixture boils. Stir once.
3. Serve either hot or cold.

Butterscotch Fondue

2 (6-ounce) packages butterscotch pieces
½ cup hot water
¼ cup butter or margarine
½ cup light corn syrup
1 teaspoon vanilla
Dash salt
Ladyfingers, split
Marshmallows
Banana chunks, sprinkled with
   lemon juice

Serves 6

1. Combine butterscotch, hot water and butter in a deep, 1-quart, heat-resistant, non-metallic casserole or fondue pot.
2. Heat, uncovered, on FULL POWER for 5 minutes or until butterscotch is melted. Stir frequently.
3. Add corn syrup, vanilla and salt.
4. Set fondue pot over low heat.
5. Arrange ladyfingers, marshmallows and banana chunks on a platter.
6. Place a ladyfinger, marshmallow or banana chunk on a fondue fork and dip it into butterscotch mixture.

Raspberry Rum Fondue

Raspberry Jam Plus, (see recipe
   page 245)
2 tablespoons rum
Square of pound cake or angel
   food cake
Marshmallows
Bananas

1. Prepare Raspberry Jam Plus recipe adding 2 tablespoons rum after last cooking period.
2. Keep warm while serving.
3. Serve with squares of pound cake, angel food cake, marshmallows and bananas.

19

Chocolate Fondue

1 (6-ounce) package semi-sweet
   chocolate pieces
2 tablespoons butter or margarine
¼ cup hot water
¼ cup light corn syrup
1 teaspoon vanilla
Dash salt
Ladyfingers, split
Marshmallows

Serves 2

1. Combine chocolate, butter or margarine, water and corn syrup in a deep, 1-quart, heat-resistant, non-metallic casserole or small, heat-resistant, non-metallic fondue pot.

2. Heat, uncovered, on ROAST for 2 minutes or until chocolate is melted. Stir frequently.

3. Add vanilla and salt; stir to blend.

4. Set fondue pot on a stand over low heat.

5. Arrange ladyfingers and marshmallows on a platter.

6. Place a ladyfinger or a marshmallow on a fondue fork and dip it into the chocolate mixture.

Variation: You may use nearly any kind of day-old cake or fruit and many kinds of candy in place of ladyfingers and marshmallows. Use your imagination.

Tip: Any remaining sauce may be placed in a tightly covered jar and stored in refrigetator to be used over ice cream or cake.

Pictured: Blueberries and Vanilla Cream

Fruit Desserts

Cooking Hints

Your favorite fruit desserts will be even more flavorful when prepared in the Microwave Oven. Fruits taste and look better since the vitamin and nutrient losses are reduced. Cooking times may vary due to the age, size, freshness, variety and temperature of the fruit. The Microwave Oven is also handy to bring refrigerated fruits to room temperature.

Frozen fruits may be thawed very successfully on the DEFROST Setting.

12—16 ounces Frozen Fruit — 3 minutes on DEFROST

Stewed Apricots

1 (8-ounce) package dried
   apricots
1 cup water
¼ cup sugar

Serves 4

1. Place apricots and water in a deep, 1-quart, heat-resistant, non-metallic casserole.
2. Let stand at room temperature at least 1 hour or until apricots are softened. Stir in sugar.
3. Heat, covered, on FULL POWER 4 minutes. Stir occasionally.
4. Let stand, covered, until cool.

Variation: Stewed prunes: Substitute prunes for apricots and follow recipe above omitting the the sugar and increasing water to 1½ cups.
Stewed peaches: Use recipe above substituting peaches for apricots.

Brandied Peaches

1 (29-ounce) can peach halves,
   undrained
⅔ cup pineapple preserves
⅓ cup brandy
1 teaspoon lemon juice
¼ cup toasted coconut

Serves 4

1. Drain peach halves and reserve ½ cup syrup.
2. In a small bowl, combine reserved syrup, pineapple preserves, brandy and lemon juice.
3. Arrange peaches in a shallow, heat-resistant, non-metallic baking dish.
4. Pour sauce over peaches. Sprinkle with coconut.
5. Heat, uncovered, on FULL POWER 4 to 5 minutes.
6. Serve either warm or chilled.

Fruit Compote

2 medium apples, peeled,
   cored and thinly sliced
3 tablespoons sugar
1 (17-ounce) can peach slices,
   undrained
½ cup whole-berry cranberry
   sauce
¼ teaspoon cinnamon
⅛ teaspoon allspice
⅛ teaspoon cloves
⅛ teaspoon nutmeg
Whipped cream

Serves 4

1. In a deep, 1½-quart, heat-resistant, non-metallic casserole, place apples and sprinkle with sugar.
2. Heat, covered, on FULL POWER 3 minutes.
3. Add remaining ingredients; stir to combine.
4. Heat, uncovered, on FULL POWER 4 minutes or until apples are tender.
5. Serve with dollops of whipped cream.

Variation: Pineapples, apricots, pears or plums may be substituted for apples or peach slices. If desired, ½-cup walnut or pecan pieces may be added to compote in Step 3.

20

Baked Apples With Mincemeat Stuffing

6 medium baking apples
3 tablespoons butter or margarine
6 tablespoons prepared mincemeat

Serves 6

1. Wash and core apples. Peel a narrow strip of peel from around the top of the apple.

2. Place apples in a shallow, heat-resistant, non-metallic baking dish.

3. Place ½ tablespoon of butter or margarine and 1 tablespoon of mincemeat in the center of each apple. Heat, uncovered, on FULL POWER 7 to 8 minutes or until apples are tender.

4. Allow apples to stand, covered, about 5 minutes.

Variation: If desired, raisins, nuts, chutney or preserves can be substituted for mincemeat.

Apple Crisp

4 cups peeled and sliced apples
2 tablespoons lemon juice
½ cup quick or old fashioned oats, uncooked
½ cup firmly packed dark brown sugar
¼ cup flour
½ teaspoon salt
6 tablespoons butter or margarine
1 teaspoon cinnamon
⅛ teaspoon nutmeg

Serves 4 to 6

1. Place apples in a 9-inch, heat-resistant, non-metallic pie plate.

2. Sprinkle with lemon juice.

3. Heat, covered, on FULL POWER 2 minutes.

4. Combine remaining ingredients in a small, heat-resistant, non-metallic bowl.

5. Heat topping mixture, uncovered, on FULL POWER 2 minutes, stirring after the first minute. Cool slightly.

6. Sprinkle topping mixture over apples.

7. Heat, uncovered, on FULL POWER 8 minutes or until apples are tender and topping is crisp.

Applesauce

4 cups peeled and sliced tart apples
½ cup water
¼ to ½ cup sugar
¼ teaspoon cinnamon

Serves 4 to 6

1. Place apples, water and sugar in a deep, 1½-quart, heat-resistant, non-metallic casserole.

2. Heat, covered, on FULL POWER 8 to 9 minutes or until apples are tender.

3. If smooth applesauce is desired, a blender or food mill may be used. Cooked apples may be mashed with a potato masher or fork.

4. After desired consistency is reached, add cinnamon while applesauce is still hot.

5. Serve warm or chilled.

Cinnamon Baked Apples

4 large baking apples (Rome beauties or Courtlands)
4 tablespoons small cinnamon candies

Serves 4

1. Core apples without cutting through bottom skin of apple and peel about 1 inch of the peel from the stem end of each apple. If necessary, cut a thin slice from the bottom of each apple so it will stand upright.

2. Arrange apples in a shallow, heat-resistant, non-metallic baking dish.

3. Place 1 tablespoon of the cinnamon candies in the cavity of each apple.

4. Heat, uncovered, on FULL POWER 6 minutes or until apples are tender. The time will depend on the size and kind of apples used.

Variation: 1 tablespoon of sugar, fruit-flavored syrup or carbonated beverage may be substituted for the cinnamon candies. If desired, raisins or nuts may be placed in the cavities of the apples. An additional 1 to 2 minutes must be added to the heating time in Step 4.

Snowcapped Apples

4 large baking apples
4 tablespoons small cinnamon candies
2 egg whites, at room temperature
2 tablespoons sugar

Serves 4

1. Core apples and peel about 1-inch of the peel from the stem end of each apple. If necessary, cut a thin slice from the bottom of each apple so it will stand.

2. Arrange apples in a shallow, heat-resistant, non-metallic baking dish.

3. Fill cavity of each apple with the cinnamon candies.

4. Heat, uncovered, on FULL POWER 8 minutes or until apples are tender.

5. While apples are cooking, beat egg whites with electric mixer until they are foamy. Gradually add the 2 tablespoons sugar and beat until egg whites are stiff and glossy.

6. Just before serving, spoon a dollop of meringue on top of each apple.

7. Heat, uncovered, on ROAST for 1 minute or until meringue sets.

20

Blueberries And Vanilla Cream

½ cup cold water
1 envelope unflavored gelatin
1 cup light cream
¾ cup sugar
½ teaspoon vanilla
¼ teaspoon salt
1 cup dairy sour cream
2 tablespoons butter or margarine
2 tablespoons flour
2½ cups frozen blueberries, thawed and undrained
⅓ cup sugar
Dash salt
1 tablespoon lemon juice

Serves 6

1. Dissolve unflavored gelatin in cold water and set aside.

2. In a medium-sized, heat-resistant, non-metallic bowl, heat cream on FULL POWER 2 to 2½ minutes or until scalded.

3. Add dissolved gelatin to cream and stir until completely dissolved.

4. Stir in sugar, vanilla and salt, mixing well.

5. Chill until mixture begins to gel. When gelatin mixture is of desired consistency, whip with rotary beater until light and fluffy.

6. Add sour cream and beat until thick.

7. Spoon into 6 lightly-oiled, 6-ounce custard cups or any small cup. Chill until firm, about 8 hours.

8. Just before serving, in a deep, 2-quart, heat-resistant, non-metallic casserole, melt butter on FULL POWER 30 seconds.

9. Stir in flour until mixture is like paste.

10. Add liquid from blueberries, sugar and salt, mixing well.

11. Gently stir in blueberries.

12. Heat, uncovered, on FULL POWER 4 minutes or until mixture boils.

13. Add lemon juice. Heat, covered, an additional 3 minutes on FULL POWER.

14. To serve, spoon some of the Blueberry Sauce into each of 6 sherbet glasses. Run a knife around the outside edge of each custard cup to loosen Vanilla Cream. Invert one custard cup of Vanilla Cream in each sherbet glass. Spoon additional Blueberry Sauce on top.

Brazilian Bananas

4 tablespoons butter or margarine
6 medium ripe bananas, peeled
1 tablespoon lemon juice
¼ cup firmly packed dark brown sugar
⅛ teaspoon cinnamon
⅛ teaspoon allspice
⅔ cup shredded coconut

Serves 4 to 6

1. Place butter in a shallow, oblong, heat-resistant, non-metallic baking dish. Heat, uncovered, on FULL POWER 30 seconds or until butter is melted.

2. Roll bananas in butter to coat well. Sprinkle bananas with lemon juice.

3. In a small bowl, combine brown sugar, cinnamon and allspice.

4. Sprinkle over bananas.

5. Heat, uncovered, on FULL POWER 2 to 3 minutes.

6. Sprinkle with coconut and heat on FULL POWER an additional 1 to 2 minutes, or until bananas are soft.

Strawberry Soufflé

2 pints fresh strawberries,
  washed and hulled
2 envelopes unflavored gelatin
¼ cup water
1 cup sugar, divided
4 egg yolks, well beaten
⅛ teaspoon salt
1 tablespoon lemon juice
4 egg whites, at room temperature
1 cup heavy cream, chilled and
  whipped
2 to 3 drops red food coloring
  (optional)
Sweetened whipped cream
  (optional)

Serves 6 to 8

1. Pureé strawberries in an electric blender or press through a sieve or food mill.
2. In a heat-resistant, non-metallic, 1-quart measuring cup, combine 1 cup of strawberry pureé, the gelatin, water, ½ cup sugar, the egg yolks and salt. Stir to combine.
3. Heat, uncovered, on ROAST for 4 minutes or until mixture just begins to boil. Stir frequently.
4. Cool mixture slightly.
5. Add remaining strawberries and lemon juice.
6. Chill mixture until it is consistency of unbeaten egg whites.
7. While mixture is chilling, beat egg whites in a large bowl until stiff peaks form. Add the remaining ½ cup sugar, 1 tablespoon at a time, beating constantly until egg whites are stiff and glossy.
8. Fold whipped cream and chilled berry mixture into egg whites. Add food coloring until desired color is reached.
9. Pour mixture in a 2-quart mold.
10. Chill at least 3 to 4 hours to set.
11. Unmold. Garnish with whipped cream, if desired.

Blueberry Betty

1 quart fresh blueberries, washed and drained, or 2 (9-ounce)
  containers frozen blueberries
  with no sugar added
1 tablespoon lemon juice
2 to 4 tablespoons granulated
  sugar
1 tablespoon cornstarch
1 cup flour
Dash salt
¼ teaspoon cinnamon
1 cup firmly packed dark brown
  sugar
½ cup butter or margarine,
  softened

Serves 4 to 6

1. Place berries in a deep, 1½-quart, heat-resistant, non-metallic casserole.
2. Sprinkle with lemon juice and granulated sugar, to taste.
3. Heat, covered, on FULL POWER 3 minutes. (If frozen blueberries are used, heat an additional minute.)
4. Stir in cornstarch until smooth.
5. Sift flour, salt and cinnamon together into a small bowl. With a pastry blender or 2 knives cut in butter and brown sugar until mixture is crumbly.
6. Sprinkle mixture over berries.
7. Heat, uncovered, on FULL POWER 6 to 8 minutes or until topping is no longer doughy.

Tip: If a browner topping is desired, Blueberry Betty may be placed under the broiler of a conventional oven for several minutes.

20

Peach Halves With Raspberry Sauce

1 cup water
½ cup sugar
6 large, fresh peaches, peeled, halved and pitted
1 pint fresh raspberries, washed and hulled
¼ cup sugar
¼ cup water
1 teaspoon grated lemon rind

Serves 6

1. In a large, heat-resistant, non-metallic bowl, combine 1 cup water and ½ cup of sugar.

2. Heat, covered, on FULL POWER 5 minutes, stirring occasionally.

3. Add peach halves and heat, covered, on FULL POWER an additional 4 minutes, basting peaches frequently.

4. In a medium-sized, heat-resistant, non-metallic bowl, combine remaining ingredients.

5. Heat, covered, on FULL POWER 3 minutes or until berries are soft.

6. To serve, arrange peach halves on each dessert plate and spoon some of the raspberry sauce over them.

7. Serve either warm or chilled.

Tip: If serving this dish chilled, refrigerate peaches and raspberries separately.

Variations: Canned peach halves may be used. When using canned peach halves, begin with Step 4. If desired, pears, apricots, or other fruits may be substituted for peaches. Other berries may be used for sauce.

Pictured: French Chocolates, Date Nut Roll, Spiced Nuts, Chocolate Bourbon Balls, Peanut Brittle

Cooking Hints

Candy can now be made in your Microwave Oven without the worry of scorching. Cooking occurs on all sides rather than just the bottom. As with conventional candy making, the cooking dish should be two to three times as large as the volume of the candy mixture to allow sufficient boiling space. A candy thermometer may be used after the candy is removed from the Microwave Oven. NEVER USE A CANDY THERMOMETER IN THE MICROWAVE OVEN.

When cooking a large number of individual cookies, you may use your conventional oven more frequently to save time and also because the texture of individual cookies is often different when cooked by microwaves. The next time you bake individual cookies conventionally, test a couple of them in your Microwave Oven to see how well that particular recipe works.

Timing Guide for Cookies:

3 cookies	1 minute on FULL POWER
6 cookies	1½ to 1¾ minutes on FULL POWER
9 cookies	2 to 2½ minutes on FULL POWER

Many cookie recipes benefit from chilling the cookie dough before baking. Form into 1-inch balls and place on wax paper. Flatten with a drinking glass or the tines of a fork.

Cook chilled cookies until there are no doughy spots. If cookies are overbaked, brown spots will appear in the interior. Allow cookies to cool on the wax paper to become firm before removing them.

Cookie dough can be formed into rolls, 2 inches in diameter. Slice ¼ inch thick and cook, 9 cookies at a time, about 1¼ to 1¾ minutes on FULL POWER. Bar cookies will normally save the greatest amount of time when you are preparing cookies in the Microwave Oven.

Chocolate Bourbon Balls

1 cup finely chopped pecans
¼ cup bourbon
½ cup butter or margarine
4 cups sifted confectioners' sugar
3 (8-ounce) packages semi-sweet chocolate pieces

Makes 1½ dozen

1. Combine chopped pecans with bourbon and refrigerate overnight.

2. Melt butter in small, heat-resistant, non-metallic bowl on FULL POWER 1 minute.

3. Add confectioners' sugar, 1 cup at a time, to melted butter. Add nuts and bourbon, mixing well.

4. Place in refrigerator to harden. Mixture should be stiff enough to hold its shape for dipping. If necessary, more confectioners' sugar may be added to obtain the desired stiffness.

5. In a medium-sized, heat-resistant, non-metallic bowl, place the chocolate pieces. Heat, uncovered, on FULL POWER 4 minutes or until melted.

6. While chocolate is melting, shape candy into balls. Place on tray with waxed paper and return to refrigerator to harden.

7. Put a wooden pick in each ball and dip into melted chocolate. Place on waxed paper and refrigerate to harden.

Tip: Dip only a few bourbon balls at a time, leaving the rest in the refrigerator. If balls become too soft, return to the refrigerator to harden. If chocolate becomes too stiff, return to Microwave Oven for 1 minute to soften.

Peanut Brittle

1½ teaspoons baking soda
1 teaspoon water
1 teaspoon vanilla
1½ cups sugar
1 cup water
1 cup light corn syrup
3 tablespoons butter or margarine
1 pound shelled raw peanuts

1. Combine baking soda, water and vanilla in a small dish and set aside.

2. Place sugar, water and corn syrup in a deep, 3-quart, heat-resistant, non-metallic casserole; stir to blend.

3. Heat, uncovered, on FULL POWER 20 minutes or until candy thermometer registers 240°F. If a candy thermometer is not available, drop a small amount of the mixture into very cold water. The mixture should form a soft ball which flattens when removed from the water. DO NOT PLACE CANDY THERMOMETER IN MICROWAVE OVEN OR USE TEMPERATURE PROBE.

4. Stir in butter until melted. Add peanuts and heat, uncovered, on FULL POWER 12 minutes or until candy thermometer registers 300°F. If a candy thermometer is not available, drop a small amount of mixture into very cold water. The mixture should separate into threads which are hard and brittle. Stir occasionally with a wooden spoon.

5. Grease 2 cookie sheets and warm in a conventional oven at 250°F while peanut mixture is heating.

6. Stir reserved baking soda mixture into hot candy mixture. Pour hot peanut brittle onto prepared cookie sheets and spread to ¼-inch thickness.

7. When peanut brittle has cooled, break into bite-sized pieces.

21

Date Nut Roll

2 cups sugar
1 cup milk
1 tablespoon butter or marga
   rine, melted
1 cup chopped dates
1 teaspoon vanilla
1 cup coarsely chopped pecans
   or walnuts
½ cup finely chopped pecans
   or walnuts

1. In a deep, 2-quart, heat-resistant, non-metallic casserole, combine sugar, milk and butter or margarine. Heat, uncovered, on ROAST for 8 minutes or until sugar is dissolved and mixture is boiling. Stir.

2. Heat, covered, on ROAST for 12 to 14 minutes or until mixture reaches 234°F on a candy thermometer. If a candy thermometer is not available, drop a small amount of the mixture into very cold water. The mixture should form a soft ball which flattens when removed. DO NOT PLACE CANDY THERMOMETER IN MICROWAVE OVEN OR USE TEMPERATURE PROBE.

3. Add dates and stir well.

4. Heat, covered, on ROAST for 5 minutes, or until candy again reaches 234°F. If a candy thermometer is not available, drop a small amount of the mixture into very cold water. The mixture should form a soft ball which should flatten when removed from the water. Add vanilla. Set aside.

5. Cool candy without stirring until lukewarm (110°F). Beat until very thick.

6. Add 1 cup chopped nuts and stir until mixture becomes solid. Knead until smooth.

7. Divide into 3 equal portions. Form each portion into a roll. Coat each roll with the ½ cup chopped nuts. Wrap in waxed paper and chill.

8. To serve, cut into slices.

> **Variation:** If desired, after kneading candy may be served by forming into patties and placing a pecan half on top.

French Chocolates

1 (12-ounce) package semi-
   sweet chocolate pieces
1 cup walnuts, ground
¾ cup sweetened condensed
   milk
1 teaspoon vanilla
Dash salt
Chocolate sprinkles
Shredded coconut
Chopped nuts

Makes about 50 chocolate balls.

1. Place chocolate pieces in a medium-sized, heat-resistant, non-metallic mixing bowl.

2. Heat, uncovered, on FULL POWER 4 minutes or until melted.

3. Stir in ground walnuts, condensed milk, vanilla and salt.

4. Cool 5 minutes.

5. Roll into balls and dip into chocolate sprinkles, coconut or nuts, as desired.

6. Place on greased cookie sheet and refrigerate until set.

Spiced Nuts

½ cup firmly packed dark
    brown sugar
1½ tablespoons water
½ teaspoon salt
½ teaspoon cinnamon
¼ teaspoon allspice
⅛ teaspoon nutmeg
⅛ teaspoon cloves
1½ cups walnut halves, pecan
    halves, cashews or a combi-
    nation of these

Makes 1½ cups

1. In a deep, 2-quart, heat-resistant, non-metallic casserole, combine first 7 ingredients.
2. Heat, uncovered, on FULL POWER 1½ minutes; stir occasionally.
3. Add ½ cup nuts at a time to syrup mixture. Stir until well coated. With a slotted spoon lift out nuts; drain extra syrup. Place nuts in a shallow, 1½-quart, heat-resistant, non-metallic baking dish. Repeat with remaining nuts.
4. Heat coated nuts, uncovered, on FULL POWER 5 minutes or until syrup begins to harden slightly.
5. Transfer nuts to greased wax paper and allow to cool and harden.

Party Mix

½ cup butter or margarine
2 tablespoons Worcestershire
    sauce
Few drops Tabasco sauce, to
    taste
½ teaspoon salt
2 cups bite-sized shredded corn
    biscuits
2 cups bite-sized shredded
    wheat biscuits
2 cups bite-sized shredded rice
    biscuits
1 cup salted nuts
1 cup thin pretzel sticks

Makes 8 cups

1. In a deep, 3-quart, heat-resistant, non-metallic casserole, melt butter or margarine on FULL POWER 45 seconds.
2. Add Worcestershire sauce, Tabasco sauce and salt. Stir to combine thoroughly.
3. Mix remaining ingredients together and stir into butter mixture.
4. Heat, uncovered, stirring frequently, on FULL POWER 6 minutes or until cereal is well coated and crisp.
5. Turn mixture onto a paper-towel-lined tray and spread evenly.
6. Allow to cool.

Fudge

1 pound confectioners' sugar
½ cup cocoa
¼ pound butter or margarine
¼ cup milk
½ cup chopped nuts
1 teaspoon vanilla

Makes 2 to 3 dozen squares.

1. Lightly grease an 8-inch square dish. Set aside.
2. Place confectioners' sugar and cocoa in a medium-sized, heat-resistant, non-metallic mixing bowl. Stir to combine.
3. Add butter and milk to sugar-cocoa mixture. DO NOT STIR.
4. Heat, uncovered, on FULL POWER 2 minutes.
5. After cooking, stir just to combine ingredients.
6. Add nuts and vanilla. Stir until blended.
7. Pour into prepared dish and refrigerate for 1 hour before cutting and serving.

21

White Fudge

2 tablespoons butter or margarine
½ cup chopped unblanched almonds
2 cups sugar
½ cup butter or margarine
1 cup evaporated milk
1 (8-ounce) bar white chocolate, with whole almonds or ½ pound of white chocolate pieces with almonds
1 cup miniature marshmallows
1 teaspoon vanilla

Makes 1½ pounds

1. In a shallow, heat-resistant, non-metallic baking dish melt the 2 tablespoons butter on FULL POWER 30 seconds. Add ½ cup almonds and heat, uncovered, on FULL POWER 3 to 4 minutes, or until almonds are toasted. Stir each minute of heating. Set aside.

2. In a deep, 3-quart, heat-resistant, non-metallic casserole combine sugar, the ½ cup butter and evaporated milk. Heat, uncovered, on ROAST for 18 to 20 minutes, or until mixture reaches 234°F with candy thermometer. If a candy thermometer is not available, drop a small amount of mixture into cold water. The mixture should form a soft ball which flattens when removed from the water. Stir every 4 minutes of heating time. DO NOT PLACE CANDY THERMOMETER IN MICROWAVE OVEN OR USE TEMPERATURE PROBE.

3. Add broken pieces of white chocolate and miniature marshmallows. Beat until melted.

4. Add toasted almonds and vanilla. Beat until candy thickens.

5. Pour candy into a buttered, shallow, heat-resistant, non-metallic baking dish.

6. Cool before cutting into squares.

Rocky Road Candy

1 (6-ounce) package semi-sweet chocolate pieces
1 tablespoon butter or margarine
2 eggs, beaten until foamy
1¼ cups confectioners' sugar
½ teaspoon salt
1 teaspoon vanilla
2 cups miniature marshmallows
1½ cups shelled, chopped walnuts, peanuts or pecans
1 cup shredded coconut

Makes 2 to 3 dozen

1. In a large, heat-resistant, non-metallic bowl, melt chocolate and butter on FULL POWER 1½ to 2 minutes.
2. While chocolate and butter are melting, in small bowl combine beaten eggs, confectioners' sugar, salt and vanilla until well blended.
3. Stir marshmallows, nuts and coconut into chocolate mixture.
4. Add egg mixture; stir until well blended. Add marshmallows.
5. Drop by teaspoonfuls onto greased wax paper.
6. If mixture becomes too stiff, return to Microwave Oven for 30 seconds on FULL POWER.
7. Chill candies to set.

Peanut Butter Cookies

¾ cup peanut butter
¼ cup butter or margarine, softened
½ cup granulated sugar
½ cup firmly packed dark brown sugar
2 eggs
1½ cups flour
¾ teaspoon baking soda
½ teaspoon salt

Makes 4 dozen

1. Cover 2 pieces of cardboard, cut into the shape of the glass turntable with wax paper to use as cookie sheets.

2. In a large mixing bowl, cream peanut butter and butter together until smooth. Add sugars and beat until fluffy.

3. Add eggs, one at a time, beating well after each addition.

4. Add remaining ingredients and beat until well combined.

5. Chill dough 1 hour.

6. Roll dough into 1-inch balls and place on cookie sheets in a circle. Place 12 balls on each sheet.

7. Press each dough ball with a 4-tined fork in two directions to flatten.

8. Bake on FULL POWER 2 to 2½ minutes or until no longer doughy.

Jam Crumble Bars

¾ cup butter or margarine
1 cup firmly packed dark brown sugar
1¾ cups flour
1½ cups quick oats, uncooked
1 teaspoon salt
½ teaspoon baking soda
¾ cup raspberry jam

Makes 32 small bars

1. Lightly grease an 8-inch, heat-resistant, non-metallic baking dish.

2. In a medium-sized bowl, cream butter and sugar together until fluffy. Stir in flour, salt, baking soda and oats. Combine until well blended.

3. Press one-half of mixture into bottom of prepared baking dish.

4. Heat, uncovered, on ROAST for 5 minutes.

5. Spread jam evenly over baked oat mixture.

6. Crumble remaining oat mixture over jam and press lightly.

7. Heat, uncovered, on ROAST an additional 7 minutes. Test for doneness with a wooden pick.

8. Allow to cool and cut into bars.

Chocolate Candy Chip Cookies

1 (23-ounce) package double fudge brownie mix (with chocolate flavor packet)
¾ cup flour
6 tablespoons vegetable oil
2 eggs
2 tablespoons water
¾ cup coarsely chopped nuts
1 (6-ounce) package candy-coated chocolate bits

Makes 5 to 6 dozen

1. Cover 2 pieces of cardboard, cut in the shape of the glass turntable, with wax paper. These will serve as cookie sheets.

2. In a medium-sized bowl, combine brownie mix, chocolate flavor packet, flour, oil, eggs and water. Mix well.

3. Fold in chopped nuts and chocolate bits.

4. Drop by teaspoonfuls onto prepared cookie sheets, placing cookies 1-inch apart on outside edge. Leave center of turntable empty.

5. Bake 8 to 10 at a time on FULL POWER for 2½ minutes.

21

243

Mile High Cookies

Butter or margarine
1 (18-ounce) package fruit bar
   cookie mix
Ingredients called for on
   package label
2 tablespoons rum
2 egg whites, at room temperature
⅛ teaspoon cream of tartar
4 tablespoons sugar
¼ teaspoon vanilla
Pinch of salt

Makes 32 small bars

1. Lightly grease an 8-inch, heat-resistant, non-metallic square baking dish. Set aside.

2. In a small, heat-resistant, non-metallic bowl melt butter, on FULL POWER 1 minute.

3. Place crunchy topping mix in a small bowl. Add 1½ table-spoons of the melted margarine to topping and mix well. Set aside.

4. In a medium-sized bowl combine base mix, remainder of melted margarine and egg as package directs. Mix thoroughly.

5. Spread batter evenly over the bottom of the baking dish.

6. Spread fruit filling over batter.

7. Sprinkle 2 tablespoons of rum over fruit filling.

8. Sprinkle crunchy topping over entire surface.

9. Heat, uncovered, on FULL POWER 5 minutes.

10. While cake is baking, beat egg whites until foamy. Add cream of tartar. Gradually add sugar, beating until meringue holds stiff peaks. Add vanilla and the pinch of salt.

11. Spread meringue evenly over crunchy topping.

12. Heat, uncovered, on FULL POWER 2 minutes or until meringue is set.

13. Cool and then cut into squares.

Cherry Filled Squares

¾ cup butter or margarine
1 cup sugar
1 egg
1 teaspoon vanilla
2 cups sifted flour
1 cup chopped walnuts
⅛ teaspoon allspice
⅛ teaspoon nutmeg
¾ cup cherry preserves
4 tablespoons confectioners'
   sugar

Makes 2 dozen

1. Lightly grease an 8-inch, square, heat-resistant, non-metallic baking dish. Set aside.

2. Beat butter until light and fluffy. Add sugar gradually. Beat until light and fluffy.

3. Beat in egg and vanilla.

4. Stir in flour, walnuts, allspice and nutmeg.

5. Press ½ of mixture into the prepared baking dish.

6. Spread with cherry preserves.

7. Top with remaining dough.

8. Heat, uncovered, on ROAST for 10 minutes or until top looks dry.

9. Cool in pan and sprinkle with confectioners' sugar. Cut into squares.

Apple Jam

2 medium apples, washed, cored and peeled
1½ cups sugar
1 teaspoon lemon juice

Makes 1 cup

1. In a medium-sized, heat-resistant, non-metallic bowl, place the 2 apples. Add sugar. Do not mix. Heat, uncovered, on FULL POWER for 5 minutes.

2. With electric mixer beat apples until apples and sugar are well blended.

3. Heat, uncovered, on FULL POWER for 3 minutes.

4. Stir in 1 teaspoon lemon juice.

5. Cool before serving.

Raspberry Jam Plus

2 (10-ounce) packages frozen raspberries
3½ tablespoons liquid pectin
2½ cups sugar
1 tablespoon lemon juice

Makes 3 cups

1. Place 2 packages of frozen raspberries in a 3-quart, heat-resistant, non-metallic mixing bowl.

2. Heat, uncovered, on FULL POWER 4 minutes.

3. Stir in liquid pectin and mix well.

4. Heat, uncovered, on FULL POWER 4 minutes. Stir and heat for an additional 2½ minutes.

5. Add sugar and lemon juice. Stir until well combined.

6. Heat, uncovered, on FULL POWER 2 minutes. Stir and heat an additional 4 minutes or until the jellying point has been reached.

7. Pour into prepared jars and seal.

Test for jellying point: Sheet test: Dip a large metal spoon into the boiling syrup; tilt spoon until syrup runs from the side of the spoon. When the jellying point is reached, liquid will not flow in a stream, but will divide into distinct drops which run together and flake or sheet from the spoon.

21

245

Recipe Index

—A—

—B—

—— E ——

—— F ——

---G---

---H---

---I---

---J---

---K---

---L---

—M—

Guide to Proper

USE
and
CARE

OF YOUR
NEW SHARP CAROUSEL™
MICROWAVE OVEN

MODEL R-5600

SHARP®

Featuring:
Carousel™ Cooking System
Variable Cooking Control

FOR YOUR PROTECTION...

To aid in reporting this microwave oven in case of loss or theft, please record below the model number and serial number located on the back of the unit. We also suggest you record all the information listed and retain for future reference.

MODEL NUMBER _____ SERIAL NUMBER _____
DATE OF PURCHASE_____
Dealer_____
Address_____ City_____
State_____ Zip_____ Telephone_____
Address_____ City_____
Service Station _____
State_____ Zip_____ Telephone_____

TOLL FREE SERVICE INFORMATION

For your nearest Sharp Authorized Service Station, call toll free:

800-447-4700
In Illinois: 800–322–4400
In Hawaii or Alaska, contact your local dealer.

WARRANTY VALIDATION

Dealers who sell Microwave Ovens are required to register the location of all ovens sold with the manufacturer.

The warranty registration card and the U.S. Department of Health and Human Services (DHHS) recordkeeping card provided on the outer carton of your Sharp Microwave Oven should be completed and returned by your dealer to register your purchase. If your dealer should fail to return these cards, please send them to Sharp Electronics Corporation. If you sell a Microwave Oven or purchase one through an original owner, you are required to notify the manufacturer.

LIMITED WARRANTY • MODEL R-5600 Home Usage Warranty

Sharp Electronics Corporation warrants this product to the original purchaser to be free from defective materials and workmanship and agrees to remedy any such defect or to furnish a new or equal part in exchange, (except appearance items, gaskets, rubber or plastic parts, light bulbs or glass parts, or printed materials,) through an authorized Sharp Service Dealer or Station.

This warranty does not apply to any product whose exterior has been damaged or defaced, nor to any product subjected to misuse, abnormal service or handling, nor to any product altered or repaired by other than an authorized Sharp Service Dealer or Station. This warranty does not apply outside the United States, its territories or possessions.

The period of this warranty covers seven (7) years on the magnetron tube and two (2) years on other parts, and two (2) years labor to replace any defective parts (including magnetron tube) from date of purchase.

This warranty entitles the original purchaser to have the magnetron tube repaired or replaced within seven (7) years from date of purchase and other parts, except those indicated above, repaired or replaced within two (2) years from date of purchase. This warranty further entitles the original purchaser to have warranteed labor rendered in the home at no cost for the period of two (2) years from date of purchase in connection with such repair or replacement, providing proof of purchase is presented and this product is operated solely for home and not commercial usage.

This shall be the exclusive written warranty of the original purchaser and neither this warranty nor any other warranty expressed or implied shall extend beyond the period of time listed above. In no event shall Sharp be liable for consequential economic damage or consequential damage to property. Some states do not allow a limitation on how long an implied warranty lasts or an exclusion of consequential damage, so the above limitation and exclusion may not apply to you. In addition, this warrantly gives specific legal rights, and you may have other rights which vary from state to state.

2

SHARP MICROWAVE OVEN TEST KITCHEN

SHARP ELECTRONICS CORPORATION

10 Keystone Place, Paramus, New Jersey 07652

Dear Sharp Customer:

Congratulations on your choice of a Sharp Carousel Microwave Oven. Now that you have decided to join the millions of microwave oven owners, we at Sharp want you to get the maximum enjoyment and use from your Sharp oven.

Before you use your oven for the first time, please read this book carefully. It is very important that you understand and follow this Guide to Proper USE and CARE. Your entire family should know how to operate the oven correctly so that each of you can easily use the oven and benefit from it.

This guide is a companion to your Sharp Carousel Microwave Oven Cookbook. Refer to both frequently as you learn to use your oven.

Sharp has a staff of home economists who are eager to help you if you have questions. Please indicate the model number of your oven, your complete mailing address and telephone number on any correspondence.

Best Wishes!

Susan Edwards

Susan Edwards
Sharp Test Kitchen
10 Keystone Place
Paramus, NJ 07652

3

CONTENTS

PRECAUTIONS FOR PROPER USE — READ CAREFULLY

In order to familiarize yourself with your new SHARP Microwave Oven, it is important to read the following instructions. Proper operation will insure continued protection against excessive exposure to microwave energy or electrical shock.

1. Visual check after unpacking:
   Remove all packing material from the oven cavity.
   Check the oven for any damage, such as misaligned door, damaged gaskets around door or dents inside the oven cavity or on the door. If there is any damage, please do not operate the oven until it has been checked by an Authorized SHARP Service Station and any repairs made, if necessary.

2. Electrical grounding instructions:
   Your SHARP Microwave Oven is equipped with a three-prong grounding plug for your protection against possible shock hazards.
   This oven must be fully grounded at all times. If you move the unit from area to area, the receptacle you use must be a fully grounded, single phase A.C. 115 —120 volt, 15 amp or more circuit.
   Where a two-prong wall receptacle is encountered, it is the personal responsibility and obligation of the customer to contact a qualified electrician and have it replaced with a properly grounded three-prong wall receptacle or have grounding adapter properly grounded and polarized.
   If an extension cord must be used, it should be a 3-wire, 15 amp or more cord.

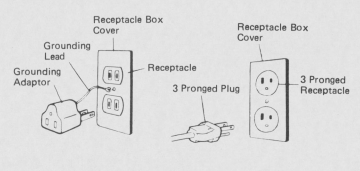

120V 15A

DO NOT UNDER ANY CIRCUMSTANCES CUT OR REMOVE THE ROUND GROUNDING PRONG FROM THIS PLUG.

3. The voltage used must be the same as specified on this Microwave Oven.

4. Be sure to read the remainder of the precautions and the operating instructions before operating the unit to get full value from your SHARP Microwave Oven.

5. If at any time the microwave oven is not working properly, contact an Authorized SHARP Service Station to have the unit checked and any needed repairs made.

PRECAUTIONS TO AVOID POSSIBLE EXPOSURE TO EXCESSIVE MICROWAVE ENERGY

(a) Do not attempt to operate this oven with the door open since open-door operation can result in harmful exposure to microwave energy. It is important not to defeat or tamper with the safety interlocks.

(b) Do not place any object between the oven front face and the door or allow soil or cleaner residue to accumulate on sealing surfaces.

(c) Do not operate the oven if it is damaged. It is particularly important that the oven door close properly and that there is no damage to the: (1) door (bent), (2) hinges and latches (broken or loosened), (3) door seals and sealing surfaces.

(d) The oven should not be adjusted or repaired by anyone except properly qualified service personnel.

GENERAL INSTRUCTIONS AND FEATURES

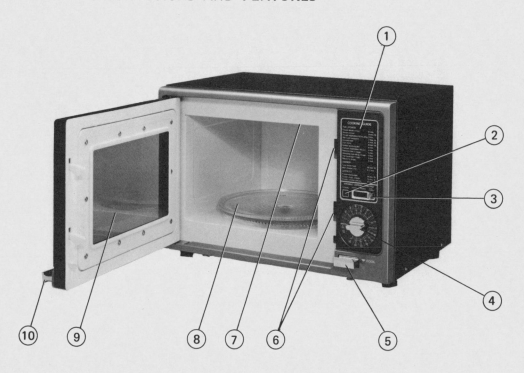

1. Recipe guide.
2. COOK indicator light.
3. Variable Cooking Control lever. Move lever to desired setting.
4. Timer, 0–15 minutes for FULL POWER setting.
          0–45 minutes for SIMMER or DEFROST setting.
5. COOK lever. Press down for cooking, after door is closed and timer is set.
6. Door latches. The oven will not operate unless the door is securely closed.
7. Cavity lamp. The lamp will light when timer is set or when door is opened.
8. Removable Carousel turntable.
9. Oven door with see-through window.
10. One touch door latch bar. Press to open door.

SHARP CAROUSEL MICROWAVE OVEN R-5600

FEATURES:

* Removable Carousel^{TM} turntable to provide more uniform cooking than ever before possible.
* Variable Cooking Control for choosing rate of microwave cooking: FULL POWER, SIMMER and DEFROST.
* 15 minute single timer for FULL POWER setting; converts to 45 minute timer for SIMMER or DEFROST setting.
* Recipe guide for many common foods.
* One-touch door latch bar with built-in safety and convenience.
* Double-safe Microwave Oven door (two separate safety switches, door interlocks and concealed interlocks).
* Oven light to view foods as they cook.
* End of cooking bell to signal when food is ready.

SPECIFICATIONS:

AC Line Voltage	Single phase 120V, 60Hz, A.C. only
AC Power Required	1.0 kW 8.5A
Output Power	500W (2000cc water load)
Frequency	2450 MHz
Outside Dimensions	19⅝"(W), 13¼"(H), 14⅝"(D)
Cavity Dimensions	11⅝"(W), 7⅛"(H), 12⅜"(D)
Weight	Approx. 45 lbs.

In compliance with standards set by:

FCC — Federal Communications Commission Type Approved.

DHHS — Department of Health and Human Services. Complies with Department of Health and Human Services (DHHS) rule, CFR, Title 21, Chapter I, Subchapter J.

UL — This symbol on the nameplate means the product is Listed by Underwriter' Laboratories, Inc.

OPERATION CHECK

1. Plug the power cord into a three-pronged electric outlet, (120V, 60Hz, A.C. only). See page 5.
2. Place turntable inside the oven cavity. When door is opened, oven light comes on automatically.
3. Place one cup of room temperature water on the turntable inside the oven.
4. Close door securely. Oven light will go out.
5. Move Variable Cooking Control lever to FULL POWER.
6. Set timer to four minutes. Oven light will come on automatically.
7. Press the COOK lever down for cooking. The cooling fan will start and the turntable will begin to rotate.
8. After four minutes, a bell will ring and the unit will turn off.*
9. The water should be bubbling if operating normally.
* When the door is opened during the cooking process, the timer automatically stops. The timer starts again when the door is closed and the COOK lever is pressed down.

SERVICE CALL CHECK

Please check the following before calling for service!!!

1. When the door is opened, does the oven lamp light?   YES____ NO____
2. Place one cup of water in the oven and close the door securely.
   Set the timer for four minutes.
   A. Does the oven lamp light?   YES____ NO____
   B. If "NO", please check your wall socket and fuse. If both the wall socket and the fuse are functioning properly, contact your nearest Sharp Authorized Service Station.
3. Press the COOK lever.
   A. Does the cooling fan work?   YES____ NO____
   (Put your hand over the ventilating opening at the rear of the oven.)
   B. Does the turntable rotate?   YES____ NO____

IF SERVICE IS NEEDED, PLEASE CONTACT YOUR NEAREST SHARP AUTHORIZED SERVICE STATION. For the location of your nearest Sharp Authorized Service Station, see page 1 for toll free number.

TURNTABLE NOTE

The turntable of your Sharp R-5600 is designed to move up and down slightly as it rotates. This is a normal condition and further improves the cooking performance of the oven.

STEPS FOR COOKING

Throughout your Sharp Carousel Microwave Oven Cookbook, you will find step by step instructions for each recipe. Basic instructions follow.

1. Make sure the oven is plugged into a 3-pronged, grounded 115–120 volt, 15 amp household circuit. Press "latch" bar on the lower right-hand side of door to open. The interior light comes on whenever the door is opened.

note (

2. The glass turntable should be seated in the oven. Always make certain the turntable is in place when using your Microwave Oven. The oven should not be used without the turntable in place, and it should never be restricted so that it cannot rotate.

3. The Variable Cooking Control on your Sharp Microwave Oven allows you to select the amount of microwave energy and the rate of cooking or defrosting. There are three power levels or settings:

	approximate percentage
FULL POWER	100%
SIMMER	50% of full power
DEFROST	30% of full power

The Chapter on Variable Cooking explains the use of this feature.

4. Be sure to select the recommended power level before beginning to cook by moving the Variable Cooking Control lever to the recommended setting.

5. If food does not seem to be heating properly, check the Variable Cooking Control to make sure it is on the setting you need.

6. Set the timer for the appropriate cooking time. Whenever setting a mechanical timer for less than 2 minutes, turn the timer past 2 minutes and then back to the correct time. When the Variable Cooking Control lever is set on FULL POWER, the timer will time up to 15 minutes. When the lever is set on SIMMER or DEFROST, the timer will time up to 45 minutes automatically.

7. Press the COOK lever down. The COOK indicator light will go on and stay on throughout the microwave cooking activity. The cooling fan will start whenever the COOK lever is engaged. This is a fan which cools the interior of the oven and the magnetron tube. The interior oven light should be on whenever the timer is set or when the oven door is opened.

8. The oven door may be opened anytime during the cooking process. The timer will automatically stop so that you will always know how much cooking time is left. If you wish to continue cooking, close the door and press the COOK lever. If you wish to alter the cooking time at any time during the operation, just turn the timer ahead or back as desired.

9. The signal bell will ring to indicate when cooking time is finished, and the oven will turn off automatically. The fan and lights will also turn off. After cooking time is completed, the timer will return to zero. If you wish to stop cooking before the cooking bell goes off, turn the timer back to zero or simply open the door. Anytime the door is opened, all microwave activity stops immediately.

CLEANING AND CARE

Exterior:

The outside surface of the unit is painted metal and plastic. The outside may be cleaned with mild soap and warm water; rinse and dry with a soft cloth. Do not use any type of household cleaner or abrasive cleaner.

Interior Walls:

Cleaning the SHARP Microwave Oven is very easy because no heat is generated to the interior surfaces, baking and setting spills or causing spatters. To clean the interior surfaces, bring a container of water to a boil. Let boil 2 minutes. Wipe the resulting condensation from the interior surfaces with a soft, dry cloth. DO NOT USE ABRASIVE OR HARSH CLEANERS OR SCOURING PADS. For heavier soil, use baking soda or a mild soap; rinse thoroughly with hot water.

Turntable:

Occasionally it will be necessary to remove the turntable for cleaning or in order to clean the floor of the oven. Wash the turntable in mild, sudsy water. Dry with a soft cloth. The turntable is dishwasher-proof. Be sure to replace the turntable before cooking.

Be cautious when cleaning the floor of the oven so as not to get water into the motor shaft.

Door:

Wipe the window on both sides with a damp cloth to remove any spills or spatter. Metal and plastic parts will be easier to maintain if wiped frequently with a damp cloth.

CONDENSATION

Occasionally you may find that some foods will cause the Microwave Oven to "sweat"; others will not. The humidity and the moisture in the food will influence the amount of moisture you find in your oven. Generally, covered foods will not cause as much condensation as uncovered foods. Be sure that the vent of your oven is not blocked.

Condensation is a normal part of microwave cooking.

The door seal on your microwave oven is designed to prevent the leakage of microwave energy from the oven during cooking. The door seal does not need to be air-tight in order to accomplish this function. Occasionally moisture may appear around the oven door. You may also be able to see some small areas of light or feel warm air movement around the oven door. None of these situations is abnormal or necessarily indicates that your oven is leaking microwave energy.

USING YOUR SHARP CAROUSEL MICROWAVE OVEN COOKBOOK

Recipes in your Sharp Carousel Microwave Oven Cookbook were developed for 650 watt microwave ovens. Model R-5600 has an output wattage of 500 watts. Cookbook recipes will require slightly longer cooking times in the R-5600, but are easily adapted for use in the R-5600 by using the chart below. Compare the COOKBOOK VARIABLE COOKING CONTROL SETTING to the R-5600 VARIABLE COOKING CONTROL SETTING and make these simple adjustments.

COOKBOOK VARIABLE COOKING CONTROL SETTING		R-5600 VARIABLE COOKING CONTROL SETTING
FULL POWER	=	FULL POWER plus 15% additional cooking time *
ROAST	=	FULL POWER **
SIMMER	=	SIMMER plus 20% additional cooking time ***

*   If a cookbook recipe cooks for 10 minutes on FULL POWER, the recipe would cook for 11½ minutes on FULL POWER in the R-5600.
(10 minutes x .15 or 15% = 1.5 minutes.   10 + 1.5 = 11.5 or 11½ minutes)

**   If a cookbook recipe cooks for 5 minutes on ROAST, the recipe would cook for 5 minutes on FULL POWER in the R-5600.

*** If a cookbook recipe cooks for 5 minutes on SIMMER, the recipe would cook for 6 minutes on SIMMER in the R-5600.
(5 minutes x .20 or 20% = 1.0 minute.   5 + 1.0 = 6 minutes)

Times stated in the cookbook are approximate and several factors will determine the exact cooking times. REMEMBER, it is always better to undercook foods rather than to overcook them. If a range of times is stated in a recipe, cook the minimum suggested time, check for doneness, and then cook slightly longer if necessary.

DEFROSTING IN THE R-5600

Defrosting instructions and cooking times in your cookbook were developed for 650 watt microwave ovens. Model R-5600 has an output wattage of 500 watts, so defrosting will require slightly longer in the R-5600. To defrost in the R-5600 increase approximate cookbook defrosting time 50% to 75%. Standing time will remain the same. For faster defrosting, foods can be defrosted on SIMMER in the R-5600. Defrosting on SIMMER will be similar to the cookbook defrosting times.

COOKBOOK DEFROST		R-5600 DEFROST	STANDING TIME
DEFROST	=	DEFROST plus 50% to 75% additional cooking time*	Same
DEFROST	=	SIMMER	Same

*   If a food defrosts for 8 minutes according to cookbook time, the food would defrost for approximately 12 to 14 minutes in the R-5600.
(8 minutes x .75 or 75% = 6.00 minutes. 8 + 6 = 14 minutes)

SUGGESTED COOKWARE SIZES

Although Cookware Utensils are discussed in detail in the introduction of your cookbook, below is a chart of suggested cookware sizes that are appropriate for use in the R-5600.

DISH		SIZE
Pie Plate		8-inch, 9-inch, 10-inch
Loaf Dish		8½ x 4½-inch, 9 x 5-inch
Round Cake Dish		8¼ x 1½-inch
Soufflé Dish		1-pint, 1-quart, 2-quart
Round Covered Casserole		1-quart, 1½-quart, 2-quart
Square Covered Casserole		1-quart, 1½-quart
Mixing Bowl		1½-quart, 2½-quart
Dinner Plate		10-inch
Browning Dish		8-inch

INSTALLATION INSTRUCTIONS

Your SHARP Microwave Oven may be most convenient for you when located on the countertop in your kitchen. It can be placed anywhere you have a 3-pronged grounded 115—120 volt, 15 amp. outlet.

1. Exhaust vents are provided on the back of the unit for proper cooling and air flow in the cavity. To permit adequate ventilation, be sure to install the unit so as not to block these vents. There should be some space for air circulation.

2. The unit should not be installed in any area where heat and steam are generated. The unit should not be installed, for example, next to a conventional surface unit.

PORTABLE WHEELED CART

Many SHARP dealers stock portable roli-about Microwave Oven carts. Placing the SHARP Microwave Oven on a wheeled cart makes it a portable cooking center. This will allow you to move the unit from place to place; from the kitchen to the family room or to the patio or terrace.

BEFORE YOU BEGIN COOKING . . . .

This Use and Care Guide is a companion to your new Sharp Carousel Microwave Oven Cookbook. Before you begin cooking, read the Introduction Chapter of your cookbook. Topics discussed there include:
- What is Microwave Energy? How does it work?
- Microwave Utensils
    Dish Test
    Glass, Ceramic and China
    Paper Goods
    Plastic Utensils and Accessories
    Wicker, Wood and Straw
    Browning Dishes
    Metal Utensils
- Thermometers
- General Cooking Hints

CAUTIOUS REMINDERS:

1. Do not operate the oven empty. Either food or water should always be in the oven during operation to absorb microwave energy.

2. Limit use of metal to those specific examples given in the Introduction Chapter of your cookbook. Generally speaking, metal should not be used in the microwave oven during operation.

3. Do not cook eggs in the shell. Pressure will build up inside the shell and it will explode. Do not reheat cooked eggs unless they are scrambled or chopped. Puncture the yolk before cooking eggs.

4. Avoid popping popcorn in your microwave oven. Microwave popcorn poppers are designed to be used in ovens with 600 to 700 watt output and results are not satisfactory in ovens with 500 watt output.

5. Avoid canning in your microwave oven.

14

6. Do not heat oil or fat for deep fat frying.

7. Pierce the "skin" of potatoes, whole squash, apples or any fruit or vegetable which has a skin covering before cooking.

SHARP

SHARP ELECTRONICS CORPORATION

10 Keystone Place, Paramus, New Jersey 07652 Phone (201) 265-5600

56R-UC003 Printed in Japan